S0-BPI-674

Quantitative Methods for Market-Oriented Economic Analysis over Space and Time

Edited by
WALTER C. LABYS
West Virginia University
TAKASHI TAKAYAMA
University of Western Australia
NOEL D. URI
US Department of Agriculture

Avebury

Aldershot · Brookfield USA · Hong Kong · Singapore · Sydney

Published by

Avebury

Gower Publishing Company Limited,
Gower House, Croft Road, Aldershot,
Hants, GU11 3HR, England

Gower Publishing Company,
Old Post Road, Brookfield, Vermont 05036
USA

Printed and Bound in Great Britain by
Athenaeum Press Ltd., Newcastle upon Tyne.

ISBN 0 566 07024 3

Contents

Preface

In recent years we have seen a persistent interest in the use of economic models for investigating the processes of and policies for economic growth and development as well as providing an objective framework for planning or evaluative purposes. There thus is a renewed interest in systematic and comprehensive quantitative analysis at the regional, national and international levels. This collection of papers is devoted to research results concerned with economic decision problems over space and time; they also suggest how the methodology may be applied and how useful inferences might be drawn regarding this new spatial and temporal price equilibrium focus.

The plan of this volume is to present to researchers and to policy decision makers the state-of-the-art in the applications of market oriented policy decision making and evaluation models. Even though imperfect, the market is the best place to resolve economic forces and counterforces generated in the economy in the regional, national or international context. The basic modeling strategies we consider relevant for such market analysis include the linear or quadratic programming and linear complementarity programming approaches that have recently been applied to decentralised pricing and quantity allocation within commodity markets.

This volume is divided into three parts: (I) Review of Methodologies and Applications; (II) Mineral and Energy Models; and (III) Agricultural Models. Such a division has been made to provide the requisite framework in which to consider the issues and then to focus on the areas that have witnessed the greatest applications in the literature.

We would like to thank those individuals who helped with the preparation of the manuscript, namely graduate students of the Department of Mineral and Energy Resource Economics at West Virginia University. Thanks are also due to Mrs. Angela Durham, who patiently and proficiently typed the various drafts.

A large number of contributors are represented here. In each instance the views expressed are those of the respective individuals and do not necessarily represent the policies of the institutions with which they are affiliated or the organisations that funded their research.

PART I
REVIEW OF METHODOLOGIES AND APPLICATIONS

1 Introduction

NOEL D. URI *US Department of Agriculture*

Over thirty years ago, Stephen Enke (1951) considered in a purely descriptive framework how one good could be traded among several spatially separated markets. His argument depended on three major assumptions: (1) regions are separated but not isolated by a volume-dependent transportation cost per physical unit; (2) there are no legal restrictions to limit the actions of the profit seeking traders of each region; and (3) for each region the functions relating to local production and local use are given and transportation costs are known. From these assumptions and certain exogenous information, he concluded that one could determine: (1) the net price in each region, (2) the quantity of exports or imports for each region, (3) which regions export, import, or do neither, and (4) the volume and direction of trade between all possible regions.

Samuelson (1952) considered this spatial problem, casting Enke's descriptive formulation mathematically into a maximum problem and related this specification to a standard problem in linear programming, the so-called Koopmans-Hitchcock minimum-transport-cost problem. Samuelson then suggested that after the problem in descriptive price behaviour is converted into a maximum problem, it can be solved by trial and error or by a systematic procedure of varying shipments in the direction of increasing social payoff, which is defined for a given region as the algebraic area under its excess-demand curve.

Takayama and Judge (1964a and b) restated the Samuelson partial-equilibrium (one commodity) formulation, disregarding the interdependencies with other commodities and concentrating on the interdependencies that exist between the different markets in production, pricing and the use of the one commodity. They thus established appropriate linear dependencies between regional supply, demand, and price and converted the Enke-Samuelson specification into a quadratic programming problem. The existence of aggregate linear regional demand and supply relations was assumed. The formulation was restated by Takayama and Woodland (1970), clarifying the relationship between various price and quantity formulations. The problem was stated in its primal and "purified" dual form. i.e., entirely in terms of either price variables or in terms of quantity variables.

Noting that economic relations in time have many of the properties of economic relations in space, Samuelson (1957) in subsequent work discussed the problem of intertemporal price equilibrium and suggested how the tools for analyzing spatial competitive relations might be applied to the more complex problems of equilibrium commodity prices over time. This problem is much more complex because the theory is inextricably bound up with uncertainty. It is assumed for simplicity's sake that future conditions are foreseeable and foreseen.

Operating under these considerations, Takayama and Judge extend their spatial formulation to obtain the competitive price and product allocation when markets are separated by both space and time. This approach has come to be known as the spatial and temporal price and allocation (STPA) model. In particular, the concept of net social payoff is used as a basis for deducing the conditions of spatial and intertemporal equilibrium and, given linear dependencies between regional supply, demand, and prices for each time period and given transportation costs among regions and storage costs from time period t to time period t+1, the problem is converted to a quadratic programming problem that can be solved directly for a competitive solution.

It is against the backdrop of this historical development that the contributions to this volume must be considered. Subsequent to the theoretical developments, a wide range of applications in the fields of minerals, metals and energy and agriculture has been seen. Moreover, these developments continue. Since the literature is quite diverse, it was deemed appropriate that a collection of papers be made available that not only reviewed the relevant literature but also offered applications of some of the more recent extensions of the methodology. The volume thus begins with reviews of the state-of-the-art developments and applications of the methodologies. It then continues with specific applications in the minerals, energy and agriculture areas.

Reviews of Methodologies

Two separate reviews of the methodologies are provided. In the first, Walter Labys surveys applications of spatial equilibrium and related programming methods to the modeling of mineral and energy markets and issues. It traces the development of the methodology from linear programming (LP) applications through to the linear complementarity (LCP) approaches currently being developed and implemented. It is emphasized that as developments have taken place, each step in the process has permitted the introduction of greater realism in spatial equilibrium models.

Robert Thompson then provides a detailed survey of the various attempts to model agricultural markets and sectors using the spatial equilibrium approach. Reference to most of the research, including that contained in various doctoral dissertations, is made and each work is put into its proper perspective in the overall context of spatial price equilibrium modeling. Thompson, moreover, extends the review by Labys in that he discusses the advantages and disadvantages of the methodologies and provides some advice on the direction that model improvements should take.

Mineral and Energy Model Applications

Turning to specific applications, Walter Labys and Chin-wei Yang look at Appalachian steam coal. They demonstrate the usefulness of the linear complementarity programming spatial equilibrium model. The basic distinction between the LCP and the quadratic program (QP) is that both are dealing with a set of equilibrium conditions in terms of inequalities. When the cross-regression coefficients are symmetric, the QP is equivalent to the LCP. However, one major problem of the LCP, as experienced in the Appalachian energy market, is its limited capability to model the large-scale spatial equilibrium problem. Model-builders must either aggregate economic regions or reduce the number of commodities in order to accommodate the "dimensionality" problem. A brief sensitivity analysis is provided for this model. However, such analysis is valid only for a given base or trade pattern. For some small changes in parameters, the sensitivity of the solution vectors is largely dependent on the relative size of characteristic roots of the coefficient matrices, a well known property. Lastly, changes in slopes and intercepts are shown to have important policy implications especially in the case of the ad valorem tariff.

Charles Kolstad is concerned with the computation of market equilibrium in imperfectly competitive markets. His contribution serves to demonstrate how conventional spatial equilibrium theory can be extended to non-competitive markets, specifically reaction-function type oligopolies. In developing the mathematics of computing such market equilibria it is shown that it is straightforward to formulate oligopolistic spatial equilibrium models. In fact, the complementarity approach presented could be considered an alternative to optimizátion methods for solving competitive spatial equilibrium models.

To demonstrate the applicability of the methodology, an example of the international steam coal market is presented. Although the model of the coal market was quite large, it is relatively easy from a computational point of view to find equilibrium solutions. Unfortunately, it does not appear that for this market, the duopoly market conduct assumptions give particularly good results, at least given the assumptions of the model. Nevertheless, it is demonstrated that the potential applicability of spatial models of imperfect competition is worth developing.

Air quality standards and steam electric coal uses are studied by Alan Schlottman and Robin Watson. In particular, the use of Western coal is shown to be significantly affected by sulfur emissions policies. The issue of adequate surface mine reclamation in the West would receive new emphasis if public policies were seriously undertaken to lower current levels of sulfur emissions at coal-fired power plants. These results would only be intensified with coal conversion policies at power plants currently using oil and natural gas as their main boiler fuel. Midwestern high sulfur coal can compete with Western coal only if operating costs for sulfur reducing technologies are moderate. Perhaps the main point to be learned through the analysis is that public policy towards alternative energy-environmental issues can have important interactions. Air quality policies which decrease sulfur emissions can stimulate surface mining and regional land use controversies. Simply banning the use of high sulfur coal may be difficult given current regional production capabilities; coal conversion at power plants does reduce oil use but overall it cannot easily meet low sulfur emission standards. Pressure by government agencies for stack gas scrubbing or similar technology to be installed at power plants without consideration for the prices of substitute fuels may aggravate the surface mining controversy even further. In short, the interrelationships among energy policies in the United States concerning coal use and its environmental impacts must be recognized.

The world aluminum and bauxite markets are examined via LCP and LP models by Takashi Takayama and Hideo Hashimoto. The comparative analysis provided yields three conclusions in particular.

(1) The LCP model has a mechanism to solve for regional market demand quantitites which are consistent with market prices, while this mechanism is missing in the LP model. The implication of this difference is straightforward. If the regional market demand functions can be approximated by the linear form, LCP modeling enables analysts to project the market clearing prices as well as the corresponding quantities consumed. In LP modeling, however, the dual LP solutions (that is, the shadow prices) may not be consistent with market clearing prices. Because such a market (Marshallian) operates in reality in many free market economies, socially suboptimal pricing and allocation policy decisions may be made if policy decisions are taken on the basis of LP methods.

(2) Due to the representation in functional form of regional demands for final products, operating costs and investment costs in the LCP model, quantity and price variables respond continuously to continuous parameter perturbations. In the LP model, parameter perturbations result in some discrete jumps in the quantity solutions. In particular, drastic changes occur in investment, which often shifts from zero to a large quantity and vice-versa. This characteristic limits the applicability of the LP model for investment planning.

(3) The LCP approach is useful for solving prices of primary commodities and their downstream (or final) products, particularly when the supplies of primary commodities are globally tight or are fixed by the producers. This is

because the Lagrangean multipliers of the given constraints in the LCP approach can be interpreted as economic rents, which can be passed on to the prices of both primary and final products. However, in such a situation, the LP approach may prove to be either infeasible, as shown by the authors, or some ingenuous calibration of the regional demand equations is required to derive feasible solutions.

In sum, though the basic structure of the LCP and LP investment models are very similar, the LCP model is capable of dealing with a wider range of policy questions. The above LCP model can be effectively applied to the evaluation of national or regional economic policy issues such as the pricing or taxing (subsidizing) of commodities, or the determination of future refining (or smelting) capacity expansion.

Noel Uri in his study, sets out a development planning model that can aid in formulating suitable policies for performing the activities of generating, transmitting and distributing, and consuming electrical energy in the United States over space and over time. As is implicitly and explicitly observed, costs are a most significant consideration in the analysis of determining the least-cost investment in electrical energy generation. Because of their lower costs, coal and nuclear capacity are expected to exhibit the largest increases. Oil generating capacity is expected to decline due to the requirements of the Power Plant and Industrial Fuel Use Act (PIFUA). This is most noticeable in the Middle Atlantic region and the East North Central region both of which had considerable oil generation at the start of the 1980s. Natural gas generating capacity in general will not be affected. The exception is the West South Central region that finds almost 69 percent of its 1980 generating capacity being natural gas-fired. Had the analysis extended beyond 1990, however, there would be a significant decline in natural gas generating capacity due to PIFUA. Hydroelectric capacity will expand primarily in the western portion of the United States, where the development potential continues to be the greatest. Finally, it is important to realize that the process is dynamic in that demands, costs, and environmental and energy related legislation continually change. This will necessarily affect the exact evolution of, for example, the optimal configuration of generating capacity. Thus, for example, if political and institutional considerations continue to weigh heavily with regard to the addition of nuclear capacity as they have in the last years of the decade of the seventies, then one would expect to realize a larger addition to coal-fired generating capacity and considerably smaller additions to nuclear capacity.

George Provenzano uses spatial equilibrium analysis to address the issue of the location patterns of energy-producing facilities. His paper demonstrates that a multiperiod, multiplant, multimarket linear programming model can provide information that is useful to planners in coordinating regional development of energy and water resources. The model generates information on optimal spatial and temporal patterns of energy facility construction and operation subject to regional constraints on water for energy. Because of the spatially disaggregated nature of this information, it facilitates coordinating location specific options for providing needed water supplies with construction opportunities for new energy production facilities. The model provides information in a manner that is consistent with a minimum-cost strategy for regional energy development and in a manner in which cumulative regional energy related water demands do not exceed the water resources available for energy production.

An application of the model to a coal rich production region indicates that optimal energy facility location patterns are quite sensitive to changes in energy and water resources development policies. An analysis of several hypothetical development scenarios reveals that major differences in locational and, hence, environmental impacts may be associated with policy initiatives calling for rapid synfuels development, a nuclear moratorium and energy-related water withdrawal limitations. Although the analysis indicates that these policy changes will not result in substantial increases in the cost of electricity to the consumer, many of the negative environmental spillovers associated with energy development cannot be included in the estimated average costs.

Agricultural Model Applications

The first paper in the section on agricultural modeling is by T. Takayama, H. Hashimoto, D.A. Nguyen, and R.C. Whitacre. Its focus is on applying the STPA framework to the world food economy. A number of important features are captured in this model. The first important feature of the world feed economy model presented is that the multi-commodity linkages among major farm products (except for some specialty crops and fruit) are established, even though the linkages are the first rough-cut representation in the linear functional form. This approach can be termed as an "integrated agricultural commodity systems approach" or "systems approach" for short. So far, a large number of single commodity policy studies have been published with an important caveat that further study should systematically include other commodities than the one in the study in order to reach more balanced policy conclusions. However, no really operational modeling system for policy analysis had been developed until now. Nine commodities are connected with each other (with different degrees of substitutability). These connections play an important role in some policy analysis.

Secondly, the systems appoach is extended to cover the time dimension where the stability and instability of the system are examined based on the food economy of the United States. Commodity-by-commodity examinations reveal that the wheat market is stable, while the maize market and the soybean market are unstable. The degree of instability of the soybean market is found to be higher than the maize market. There is, however, some hope that the whole nine-commodity system might produce relatively stable development over time. But this hope is not warranted, as shown in the recursive simulation exercises. If the system is stable, that is, either monotonically converging or cyclically converging then, no stabilization policy (intervention) is needed. In the case of the U.S. food economy, in cases where system stability is found to be non-existent, it is concluded that some stabilization scheme is needed.

The modeling system developed does provide for some innovation. The first and most important issue considered in the modeling system is the proper recognition of the difference in the North and South cropping seasons. For short-run analysis, this has proven to be crucially important. A modeling framework that can differentiate the cropping seasons is already available in the STPA dynamic models. Only estimation of the requisite demand functions is the remaining problem. The second issue relates to the linear system and the related estimation of parameters. Linear demand and supply functions employed in the STPA models are a first approximation to reality. The linear system is not required if more efficient (and less costly) algorithms in solving non-linear programming problems are developed. At this stage it is still recommended that this STPA approach or iterative STPA approach be used over others available for the modeling framework on the basis of their computational efficiency.

The last issue discussed is more fundamental and philisophical than technical. Modeling activities such as those presented by Takayama, et al., must serve some purpose(s) of a policy decision-maker(s) in the real world. Policy changes, such as on-going trade liberalization of agricultural commodities in Japan, require detailed impact studies of the policy changes and careful vigilance over the affected parties by the policy changes over some period of time. This chapter thus presents some prototypical approaches in analyzing market situations and evaluating economic policies related to farm products in the United States, Europe, Australia, Japan, Canada and the rest of the world. It is hoped that this type of modeling framework will be pursued continously by the trade and/or agriculture ministries in major trading governments and international organizations for similar or wider purposes.

Farm and sector model linkages with spatial equilibrium commodity models is the topic of the chapter by Bruce McCarl, Deborah Brown, Richard Adams, and James Pheasant. While the primary focus of the paper is methodological, an empirical case study does provide some insight into performing environmental benefit assessments. This study features both methodological and empirical advances. Regarding methodological developments, this paper implements the procedures using a linear programming model to generate crop-mix activities which in turn are integrated into a sector model. In this application, the procedure needs some modification to adjust for the yield changes which accompany changes in crop mix (due to less timely operations when planting and harvesting a crop). Although not attempted here, it may also be desirable to incorporate changes in factor-usage which could accompany such changes in yields or changes in the intensity of cropping. The procedure works satisfactorily, although no detailed attempt is made to appraise the adequacy of this procedure vis-a-vis traditional policy analysis procedures. The authors believe researchers should consider using this approach as it provides a desirable theoretical link between microeconomic behaviour and sectoral modeling.

Concerning empirical developments, the assessment of the ozone control benefits reveals relatively minor gains to society from reductions in ozone, but substantial losses with further degradation of quality air (i.e., an estimate of $1 billion in losses from the relaxed ozone scenario). At a sectoral level, an increase in ozone is an effective form of supply control and when acting against the somewhat inelastic demand curves of the included commodities results in an increase in agriculture's welfare (producer quasi-rents), although society's welfare falls. It also appears from the analysis that there is clear tradeoff between air pollution and exchange earnings with increases in air pollution leading to decreases in the amount and value of agricultural exports. In summary, spatial equilibrium analysis and the sector modeling based on the Dantzig-Wolfe decomposition procedure proves to be an adequate method for appraising agricultural adjustments in the context of environ- mental policy analysis.

The final paper in this volume by Forest Holland and Jerry Sharples addresses the question of the appropriate estimate of the elasticity of demand for U.S. exports of wheat to use in short run models. Different assumptions about the real world wheat market lead to different estimates of this elasticity. For the base period, 1979/80 to 1981/82, the twenty-region model yields an elasticity estimate of -0.7. Bilateral agreements appear to have no impact upon this estimate at the quantities traded in the base period, but do show an impact at slightly lower quantity levels.

Two characteristics of the wheat trade model suggest that the discovered value of -0.7 overestimates the true elasticity of demand for U.S. wheat exports for two reasons in particular:

(1) The model includes the assumption that trade flows will adjust immediately to a new equilibrium in response to a change in U.S. exports. To the extent that trading patterns tend to be more stable than those determined in modeling exercises, adjustment to a change in U.S. exports would be fewer, i.e., it would take a larger price increase to induce a given quantity change. This is likely to be a significant factor. Trade channels once established tend to persist because of political reasons as well as for economic reasons omitted from this study. The United States, for example, shipped some wheat to each of the importing regions during the base period. This may reflect the desire of importers to diversify their sources; it may indicate that wheat from the United States has some unique characteristics; or it may reflect wheat shipments under Public Law 480. Each factor would make short-run demand for U.S. wheat exports less elastic.

(2) The transportation rates are assumed constant no matter what volume is transported. If transportation rates were to increase with increased volume shipped, then a larger price drop to the exporter would accompany a given increase in world wheat trade, because the price wedge between the exporter and importer would increase. Both of these factors, if put into the model, would make the U.S. export demand curve less elastic than shown.

The price equilibrium model used to derive the export demand elasticity includes only wheat; it does not allow for any cross-price effects with substitute commodities. Demand substitution may be an important factor in determining the elasticity of wheat excess demand faced by U.S. exports. Substitution seems most likely in very low income countries where wheat and other grains are dietary staples and in wealthy nations where wheat is used as a livestock feed. The procedures employed in this study could be used with a multiple commodity spatial price quilibrium model to improve upon this elasticity estimate.

The Future

In the domain of individual firm management, the theoretical and operational modeling of inventory control and capital investment decisions have been routinely accomplished. However, interregional and/or international competition of firms in a commodity market or a set of markets of interrelated commodities has rarely explicitly entered into their theory or their models.

The 1972/73 grain shortage and the 1973/74 OPEC exercise of power in the face of the then fast-growing demand for petroleum called attention to the importance of global analysis of primary commodity markets. For national or regional planning and economic decision-making, international and interregional economic policy analysis models, with specific national or regional policies properly incorporated, can be employed by various private, national, or international research institutions and governmental policy decision-making agencies. Linear programming and non-linear programming models have been widely used in this context. QP and LCP models can be looked upon as a natural extension of the LP models in the sense that the price-quantity relationship in the markets is captured in its simplest form. In this book, we briefly and selectively review and extend modeling efforts in the LP, QP and LCP areas.

The future research that must follow from what is presented here can be divided into two areas: The first area is in the theoretical investigation of existence, uniqueness, and stability of optimal investment (and capital earning stream) leading, for instance, toward (infinite time horizon) a time invariant optimal investment profile. The second area is in the further applications of the types of models presented here to investigate policy effectiveness in national and international contexts. The first area can be expanded to incorporate a more general modeling framework. The second area will be naturally tried by many researchers and some useful results can be expected in the future.

Author

Noel D. Uri
U.S. Department of Agriculture
1301 New York Avenue, NW
Washington, D.C. 20005

References

Enke, S., (1951). "Equilibrium Among Spatially Separated Markets: Solution by Electric Analogue," Econometrica, 19: 4047.

Samuelson, P.A., (1952). "Spatial Price Equilibrium and Linear Programming," American Economic Review, 42: 283-303.

Samuelson, P.A., (1957). "Intertemporal Price Equilibrium: A Prologue to the Theory of Speculation," Weltwirtschaftliches Archives, 79: 181-221.

Takayama, T. and G.G. Judge, (1964a). "Equilibrium Among Spatially Separated Markets: A Reformulation," Econometrica, 32: 510-524.

Takayama, T. and G.G. Judge, (1964b). "An Intertemporal Price Equilibrium Model," Journal of Farm Economics, 46: 477-486.

Takayama, T. and A.D. Woodland, (1970). "Equivalent of Price and Quantity Formulations of Spatial Equilibrium: Purified Duality in Quadratic and Concave Programming," Econometrica, 38: 889-906.

2 Spatial and temporal price and allocation models of mineral and energy markets

WALTER C. LABYS *West Virginia University*

Introduction

Applications of spatial equilibrium programming methods to the modeling of mineral and energy issues have recently expanded considerably. The term "mineral" models refers to models of non-fuel mineral markets. "Energy" models applies to models of fuel mineral markets. Examples of mineral commodities in either category appear in Table 2.1 and a complete list of models can be found in Labys (1987). While the modeling of agricultural issues led naturally to major developments in this area, the modeling of minerals and energy issues was much less extensive. Recent circumstances, however, have led to a redisposition of this interest. First, OPEC's actions against the West have caused an unprecedented amount of economic research to be directed to energy modeling. Secondly, this occurence has led to an awareness of possible resource scarcity for other key minerals and thus to a recognition of geographical or spatial modeling as a means of analyzing geopolitical mineral issues. Thirdly and independent of this situation, mineral and energy economics has become more sophisticated as a professional field. Thus, older and more qualitative approaches have been replaced by newer and more quantitative ones.

The purpose of this chapter is thus to explain the model developments which have recently occurred in the mineral and

Table 2.1

PRINCIPAL MINERAL AND ENERGY COMMODITIES

Nonfuel Mineral Commodities		Fuel Minerals or Energy Commodities
Metals	Nonmetals	
Iron:	Building:	Fossil:
iron ore	sand/gravel	bituminous coal
Iron Alloy:	limestone	and lignite
manganese	cements	anthracite
chromite	Chemical:	petroleum
nickel	sulfur	natural gas
molybdenum	salt	Nonfossil:
cobalt	Fertilizer:	uranium
vanadium	phosphate	Processed:
Base:	potash	electricity
copper	nitrates	refined oil products
lead	Ceramic:	synthetic fuels
zinc	clay	
tin	feldspar	
Light:	Defractory and Flux:	
aluminum	clay	
magnesium	magnesia	
titanium	Abrasive:	
Precious:	sandstone	
gold	industrial diamonds	
silver	Insulant:	
platinum	asbestos	
Rare:	mica	
radium	Pigment and Filler:	
beryllium	clay	
	diatomite	
	borite	
	Precious and Gem:	
	gem diamonds	
	amethyst	

energy areas beyond that of Labys, Field and Clark (1985) and Labys and Wood (1985). Some of these modeling efforts have resulted from a consideration of conventional fuel and non-fuel mineral trade problems which recognized the importance of transport costs and political constraints in the formulation of an equilibrium approximating competitive trade. It is intuitively obvious that a mineral produced in several regions will probably have different factor requirements in each location. These disparities will lead to measurable cost differences, which are likely to influence the comparative advantage of each producer. Both the classical and the Hecksher-Ohlin theories of international trade recognize this cost difference as well as spatial demands to explain trade flows. Consideration of location theory requires an explicit recognition of the importance of transporation costs, particularly in the analysis of movement of relatively low-value goods such as mineral ores or primary energy fuels where transportation costs are a significant cost component.

Other modeling efforts have stemmed from the engineering processes required to transform primary mineral ores or fuels to their more useful processed stages. Not only does mineral processing involve cost minimization production techniques, it also requires optimization in the vertical integration of the stages of process and their location. For example, optimization is important in the evaluation of nonfuel mineral investments. It also lends itself to the optimal selections of fuels for electricity generation as well as to the optimal configuration of electricity transmission networks.

Although the modeling solution to any of the above issues or problems can be accomplished by adopting some version of generalized nonlinear programming, mineral and energy modeling has developed around the use of particular programming algorithms. This review of applications is thus similarly organized. They are presented below in the following sequences: linear programming, process programming, quadratic programming, recursive programming, mixed integer programming, and linear complementarity programming. A more complete history of the evaluation of these approaches can be found in Labys and Pollack (1984).

Linear Programming

This basic method still provides considerable incentive for spatial and programming modeling in this area. A more complete description of the method appears in Takayama and Labys (1986). The construction of an n-region mineral trade model derives from the basic Koopmans-Hitchcock transportation cost minimization LP model. This model normally involves the following components: (1) a set of demand points or observations and a set of supply points, (2) the distributive activities over space, and (3) the spatial equilibrium conditions. These components are represented in the following mathematical definition.

$$\text{Minimize } L = \sum_{i=1}^{n} \sum_{j=1}^{n} T_{ij} Q_{ij} \qquad (1)$$

Subject to

$$D_i \leq \sum_{j}^{n} Q_{ij} \qquad i = 1, \ldots, n \qquad (2)$$

$$S_j \geq \sum_{j}^{n} Q_{ij} \qquad j = 1, \ldots, n \qquad (3)$$

$$T_{ij}, Q_{ij} \geq 0 \qquad \text{all } i, j \qquad (4)$$

Definition of variables:

D_i = Commodity demand in region i

S_j = Commodity supply in region j

T_{ij} = Transportation cost of shipping a commodity between region i and region j

Q_{ij} = Quantity shipped between region i and region j.

The model operates such that transportation costs are minimized by allowing commodities to transfer until demand equals supply in every spatially separate market. The cost minimization process is established by the objection function (1). The constraint relations (2 and 3) reflect the conditions that regional consumption cannot exceed the total shipment to the region and that the total shipments from a region cannot exceed the total quantity available for shipment. Relation (4) assures the lack of negative shipments.

Regarding specific mineral applications of linear programming, two early models built by Copithorne dealt with nickel (1973) as well as with gold (1976). While both of these had a regional and spatial configuration, it was Kovisars who greatly extended the modeling application by including stage of process as well as temporal considerations in the case of copper (1975) and of zinc (1976). These stages included mining, concentrating, recycling, smelting and refining. The temporal dimension was added through an integrating system which provided successive adjustments of the demand, cost, and capacity variables based on the results of the previous periods' simulation.

More recent applications have attempted a stronger integration with econometric equations particularly on the demand side and have emphasized dynamic model solutions. For example, such a model has been constructed by Hibbard, et al. (1979) for generating long run forecasts of important aluminum industry variables. This model simulates the overall supply and demand balance of the major regions constituting the world aluminum industry. The U.S. supply model is spatial and process-oriented, time-dynamic formulation of the engineering representation of the flow of material through mining, refining, smelting, scrap recycling, fabrication and distribution of final products to end-use sectors. Supply in other regions of the world as well as demand are determined using econometric relations. It is assumed that the industry operates in a purely competitive environment so that market prices of aluminum are determined by the intersection of marginal supply curves with demand curves. This objective is obtained by maximizing the sum of the consumer's and producer's surplus to obtain a partial equilibrium of supply and demand over time.

A more detailed representation of this modeling approach can be found in the Hibbard et al. (1980) model of the U.S. copper industry. This model known as MIDAS-II featured extensive disaggregation to include production characteristics about each individual mine, smelter, refinery and electrowinning facility of U.S. companies and some international companies. While such disaggregation is useful, the more interesting contribution of the model was its adaptation by Soyster and Sherali (1981), who replaced the competitive market structure with that of oligopoly. Programming models have not dealt extensively with noncompetitive market configurations. The transformation of the programming algorithm to evaluate that of a Nash-Cournot game was significant in this respect, although the oligopoly model could only be solved on a static, single period basis.

Other solution possibilities were offered by Kolstad et al. (1983) and by Kolstad in several later papers.

Whereas algorithms for finding a Nash equilibrium in economic models have usually relied on complementarity pivot approaches such as that of Lemke and Howson (1964) and Scarf (1973), the approach adopted is that of Murphy et al. (1980) which solved a sequence of convex programs delineated by a scalar representing total industry output. The results of model solution confirm the importance of incorporating noncompetitive market structure as proposed by Takayama and Judge (1971) generally and by Labys (1980) for the case of minerals.

Among the first applications of LP study spatial allocation problems in energy markets was that of Henderson (1958) who analyzed competitiveness in coal industry allocation problems. Coal demands and supplies were identified among some 14 regions in the United States. The objective function was solved to minimize the delivered costs (extraction plus transportation costs) or coal allocation patterns, subject to competitive market conditions. The solution of the model is then used to evaluate deviations from competitive efficiency by comparing the efficient model solution with the actual or existing coal allocation problems.

When coal again gained stature as a prominent energy source in the 1970's, a more elaborate LP model comparing the supply and demand potential of western and eastern coals was constructed by Libbin et al. (1977). This model expanded the regional coal supply activities to include types of surface and underground mining as well as three quality levels based on sulfur content and heating value. Heating content and sulfur value were also embodied as additional activities in regional demand allocations. The blending of coals to meet sulfur standards was also allocated in each demand region. The solution of the model minimized the discounted total cost of meeting national coal demand subject to varying sulfur burning standards up to the year 1990. The results were then interpreted in terms of the amounts of coal that could be supplied by various western and eastern states.

One of the more elaborate attempts in the late 1970's to utilize LP in spatial and process energy analysis is that of the Project Independence Energy Evaluation System (PIES) constructed for the FEA or now the EIA. This model (EIA, 1979) includes a macroeconometric model, an econometric demand model, and a LP model explaining fuel supplies, conversion and shipments. This model was started by the Nixon administration to analyze a policy of energy independence, was later shelved during the Ford administration, and was subsequently renewed by the Carter administration. This model later came under severe criticism by Commoner (1979).

The solution process of PIES depends on an integrating model -- an LP model that uses given estimates of regional demands, prices and elasticities, regional supply schedules, and resource input requirements to calculate an energy market equilibrium. The relation between the demand model and the LP submodel, which incorporates the supply schedules and conversion processes, may be summarized as follows: The demand model is used to calculate a price/quantity coordinate on the demand curve for each of the primary and derived energy products in the system. Associated with each of these coordinates are measures of the sensitivity of the quantities demanded to small changes in each of the prices in the demand model (own- and cross-price elasticities). In the actual solution, the LP problem is solved such that the minimum cost schedule of production, distribution, and transportation necessary to satisfy the given demand levels is reached. This process is continued until the demand and supply prices are equal, at which point the energy market is assumed to be in equilibrium. One aspect of the PIES effort which has proven useful is the "combined" or "integrating" model algorithm developed by Hogan and Weyant (1980). While useful in further modeling efforts, such a simultaneous solution algorithm can be obtained without integration in STPA models, e.g., see the STPA energy model design of Takayama (1979).

Among other applications of LP to energy modeling, Deam et al. (1973) in addressing the issue of petroleum trade, have built a spatial energy model in which the petroleum/natural gas component dominates, and Devanney and Kennedy (1980) have paid particular attention to world refinery location and flows. It should be noted that most of these models combine spatial, process, and demand characteristics making model hybridization one of the principal outcomes of this era of LP application.

Process Programming

These models can be considered a complement to linear programming formulations of spatial equilibrium models. They recognize an important characteristic of mineral trade that the commodities used and traded within industrial requirements normally involve different stages of process or production, e.g., see Kovisars (1976). These can include: mining, ore treatment (milling and concentration), reduction (smelting), purification (refining), and consumption by fabricators. Recycled material is an important process input for many mineral flows and may enter the supply flow at several stages. While Manne and Markowitz (1963) describe the early development of these models as an application of process analysis, they also report on the integration of this approach with spatial equilibrium analysis. In that study, Fox (1963) presented a process model of spatial equilibrium in agriculture and Marschak (1963) presented a process model of spatial equilibrium in petroleum refining. Not much has been reported on more recent developments of this methodology until the appearance of a survey article by Sparrow and Soyster (1980). More recently, the National Academy of Sciences (1982) in a state-of-the-art survey have recognized it as a distinct class of mineral and energy modeling.

The actual formulation of a process programming (PP) model is normally based on LP but other forms of mathematical programming can be used. What is important is that an intermediate step is included to better approximate the production function. The model also requires the usual objective function, activities and constraints. Model solution usually involves minimizing an objective function specified in terms of production costs, subject to such constraints as the time sequence of production, regional capacities, the demand for the product, and technical relationships among the production variables.

The activity component is the distinguishing feature of process programming. It can be considered as an intermediate step that describes how decision variables (resources in the production problem) are combined in fixed proportions by the production technologies to produce an output. This emphasis makes PP in some ways similar to the input-output approach. But instead of a single technology for every process, linear programming can allow for multiple processes or activities. These activities define technologically possible alternatives in physical terms only (e.g., different energy and material requirements and labor requirements) and do not necessarily yield economically (or socially) efficient solutions. Economic considerations are introduced by the cost function, which shows the minimum cost of producing various levels of output, given factor prices and technologies.

Referring to the LP model presented above, an example of model formulation can be given in terms of the costs (processing plus transportation) of delivering a material to a consumer. Tariffs and value-added taxes can be treated as additional transport costs incurred over a particular delivery route. For a particular mineral, this can be written as:

$$\text{Minimize } L = \sum_{i=1}^{5} (PC_i + T_{i,i+1}) \tag{5}$$

Definition of variables:

PC_i = processing cost at stage i

$T_{i,i+1}$ = transportation cost from i to the next stage

i = 1 for Mining, 2 for Concentrating, 3 for Reduction or smelting, 4 for Purification or refining, and 5 for Consumption.

For a number of minerals there may not be clear agreement over what constitutes final consumption. However, this does not have to be a practical barrier in the examination of supply flows as long as some final demand stage is selected.

Process models are well suited for conducting mineral supply analysis in a spatial context. They are usually formulated in terms of production technologies, accounting for the important inputs (labor, energy, and materials requirements) at each stage of the production sequence. This requires constructing mathematical equations that represent the various technological or engineering production possibilities. Usually the overall production flow is disaggregated into elementary process routes, and input-output parameters are derived for each stage of each route, based upon engineering data. For each process, programming techniques can be used to select from among the various production possibilities the ones that optimize a preset goal.

A process model can also lend itself to demand analysis by permitting a linkage to be made between final product demands and derived material demands. National economic activity can be used to explain final product demand. The process model then explains the product transformation process, that is, how primary products derived from materials can be transformed into secondary and then tertiary products (or greater) until final product demand is met. Sometimes the supply of material is also studied as part of the demand process.

Among examples of PP applications, Ray and Szekely (1973) have attempted to find the least-cost combination of production technologies in an integrated steel plant, subject to demand, technological, and raw material constraints. Their formulation allows the analyst to find the optimal mix of three process routes (blast furnace/basic oxygen furnace, blast furnace/open hearth furnace, electric furnace), depending on the prices of the factor inputs, such as scrap and hot metal. Such a formulation is of interest for studying the demand for materials that are used in the production sequence.

A number of other PP models have been built for the steel industry. One of these is the model of Tsao and Day (1971) which is a short-run (fixed capacity) model employed to compare the optimal and actual behaviour of the U.S. carbon steel industry over the period 1955-1968. Alternative arrangements of processes are included in the technology matrix, with optimization indicating the desirable proportion of each. In addition to the technology matrix, the model also contains a set of auxiliary activities, which represents the purchase of inputs and the sale of final outputs. The constraint on input purchases prevents the total use of a given input (such as oxygen) from exceeding the amount purchased. Sales constraints are included to insure that production of finished products meets sales requirements.

Finally, Clark and Church (1981) describe a model that represents the production of stainless steel products (bar, sheet, strip, rod, wire, etc.) by alternative technological routes, starting with basic raw materials such as carbon and stainless steel scrap, ferrochromium, ferronickel, and other materials including gases. Although not constructed explicitly as a demand model, this type of model can be used to analyze indirectly the demand for input materials required in the production process. In the case of stainless steel, it is possible to estimate the demand for input materials, such as chromium, nickel, and manganese (in various forms) as a function of the production of stainless steel by different processing routes.

Apart from the applications of Kovisars (1975, 1976) which extended process analysis to spatial equilibrium mineral modeling, most of combined process and spatial modeling has taken place within the context of the international petroleum refining industry. In the discussion of LP modeling, reference was made to the model of Devanney and Kennedy (1980). Their process activities included the production of crude oil, its transformation to refinery products, including gasoline, kerosene, distillate fuel and residual oil, and the consumption of these products. Their spatial allocation consisted of seven regions, namely the United States, Canada, Latin America, the Middle East, Africa and Asia. The model was operated to determine the optimal spatial allocation of these products, given government policies that might include tariffs, excise taxes, environmental restrictions, refinery subsidies, and policies intended to shift the supply curves or demand curves through tax measures or direct regulation.

An alternative process model of the world oil market by Deam (1974) includes fuel transportation among some 25 worldwide geographical areas. Fifty-two types of crude oil and 22 refining centers are represented along with 6 types of tankers that may be selected for transport. The LP matrix for this model is quite large (about 2500 rows and 13,500 columns). The exogenous inputs to the model include future demand for products by region, refinery technology, costs of product refining, and transport of specific crudes and products. The model is solved to determine the optimal allocation and routing of crude oil and products between sources, refineries and demand centers at some future target date. The requirements for new refineries, tankers, and production facilities to satisfy the projected level and distribution of demands are also determined. Because the model includes the transport and refining costs for crude from specific sources, it provides a basis for analyzing the relative price of these crudes in a competitive market or in a controlled market where relative prices are set to reflect the differences in transportation and refining costs among the many sources.

Quadratic Programming

This class of spatial model replaces exogenously given demand and supply quantity estimates with estimates that are endogenously determined. As developed by Takayama and Judge (1971), the quadratic programming (QP) formulation of a spatial equilibrium model features the following components: (1) a system of equations describing the aggregate demand for one or more commodities or interest in each of the included markets as well as the aggregate supply of the commodities in each of the markets, (2) the distribution activities over space, and (3) the equilibrium conditions. While the demand and supply equations imply a structure similar to that of an econometric market model, the equilibrium process is more adequately represented through the identification of the profits to be realized from the flow of commodities, i.e., the excess of a price differential between two points minus transportation costs. Profit maximization is assured through the use of a computational algorithm which allows commodities to transfer until demand equals supply in every spatially separated market. So that policy decisions can be evaluated more realistically, the equilibrium conditions and other definitional equations can be used to impose constraints on the model parameters.

The structure of an elementary spatial and temporal price and allocation model (STPA) can be viewed in the following example. To establish the quadratic objective function necessary for the QP solution, the equations follow the standard STPA form: linearity is assumed and the necessary identifying variables are embodied in the constant terms.

$$D_i = b_{oi} - b_{1i} P_i \tag{6}$$

$$S_j = b_{oj} + b_{1j} P_j \tag{7}$$

Definition of variables

D_i = commodity demand in region i

S_j = commodity supply in region j

P_i = commodity demand price in region i

P_j = commodity supply price in region j

Q_{ij} = commodity shipments between regions i and j

T_{ij} = transportation costs between regions i and j

Because the formulation of this model by Takayama and Judge (1971) expresses these equations in their inverse form, the above equations can be alternatively written as

$$P_i = a_{1i} + a_{2i} D_i \quad \text{for all i} \tag{8}$$

$$P_j = a_{3j} + a_{4j} S_j \quad \text{for all j} \tag{9}$$

where a_1, a_2, $a_3 > 0$ and $a_4 < 0$ over all observations.

The constraints imposed on the supply and demand relations are the same as in the linear programming model.

$$D_i \leq \sum_j^n Q_{ij} \qquad \text{for all } i \tag{10}$$

$$S_j \geq \sum_i^n Q_{ij} \qquad \text{for all } j \tag{11}$$

Transport costs and shipments are assumed to be non-negative.

$$T_{ij}, \; Q_{ij} \geq 0 \tag{12}$$

The objective function necessary to complete the model goes beyond the cost minimization goal of linear programming. That is, the function maximizes the global sum of producers' and consumers' surplus after the deduction of transportation costs. This form of market-oriented quasi-welfare function has been termed net social payoff (NSP) by Samuelson (1952) and is defined as follows:

$$NSP = \sum_i^n {}^{D}\!\int_0 P_i(D_i)dD_i - \sum_j^n {}^{S}\!\int_0 P_j(S_j)dS_j - \sum_i^n \sum_j^n Q_{ij}T_{ij} \tag{13}$$

The objective function for the present model is a restatement of the above after substitution of the linear demand and supply relations.

$$\text{Max (MSP)} = \sum_i^n a_{1i}D_i - \sum_j^n a_{3j}S_j - \frac{1}{2}\sum_i^n a_{2i}D^2 - \frac{1}{2}\sum_j^n a_{4j}S^2 - \sum_j^n \sum_j^n T_{ij}Q_{ij} \tag{14}$$

where D_i and $S_j \geq 0$.

Although this model can be solved relatively easily, the introduction of nonlinearities into the demand or supply equations requires other programming techniques, as explained in Chapter 3. The model can become temporal by solving it over time. Time varying parameters can also be introduced, and separable or other programming algorithms can be employed. As the size of the model increases, it is possible to break larger nonlinear programming models into smaller submodels. Finally, the models require increasing the number of constraints such as trade restrictions in the model to enlarge the number of trade flows to a realistic level. (The basic solution of the model specifies that the number of trade flows cannot exceed one less than the total number of exporting plus importing regions in the model.)

Among applications of QP to mineral and energy models, no mineral model applications have been published to date. However, energy model applications have been numerous. Uri (1975) has examined the efficiency with which electricity is generated and allocated in the United States. His model characterized the electrical industry as having separate supply and demand locations and a fixed amount of transmission capacity available at any one time. Based on the STPA, Uri selected a partial equilibrium solution, since other energy markets although exogenous to the electricity market also effect overall energy market equilibrium. His formulation also assumes that a unified authority responsible for the allocation and pricing of electrical energy acts within a competitive market structure to maximize social welfare in relation to available and future electrical energy supplies. However, one of the innovations of his application is introducing monopoly considerations by introducing a price structure which specifies differing elasticities of demand among various categories of consumers, i.e., a form of price discrimination which permits the utility to recover full costs plus its allowable rate of return. Social welfare losses (decreases in net social payoff) are thus examined in relation to this consumer pricing system. Uri later (1976, 1977) showed how industry capacity could be varied within the model solution by introducing concepts of investment and capital formation.

Among more recent developments, the domestic coal industry and the international coal market have been subject to QP applications. For example, Labys and Yang (1980) have used this approach to model the spatial allocation of Appalachian coal shipments. Their model begins with a spatial allocation limited to Appalachian steam coal supplying states and eastern steam coal demand regions. However, it advanced beyond the point supply and demand allocations of the LP models to include econometric demand and supply equations, such that coal quantitites as well as prices are solved simultaneously in the model solution. With the objective function stated to maximize net social payoff, the sensitivity of coal demand and supplies is measured in response to changes in price elasticities, transportation cost and ad valorem tax rates. This model was subsequently applied by Newcomb and Fan (1980) who expanded this supply sector to include geological factors surrounding coal deposits. An international application is that of Dutton (1982) who assessed the impact of future coal prices on import policies of selected coal consuming countries.

An application to the world oil market employing QP has been made by Kennedy (1974). The purpose of this model was to provide simulation analysis and forecasts of the oil market, based on changing exogenous factors such as tanker technology and in the cost of finding and producing oil in more remote regions; it also examined the impact of government policies on trade, environmental restrictions and taxation. For each region and fuel or refined product, the model determines the level of oil production, consumption, price, refinery capital structure, and the pattern of world oil trade flows.

Finally overall energy market assessments have been made using this approach. Takayama (1979) has confirmed the usefulness of the QP approach in his specification of a world energy model. The advantage of QP in this respect is avoiding the cumbersome integrating routines, for example, that were employed in the PIES (1979) model. An example of such an application can be seen in the Hashimoto (1977) world food and energy model. This model not only combines separate world food and energy models but generates its solutions on the basis of related macroeconomic model forecasts.

Recursive Programming

These models can be considered a special case of adaptive intertemporal spatial equilibrium models. Recursive programming (RP) can be described as a sequence of constrained optimization problems in which one or more objective functions, constraint or limitation coefficients of a given problem depend functionally on the optimal primal and/or dual solution vectors of one or more problems earlier in the sequence. To obtain this recursive dependence of the coefficients on preceding solutions, a set of feedback functions are used. The rationale behind this approach is that it emulates a decision maker who proceeds according to a succession of behaviourally conditioned, sub-optimizing decisions. The decision maker in protecting himself from errors of estimation and forecasting reviews his maximization plans each period based on current information. The sequence of "decisions" as a whole must then coverge to some desired optimum.

An example of an elementary recursive programming model can be seen in Day's (1973) generalized cobweb formulation. (For a survey of more complex models and some of the earlier results obtained, refer to Day and Nelson, 1973). Two homogenous commodities are produced by two firms or decision units, each requiring land or mineral resources and working capital. Their production levels as well as resource allocation are decided by maximizing gross short run profits. Thus the decision problem for each unit at the beginning or a period t can be described by the following linear program.

$$\max_{Q_1 Q_2} \; [V_1^*(t)Q_1 + V_2^*(t)Q_2] \quad (15)$$

subject to

$$Q_1 + Q_2 \leq L$$
$$C_1Q_1 + C_2Q_2 \leq K(t)$$
$$Q_1, Q_2 \geq 0$$

With L and K(t) representing aggregate amounts of resources and capital available, decision makers are considered identical in their behaviour and the linear program represents the sum of the decisions of all units.

Revenue values associated with L and K(t) are derived from the dual

$$\min_{R_1, R_2} \; [R_1L + R_2K(t)] \quad (16)$$

subject to

$$R_1 + C_1R_2 \geq V_1^*(t)$$
$$R_1 + C_1R_2 \geq V_2^*(t)$$
$$R_1, R_2 \geq 0$$

And recursivity is introduced through a feedback component consisting of three equations which describe anticipated unit profits per area, working capital, and prices

$$V_1^*(t) = P_1(t-1) - C_i \qquad 1 = 1, 2$$

Finally prices $P_i(t)$ are determined, assuming a temporary equilibrium in those markets where the commodities produced are also sold. Linear demand functions are used with $P_i(t)$ expressed as a function of current demand $Q_i(t)$; no commodity price substitution is assumed.

Recursive programming as a formal computer modeling algorithm appears to have enjoyed greater popularity in an earlier period before spatial and other programming models could yield efficient intertemporal solutions. Among applications of the RP approach, Nelson (1970) working with Day included regional or spatial equilibrium in developing an interregional recursive programming model of the U.S. iron and steel industry. Abe (1973) extended this analysis to include the Japanese steel industry. Investment in production facilities was constrained by an upper limit, determined solely by the industry's past performance. More specifically, the upper limit for investment was set at either the level of capacity in the preceding period (adjusted by an adoption coefficient) or at the gap between desired capacity in the current period and that in the preceding period. The desired capacity level was determined by finding what the expected demand for the commodities would be. This was in turn determined by demand activity in steel-using industries and other lagged variables. Whichever limit is reached in the solution, investment is determined by a combination of lagged price and profit variables. This approach was also generalized by Day and Nelson (1973) who saw it as a framework useful for analyzing industrial development problems in a dynamic investment context.

Regarding energy applications Tabb (1968) analyzed the influence of technological change on short and long run adjustments in the U.S. coal industry. In the short run, the question arises as to what levels to operate different types of available equipment. In the long run, it switches to that of choosing the best techniques and to invest in the capital equipment which embody them. His RP model thus analyzes processes of coal production, investment and technological change. Although this study is primarily historical, dealing with the period 1949-64, it describes the impact of technological change on capital-labor substitution and the consequent growth and demise of the coal industry. The model was shown as being capable of predicting growth, demand and supply as well as the derived demand for labor given the introduction of different coal-producing technologies.

Mixed Integer Programming Models

The multiperiod linear mixed integer (MIP) programming model of the type developed earlier by Kendrick (1967) and later by Kendrick and Stoutjesdijk (1978) combines the attributes of both the spatial and intertemporal equilibrium models. Like spatial equilibrium, it explains the flows of commodities by stage of process between regions subject to price differences and costs. Like recursive programming, it represents an application of linear programming; only the integer characteristic is introduced to accomodate combinations of 0-1 variables which can refer to the non-existence or existence of a production facility. The background to MIP stems from attempts to cope with a number of commodity-oriented analyses including shipping and transportation, industrial process, intertemporal considerations and investment project selection. Several of these functions are typically combined to study market adjustments, as exemplified in Dammert's (1980) study of copper investment in Latin America and the Brown et al. (1981) study of international aluminum patterns.

Formulating such a model begins with the transport component which resembles the spatial equilibrium transportation model studied earlier. A process component is also necessary to deal with the variety of mineral or energy products. Finally, the project selection component can be introduced by incorporating investment to augment capacity as well as economies of scale and exports.

An example of the formulation of an MIP model can be drawn from Kendrick and Stoutjesdijk (1980, pp. 50-55). This model attempts to find the minimum discounted cost of meeting specified market requirements over the period covered by the model. This search involves the selection of activity levels for the following variables: (1) increments to capacity, (2) shipments from plants to markets and among plants, (3) imports and exports, and (4) domestic purchases of raw materials, miscellaneous material inputs, and labor. Because of the relative complexity of their MIP model, the following example has been derived according to (1) the objective function, (2) the cost components, and (3) the model constraints. Definitions of the symbols and variables are provided in Table 2.2.

1. Objective Function

This function minimizes the total discounted costs of

Table 2.2

DEFINITION OF VARIABLES

Symbol	Definition
INDEXES	
i	Plant sites (I)[a]
j	Domestic market areas (J)
l	Export market areas (L)
m	Productive units (M)
q	Productive processes (Q)
λ,t	Time intervals and time periods (T)
c	Commodities used or produced in the industry, (Final products of the industry (CF), Intermediate products (CI), and Raw materials, miscellaneous inputs, and labor (CR))
VARIABLES	
Q	Process levels (production levels)
X	Domestic shipments
R	Domestic purchases materials and labor
Y	0-1 investment decisions
H	Continuous investment decisions
$\bar{H}$	Maximum capacity expansion per time period
CK	Capital costs
CR	Recurrent costs
CT	Transportation costs
TC	Total costs
D	Domestic sales
K	Initial capacity
S	Retirements of capacity
W	Market requirements
PARAMETERS	
a	Process inputs (-) or outputs (+)
b	Capacity utilization rate
ρ	Discount rate per time interval
δ	Discount factor
σm	Capital recovery factor for productive unit m
ω	Fixed charge portion of investment costs
υ	Linear portion of investment costs
β	Recurrent costs related to capacity
π	Prices
μ	Unit transportation costs

[a]Total or limit indicated within parenthesis.

production where these costs consist of three cost components: capital costs, recurrent costs, and transport costs.

$$\text{Minimize } TC_t = \sum_{t}^{T} \delta_t (CK_t + CR_t + CT_t) \tag{17}$$

2. Cost Components

2a. The capital cost component equals fixed charges plus the linear portion of capital costs.

$$CK_t = \sum_{\lambda=1}^{t} \sum_{i}^{I} \sum_{m}^{M} \sigma_m (\omega_{mi\lambda} Y_{mi\lambda} + \upsilon_{mi\lambda} H_{mi\lambda}) \tag{18}$$

2b. The recurrent costs equal recurrent costs related to capacity plus local raw materials and labor costs.

$$CR_t = \sum_{\lambda=1}^{t} \sum_{i}^{I} \sum_{m}^{M} \beta_{mi\lambda} H_{mi\lambda} + \sum_{c}^{CR} \sum_{i}^{I} \pi_{cit} R_{cit} \tag{19}$$

Here β represents the portion of recurrent costs that is not proportional to actual production levels but rather is proportional to the capacity installed. Examples are the maintenance costs and insurance payments on any piece of capital equipment.

2c. The transport cost component equals final product shipment costs, plus intermediate shipment costs. Raw materials are assumed to be prices inclusive of domestic transport cost.

$$TC_t = \sum_{c}^{CF} \sum_{i}^{I} \sum_{j}^{J} \mu_{cijt} X_{cijt} + \sum_{c}^{CF} \sum_{i}^{I} \mu_{cii't} X_{cii't} \tag{20}$$

3. Material Balance Constraints

3a. Final Commodity Constraint: The production Q of commodity c by all processes p at plant i must at least equal the shipments X of commodity c from plant i to all markets j. The typical process that provides final commodities can be assigned a coefficient $a_{cpi} = 1.0$ in the final commodities constraint (21), because the unit of capacity can be arbitrarily defined in terms of one of the inputs or outputs.

$$\sum_{q}^{Q} a_{cpi} Q_{pit} \geq \sum_{j}^{J} X_{cijt} \tag{21}$$

3b. Intermediate Commodity Constraint: The output of intermediate commodities at plant i must be greater than or equal to shipments of intermediate commodities from plant i to plant i'.

$$\sum_{q}^{Q} a_{cpi} Q_{pit} \geq \sum_{\substack{i \\ i' \neq i}}^{I} X_{cii't} \tag{22}$$

3c. Raw Materials and Labor Constraint: The production of intermediate and final products requires raw materials and labor. The coefficient a_{cpi} in constraint (23) thus will normally be negative. Purchases of raw material and labor R_{ci}, in turn, will have to be positive for the constraint to hold.

$$\sum_{q}^{Q} a_{cpi} Q_{pi} + R_{ci} \geq 0. \tag{23}$$

4. Capacity Constraints

Capacity required is less than or equal to expansion less capacity retirements

$$\sum_{q}^{Q} b_{mpi} Q_{pit} \leq K_{mi} + \sum_{\substack{\lambda \\ \lambda \leq t}}^{I} (H_{mi\lambda} - S_{mi\lambda}) \tag{24}$$

Here k_{mi} = initial capacity for productive unit m at plant i, parameter b_{mpi} = units of capacity used on productive unit m per unit of output of process p, and $S_{mi\lambda}$ = expected retirement of capacity in productive unit m at plant i in time period λ. The S variables are closed exogenously to the model. For example, if a productive unit manufactures steel, the initial capacity might include a number of open hearth furnaces that were slated for retirement during the period covered by the model. Then $S_{mi\lambda}$ would represent the capacity to be retired in each time period λ. The effect of the summation over λ for λ less than or equal to t in (23) is to permit all capacity installed in previous periods to be available for use in period t.

5. Investment Constraints

Two additional constraints are needed to complete the specification of investment in the model. These two constraints introduce the integer side conditions directly into the model

$Y = 0$ when $H = 0$,

$Y = 1$ when $H > 0$,

which are used in specifying the investment cost function. These constraints are:

$$H_{mit} \geq \bar{H}_{mit} Y_{mit}, \tag{25}$$

$$Y_{mit} = 0 \text{ or } 1, \tag{26}$$

where $\bar{H}_{mit}$ = an upper bound on the size of capacity unit that can be added to productive unit m at plant i in period t.

The effect of (25) and (26) is to prohibit any addition to capacity unless the fixed charge is incurred, and the fixed charge is only incurred if Y_{mit} is equal to 1. From (25) it follows that Y_{mit} must be placed at 1 if H_{mit} is positive for the constraint to hold. If H_{mit} is 0, Y_{mit} will be forced to 0 by the model as the cost minimization objective of the model leads to a preference not to incur the fixed charge.

6. Market Requirements

The summation of shipments from all plants i to each market j must be equal to or greater than the product requirement of market j

$$\sum_{i}^{I} X_{cij} \geq W_{cj} \tag{27}$$

7. Nonnegativity Constraints

$$Y_{cij},\ Q_{pi},\ W_{ci},\ H_{mi},\ R_{ci},\ S_{mi} \geq 0 \tag{28}$$

Applications of this model have mostly taken advantage of the integer constraint to model investment in commodity industries. Important issues that can accordingly be dealt with are the determination of efficient investment patterns, project and program evaluation, economic integration plans, and industry regulations. An example of a comprehensive application of MIP has been that of regional investment and production allocation in the world fertilizer industry, by Choksi et al. (1980). Their principal goal was to determine the optimal locations of fertilizer plants in different countries given mineral and gas feedstock availabilities. Variables optimized in this respect include not only production (by products) and shipments but also domestic demands and exports.

Another application is that of Dammert and Palaniappan (1985) which deals specifically with the world copper market and copper investment planning in Latin America. One interesting aspect of Dammert's approach is its inclusion of reserve levels and reserve limits together with mineral exhaustion. This is accomplished by including the following constraints on processing different ore grades.

$$z_{pit} \leq q_{cpit} \tag{29}$$

This constraint places an upper limit on the annual exploitation of high-grade ores and of second-grade ores where q_{cpit} = annual availability of ore grade c. This constraint can also be extended to include the total reserve limit

$$\sum_{t}^{T} z_{pit} \leq v_{pi} \tag{30}$$

where v_{pi} = total reserves of ore grade in processing area i.

The Brown et al. study (1983) which also involved Dammert, Meeraus and Stoutjesdijk as researchers provided an investment analysis of the aluminum industry similar to that of the copper model. The objective was to minimize overall investment, operating and transporation costs to meet market requirements. The stages of process included involve bauxite and alumina as well as aluminum. Investment decisions are also considered in an integer (0-1) format and depletion of bauxite mine reserves is included. In meeting long run aluminum demand in the year 2000, energy costs play an important role in determining investment location. An equivalent model of the steel industry was constructed by Kendrick, Meerus and Alatorre (1984).

Finally, several of Kendrick's students at the University of Texas have applied MIP to the energy modeling. Models were built analyzing the Gulf Coast refining complex by Langston (1983), the Korean electric power industry by Kwang-Hal (1981), and the Korean petrochemical industry by Jung Suh (1982).

Linear Complementarity Programming

These models can be considered a special class of the spatial and temporal price and allocation model solved above with the QP algorithm. The latter algorithm requires symmetry among the coefficients in the regional market demand and supply function. This symmetry condition is sometimes referred to as the "integrability condition." However, there is no theoretical reason as to why independently estimated final goods demand and/or supply functions for each region have to satisfy this condition. In actual econometric practice, the possibility of occurrence for such a symmetrical relation between each pair of commodities is fairly remote, if not impossible. Of course, linear restrictions on the coefficients could be imposed to preserve symmetry. However, by doing so, an "artificial" instead of a natural spatial equilibrium will be obtained.

To obtain a model solution under conditions of asymmetry, the linear complementarity programming (LCP) approach as previously suggested by Cottle and Dantzig (1968) can be applied. This algorithm frees the spatial equilibrium model from being normative and restrictive and leaves the model as efficient as its QP counterpart. While the LCP model does not maximize net social payoff, that concept is not always important for market optimization. Instead the LCP optimizes revenues or costs consistent with a set of operational rules, the latter of which likely follow the underlying Kuhn-Tucker (1950) conditions. An explanation of the theoretical background to LCP can be found in Takayama and Labys (1986), and in Takayama and Hashimoto (1984).

The more elementary LCP application involves the incorporation of asymmetry in the parameters of the demand equations for the commodity of interest. Most recently, Yang and Labys (1985) have examined the potential of employing linear complementarity programming solutions to modify their STPA model of the Appalachian coal industry to include natural gas. This model represents an extension of their earlier (1980) QP model; only now natural gas as well as coal are studied in the context of the spatial allocation of the Appalachian coal and gas market. The model searches for the optimal trade flows of gas and coal among the major Appalachian supply and Eastern demand regions. Although the model is static providing a solution only for 1980, full simultaneity is obtained in the determination of equilibrium quantities and prices.

The more dramatic application of LCP has been its ability to use investment determination to provide intertemporal linkages. Such an approach has been employed by Hashimoto and Sihsobhon (1981) in their model of the world iron and steel industry (WISE). The major advance of their model over the iron and steel models mentioned earlier was their incorporation of market expectations based on forward information and market dynamics. Their model has been constructed in the form of two different models A and B which make different assumptions about forward expectations. In Model A it is assumed that the steel industry plans and implements investments in production facilities rationally, with perfect foresight. In Model B, the industry is assumed to follow current investment plans. In consideration of a long lead time of investments, it is assumed in Model B, that the industry has a given maximum production capacity in 1985. Projections are then prepared for the following sets of variables: (1) investment in steel production capacities in 1975-1980, 1980-1985, and 1985-1990, (2) prices, demand and supply quantities for steel products and steel production capacities, and (3) the industry's requirements for major raw materials and inputs in 1980, 1985 and 1990. Solutions to the model based on the LCP formulation show that the two different assumptions regarding expectations provide different patterns of cyclicality in industry growth and performance.

Conclusions

In this chapter we have traced the evolution of applications of the spatial and temporal price allocation model to applications in mineral and energy problems. We have also pointed to related modeling developments such as process programming and hybrid model developments such as mixed integer programming. PP, QP, RP, MIP, and LCP models can be looked upon as a natural development of programming commodity models in the sense that the price-quantity relationship in mineral and energy markets is captured in its simplest sense. Each of these programming model developments also has permitted the introduction of greater realism in spatial equilibrium modeling. However, problems do exist in applying these models as do exist for other kinds of quantitative commodity models. Some of the related advantages and disadvantages of the STPA in mineral and energy models can be found in Labys, Field and Clark (1985) and in Labys and Wood (1985). Because many of these advantages and disadvantages are similar to those of applying agricultural models, no further discussion follows here.

Author
Walter C. Labys
Department of Mineral Resource Economics
West Virginia University
Morgantown, WV 26506-6070

Acknowledgment
This chapter appears with reprint permission from the International Regional Science Review, Regional Research Institute, West Virginia University, Morgantown, WV 26506.

References

Abe, A.M., (1973). "Dynamic Micro-Economic Models of Production, Investment and Technological Change in the U.S. and Japanese Iron and Steel Industries," in G.G. Judge and T. Takayama (eds.) Studies in Economic Planning Over Space and Time, Amsterdam: North-Holland Publishing Co., pp. 345-367.

Brown, M., A. Dammert, A. Meeraus and S. Stoutjesdijk, (1983). Worldwide Investment Analysis: The Case of Aluminum, World Bank Staff Working Paper No. 603, Washington, D.C.: The World Bank.

Choksi, A.M., A. Meeraus and A.J. Stoutjesdijk, (1980). The Planning of Investment Programs in the Fertilizer Industry, World Bank Research Publication, Baltimore: Johns Hopkins University Press.

Clark, J. and A. Church, (1981). "Process Analysis Modeling of the Stainless Steel Industry," Paper presented at the National Academy of Sciences Workshop on Non-Fuel Mineral-Demand Modeling. Airlie House, Warrenton, VA.

Copithorne, L.W., (1973). The Use of Linear Programming in the Economic Analysis of a Metal Industry: The Case of Nickel, Monograph, Department of Economics, University of Manitoba.

Cottle, R.W. and G.B. Dantzig, (1968). "Complementary Pivot Theory of Mathematical Programming," in Linear Algebra and Its Applications, New York: American Elsevier Publishing Company, pp. 103-125.

Dammert, A., (1980). "Planning Investments in the Copper Sector in Latin America," in W. Labys, M. Nadiri and J. Nunez del Arco (eds.), Commodity Markets and Latin American Development: A Modeling Approach, New York: National Bureau of Economic Research.

Day, R.H., (1973). "Recursive Programming Models: A Brief Introduction," in G. Judge and T. Takayama (eds.), Studies in Economic Planning Over Space and Time, Amsterdam: North-Holland Publishing Company.

Day, R.H. and J.P. Nelson, (1973). "A Class of Dynamic Models for Describing and Projecting Industrial Development," Journal of Econometrics, 1: 155-190.

Devanney III, J.W. and M.B. Kennedy, (1980). "A Short Run Model of the World Petroleum Network Based on Decomposition," in W.T. Ziemba, S.L. Schwartz and E. Koenigsberg (eds.), Energy Policy Modeling, Boston: Martinus Nijhoff Publishing, pp. 299-307.

Dutton, C.M., (1982). "Modelling the International Steam Coal Trade," Paper No. EDP21, Energy Research Group, Cavendish Laboratory, Cambridge University, England.

Energy Information Administration, (1979). Documentation of the Project Independence Evaluation System, Vols. I-IV, U.S. Department of Energy, Washington, D.C.: U.S. Government Printing Office.

Fox, K.A., (1963). "Spatial Price Equilibrium and Process Analysis in the Food and Agricultural Sector," in A. Manne and H. Markowitz (eds.), Studies in Process Analysis, New York: John Wiley & Sons, pp. 215-234.

Hashimoto, H., (1977). "World Food Projection Models, Projections and Policy Evaluation," Ph.D. Thesis, Department of Economics, University of Illinois.

Hashimoto, H. and T. Sihsobhon, (1981). "A World Iron and Steel Economy Model: The WISE Model," in World Bank Commodity Models, 1: II 1-46 plus three Appendices, Washington, D.C.: The World Bank.

Henderson, J.M., (1958). The Efficiency of the Coal Industry: An Application of Linear Programming, Cambridge: Harvard University Press.

Hibbard, W.R., et al., (1979). "An Engineering Econometric Model of the U.S. Aluminum Industry," Proceedings, New York: American Institute of Mining Engineers.

Hibbard, W.R., A.L. Soyster and R.S. Gates, (1980). "A Disaggregated Supply Model of the U.S. Copper Industry Operating in an Aggregated World Supply/Demand System," Materials and Society, 4: 261-284.

Hogan, W.H. and J.P. Weyant, (1980). "Combined Energy Models," Discussion Paper E80-02, Kennedy School of Government, Harvard University.

Judge, G.G. and T. Takayama (eds.), (1973). Studies in Economic Planning Over Space and Time, Amsterdam: North-Holland Publishing Company.

Jung, S.S., (1982). "An Investment Planning Model for the Refining and Petrochemical Industry in Korea," Ph.D. Thesis, University of Texas at Austin.

Kendrick, D., (1967). Programming Investment in the Process Industries: An Approach to Sectoral Planning, Cambridge: MIT Press.

Kendrick, D. and A. Stoutjesdijk, (1978). The Planning of Industrial Investment Programs, A Methodology, Baltimore: Johns Hopkins University Press.

Kendrick, D., A. Meerus and J. Alatorre, (1984). The Planning of Investment Programs in the Steel Industry, Baltimore: Johns Hopkins University Press.

Kennedy, M., (1974). "An Economic Model of the World Oil Market," Bell Journal of Economics and Management Science, 5: 540-577.

Kolstad, C., D. Abbey and R. Bivins, (1983). "Modeling International Steam Coal Trade," WP No. LA-9661-MS, Los Alamos National Laboratory, New Mexico.

Kovisars, L., (1976). "World Production Consumption and Trade in Zinc - An LP Model," U.S. Bureau of Mines Contract Report J-0166003, Stanford Research Institute, Stanford, CA

Kovisars, L., (1975). "Copper Trade Flow Model," World Minerals Availability, SRI Project MED 3742-74, Stanford Research Institute, Stanford, CA.

Kuhn, N.W. and A.W. Tucker, (1950). "Nonlinear Programming," in J. Neyman (ed.), Proceedings of the Second Berkeley Symposium on Mathematical Statistics and Probability, pp. 481-492.

Kwang, H.K., (1981). "An Investment Programming Model in the Electric Power Industry," Ph.D., Thesis, University of Texas at Austin.

Labys, W.C., (1980). Market Structure, Bargaining Power and Resource Price Formation, Lexington, MA: Heath Lexington Books.

Labys, W.C. and C.W. Yang, (1980). "A Quadratic Programming Model of the Appalachian Steam Coal Market," Energy Economics, 2: 86-95.

Labys, W.C., (1987). Commodity Markets and Models: An International Bibliography, London: Gower Publishing Company.

Labys, W.C., F.R. Field and J. Clark, (1985). "Mineral Modeling," in W. Vogely (ed.), Economics of the Mineral Industry, New York: American Institute of Mining Engineers.

Labys, W.C. and D.O. Wood, (1985). "Energy Modeling," in W. Vogely (ed.), Economics of the Mineral Industry, New York: American Institute of Mining Engineers.

Labys, W.C. and P.K. Pollak, (1984). Commodity Models for Policy Analysis and Forecasting, London: Croom-Helm.

Langston, V.C., (1983). "An Investment Model for the U.S. Gulf Coast Refining Petrochemical Complex," Ph.D. Thesis, University of Texas at Austin.

Lemke, E.C. and J.T. Howson, Jr., (1964). "Equilibrium Points of Bimatrix Games," Journal of Society of Industrial Application of Mathematics, 12: 413-423.

Libbin, J.D. and M.D. Boehji, (1977). "International Structure of the U.S. Coal Industry," American Journal of Agricultural Economics, pp. 456-466.

Manne, A.S. and H.M. Markowitz (eds.), (1963). Studies in Process Analysis, New York: John Wiley & Sons.

Marschak, T.A., (1963). "A Spatial Model of U.S. Petroleum Refining," in A.S. Manne and H.M. Markowitz (eds.), Studies in Process Analysis, New York: John Wiley & Sons.

Murphy, F.H., H.D. Sherali and A.L. Soyster, (1980). "A Mathematical Programming Approach for Determining Oligopolistic Market Equilibrium," Virginia Polytechnic Institute and State University, Blacksburg, VA.

National Academy of Sciences (NAS), (1982). Mineral Demand Modeling. Committee on Nonfuel Mineral Demand Relationships, National Research Council, Washington, D.C.: National Academy Press.

Nelson, J.P., (1970). "An Interregional Recursive Programming Model of the U.S. Iron and Steel Industry: 1947-67," Ph.D. Thesis, University of Wisconsin.

Newcomb, R.T. and J. Fan, (1980). "Coal Market Analysis Issues," EPRI Report EA-1575, Electric Power Research Institute, Palo Alto, CA.

Samuelson, S.W., (1981). "Imperfect Competition and Linear Programming," American Economic Reivew, 42: 283-303.

Scarf, H., (1973). The Computation of Economic Equilibria, New Haven: Yale University Press.

Soyster, A. and H.D. Sherali, (1981). "On the Influence of Market Structure in Modeling and U.S. Copper Industry," International Journal of Management Science, pp. 381-388.

Tabb, W.K., (1968). "A Recursive Programming Model of Resource Allocation in Technological Change in the U.S. Bituminous Coal Industry," Ph.D. Thesis, University of Wisconsin.

Takayama, T., (1979). "An Application of Spatial and Temporal Price Equilibrium Model to World Energy Modeling," Papers of the Regional Science Association, 41: 43-58.

Takayama, T. and H. Hashimoto, (1984). "A Comparative Study of Linear Complementarity Programming Models and Linear Programming Models in Multi-Regional Investment Analysis," EPDCS Division Working Paper No. 1984-1, Washington, D.C.: World Bank.

Takayama, T. and G.G. Judge, (1971). Spatial and Temporal Price and Allocation Models, Amsterdam: North-Holland Publishing Company.

Takayama, T. and W.C. Labys, (1986). "Spatial Equilibrium Analysis: Mathematical and Programming Formulations of Agricultural, Mineral and Energy Models," in P. Nijkamp (ed.), Handbook of Regional Economics, Amsterdam: North-Holland Publishing Comapny.

Uri, N., (1975). Toward An Efficient Allocation of Electric Energy, Lexington, MA: Heath Lexington Books.

Uri, N., (1976). "Planning in Public Utilities," Regional Science and Urban Economics, 6: 105-125.

Uri, N., (1977). "The Impacts of Environmental Regulations on the Allocation and Pricing of Electricity Energy," Journal of Environmental Management, 5: 215-227.

Yang, C.W. and W.C. Labys, (1985). "A Sensitivity Analysis of the Linear Complementarity Programming Model: The Case of Appalachian Steam Coal and Natural Gas Markets," Energy Economics, 7: 145-152.

3 Spatial and temporal price equilibrium agricultural models

ROBERT L. THOMPSON *Purdue University*

Introduction

The most common class of agricultural trade models, particularly for comparative static analysis of the effects of a change in policy, is comprised of the class of spatial and temporal price and allocation models (STPA). The kinds of commodities that these models embody are featured in Table 3.1 The feature that distinguishes these models is that spatial equilibrium models endogenize trade flows and market shares. These models are structured in a manner consistent with spatial equilibrium theory as specified in Chapter 2 above, such that prices are directly linked only between those pairs of regions that actually trade with each other. The data requirements for a spatial price equilibrium model are identical to those for a nonspatial price equilibrium model. Both require internal supply and demand schedules or an export supply or import demand schedule for each trading region, documentation on the levels of all policy variables, exchange rates, and a matrix of transportation costs. The fundamental difference in the way in which these models are utilized concerns the solution technique employed.

Most models of this type have been linear (in demand and supply schedules) and possess solution techniques conforming to the programming methodologies described in Chapter 2. The disadvantage of most linear configurations has been overcome

Table 3.1

PRINCIPAL AGRICULTURAL COMMODITIES

Agricultural Food Products		Agricultural Raw Materials
Beverages:	Oilseeds, Oils, Meals:	Abaca
Cocoa	Copra	Burlap
Coffee	Coconut Oil/Meal	Cotton
Tea	Corn Oil/Meal	Hides and Skins
	Cottonseed Oil/Meal	Jute
Cereals:	Fish Oil/Meal	Linseed Oil
Barley	Groundnut Oil/Meal	Rubber
Maize	Palm Kernel Oil/Meal	Sisal
Oats	Palm Oil/Meal	Timber
Rye	Rapeseed Oil	Tung Oil
Sorghum	Soybean Oil/Meal	Wool
Wheat	Sunflower Oil	
Fruits:	Vegetables:	
Apples	Manioc	
Bananas	Onions	
Dates	Peppers	
Grapes	Potatoes	
Grapefruit	Tomatoes	
Lemons		
Olives	Others:	
Oranges	Hops	
Pineapples	Nuts	
	Rice	
Meats:	Spices	
Beef	Sugar	
Lamb	Tobacco	
Pork	Wine	
Poultry		

by separable programming, Bender's decomposition, and nonlinear algorithms. The spatial equilibrium technique, nevertheless, mathematically cannot replicate all the observed trade flows. Reasons why more trade flows occur than that predicted by spatial equilibrium theory include: (1) the product may not be perfectly homogeneous, but may be differentiated by country of origin, (2) harvests occur six months out of phase in the Northern and Southern Hemispheres, (3) some countries impose quota restrictions on trade flows, and (4) importers may diversify their purchases among several suppliers to spread risk. Nevertheless, work on these models has contributed to carrying out policy analysis and to testing spatial equilibrium theory.

Historical Background

Most spatial price equilibrium models dealing with trade between regions have been formulated with linear export supply and import demand schedules for the trading regions included and have been solved using the quadratic programming formulation developed by Takayama and Judge (1964) and defined in Chapter 2. To summarize briefly, maximization of the area under all excess demand curves minus the area under all excess supply curves minus total transport costs drives such a model to a competitive (spatial) equilibrium solution. Takayama and Judge's contribution was to show that this involves maximization of a quadratic objective function subject to a set of linear constraints; that is, it is a standard quadratic programming problem (QP). Bawden (1966) and Takayama (1967) have shown how this general spatial model could be modified to introduce trade policies to make it useful for international trade applications.

The early empirical QP spatial price equilibrium models of world agricultural markets were developed by graduate students of Bawden at the University of Wisconsin in the mid-1960s, including Schmitz (1968) on wheat, Bjarnason (1967) and Chung (1972) on feedgrains, and McGarry (1968) on beef. Two earlier spatial equilibrium trade models were built at the University of California at Davis and solved by an iterative market simulation procedure to approximate a spatial equilibrium solution, i.e. see studies by Dean and Collins (1967) and by Zusman, Melamed, and Katzer (1969) on the world orange trade. A number of other applications of the QP technique have followed. These include (1) Shei and Thompson (1977) on wheat, (2) Emerson (1972), Thompson (1973) and Janjaroen (1979) on corn, (3) Mack (1973) on beef, Margin and Zwart (1975) on pork, (4) Bates and Schmitz (1969) and Edelman and Gardiner (1979) on sugar, (5) Furtan, Nagy and Storey (1979) on rapeseed, and (6) Fernandez- Cavada (1979) on oranges. Construction of this simple static equilibrium, one-commodity form of spatial price equilibrium model for trade policy analysis has been routinized by development of an input form, matrix generator, and report writer package at Purdue University by Apland, McCarl, Thompson, and Santini (1982).

Several modifications of the basic single-priced, static equilibrium QP modeling approach were made in the 1970s. Takayama and Liu (1975) constructed a world wheat trade model that not only optimized across space but also simultaneously through time to analyze alternative reserve stocks proposals. In Pieri, Meilke and MacAulay's (1977) pork trade model, supply was made a function of lagged prices and the model was solved recursively through time. At the University of Illinois, Takayama and several graduate students developed the first multiple-commodity QP agricultural trade model, i.e., see Takayama and Hashimoto (1976). Hashimoto's (1977) multicommodity two-region model was the first phase of this project. Nguyen's (1977) thesis developed the eight-commodity, 20-region version of the model, while Whitacre and Schmidt's (1980) model included nine commodities and 5 regions. These studies reflect the most advanced state of QP agricultural trade modeling technique to date.

Not all spatial price equilibrium models have been cast in a quadratic programming framework. Moore, Elassar, and Lessley (1972) cast the grain and beef trade problem as a classical transportation problem of minimizing transport costs, with fixed export and import quantities. Blakeslee, Heady, and Framingham (1973) built a linear programming model of world trade in grains, fertilizer, and phosphate rock. The model was constructed to minimize the cost of obtaining and, in the case of fertilizer, expanding the capacity to produce the commodities required to satisfy projected "requirements" for grains, nitrogen, phosphate and potash fertilizers, and phosphate rock. In Radhi's (1979) model of the world nitrogen fertilizer industry, which included international trade in feedstock, ammonia, and urea, nonlinear fertilizer demand schedules were specified. The model was formulated in the same manner as a QP trade model. It was solved, however, as a separable programming problem, using a linear programming code with grid linearization of the demand schedules, following Duloy and Norton (1975).

Two studies specified in a similar manner to the QP trade models were instead solved by reactive programming, i.e., see King and Ho (1972). These were (1) Jellema's (1972) model of trade in peanuts, peanut oil, and peanut meal, and (2) Gemmil's (1977) 76-region world sugar trade model.

The area of most recent advances in this class of trade models has been the development of the capability for solving nonlinear spatial equilibrium models. Warner (1979) has estimated a 33-region nonlinear model of world wheat economy and solved it using MacKinnon's (1976) spatial price equilibrium problem by use of a fixed-point algorithm, i.e., see MacKinnon. Similarly, Holland and Pratt (1980) have developed an iterative, nonlinear spatial equilibrium solution algorithm, which is also being applied to world wheat trade.

Model Advantages and Disadvantages

Quadratic programming has become the most common procedure for solving spatial price equilibrium models of agricultural trade. The procedure is so well established that its use has become routinized, and efficient computer codes for solving QP problems are readily available. One advantage of this approach to solving trade models over those surveyed above is the facility with which policies can be introduced. Tariff barriers are introduced in basically the same manner as in the nonspatial price equilibrium models. However, quantitative restrictions to trade are introduced directly as linear inequality constraints in the constraint set of the QP problem. This is significantly easier than introducing quantitative restrictions with "if" statements in iterative solution techniques for systems of nonlinear equations. So, even if one is not interested in trade flows per se, this flexibility provides one argument for using QP to solve any linear trade model that is not too large.

One severe limitation of the QP formulation is the fact that the export supply and import demand schedules have to be linear. As argued above, there is considerable evidence of nonlinearities in agricultural markets, particularly in the demand for stocks of commodities. One alternative is to use time-varying parameters in the linear equations in the QP formulation. Nevertheless, the separable programming approach taken by Radhi, and particularly the new algorithms for solving nonlinear spatial equilibrium problems of Warner (1976) and Holland and Pratt (1980) provide alternatives to QP with less restrictive assumptions. This appears to be one promising direction for future work to move. Use of the separable programming approach has the advantage that much larger models can be solved than most QP codes can economically handle. Polito, McCarl and Morin (1980) have shown that Benders decomposition theorem can be applied to break large nonlinear models down into a small nonlinear programming model and a large linear programming model. The two can be solved iteratively at a much lower cost than by solving a larger model using nonlinear programming.

Reactive programming as developed by King and Ho also appears to be an efficient technique for solving larger spatial equilibrium problems than most QP codes can economically handle. This was demonstrated by the ease with which Gemmil solved a 76-region world sugar trade model. A model of this size would have taxed the capacity of most available QP algorithms and would have been much more expensive to solve by that means.

One of the principal arguments for use of the spatial over the non-spatial price equilibrium formulation was that spatial equilibrium models generate trade flows and market shares, variables that are of interest to some users of the models. However, this turns out to be a questionable advantage. Spatial equilibrium models do not explain real world trade flows adequately. Using 1963-65 trade models, Teigen (1977) found correlations between the trade flows in solution and the observed data of 0.89 for rice, 0.79 for course grains, and 0.41 for wheat. Any model that explained more than 50 percent of observed trade flows was judged as "adequate," and only the wheat model was rejected on this criterion. It seems, however, that most potential users of such models desire greater reliability than this.

While spatial equilibrium models do generate trade flows in solution, in Chapter 2 it has been shown that the maximum number permitted in the basic solution is one less than the number of restrictions (rows) in the model. Unless quantitative restrictions (quotas or bilateral agreements) are introduced, there is one row for each exporting country and one row for each importing country. Therefore, in the basic solution of the model, the number of trade flows cannot exceed one less than the total number of exporting (n) plus importing (m) countries (or regions) in the model, i.e., n + m -1, out of a possible n · m flows. In the real world, most exporters ship a certain quantity each year to each importer, although in practice many of the shipments are quite small. In a perfectly competitive spatial economy, one should expect, in effect, a basic soltuion to be generated. Any trade flows in excess of this represent departures from the global welfare maximizing spatial allocation of resources, and their existence should lead the analyst to seek alternative explanations for why they should exist.

A number of hypotheses could be advanced to account for these departures, all of which concern invalid assumptions made in the spatial equilibrium formulation. For example, the product may not be perfectly homogeneous. There are many varieties of wheat, each with different principle uses, and they are not perfect substitutes for one another. Moreover, importing countries may differentiate among countries of origin on historical or political grounds. The crop is harvested out of phase in the Northern and Southern Hemispheres, and some trade flows may represent purely seasonal phenomena.

The spatial equilibrium model assumes perfect certainty, yet the real world is characterized by uncertainty associated with variability in weather conditions and in turn crop yields. In addition, export embargoes may cause importers to view the availability of supply as uncertain and therefore to diversify sources of supply by buying from multiple exporters. Such risk-averse behaviour could be reflected in trade models in the same manner as it has been introduced into agricultural sector models, following Hazell and Scandizzo (1974). This would permit more trade flows to enter the model solution. There are no known attempts to apply this procedure in trade modeling to date.

There do exist trade policies in the form of quantitative restrictions. Each such restriction added to the model brings one more trade flow into the basic solution. Nevertheless, the fact remains that without a large number of such restrictions, spatial equilibrium models generally do not do very well at accomplishing one of their most favorable properties: their ability to account for trade flows. This casts doubt on the justification for using a spatial equilibrium formulation when trade flows are of particular interest.

One advantage of the spatial equilibrium formulation of an agricultural trade model is that it is an efficient means of examining the effects of changes in transport costs on the net trade positions of the trading regions. Nevertheless, because trade flows in the solution are very sensitive to small changes in transport costs (as well as to policy variables), one must interpret the predicted effects on trade flows with caution.

Such doubts with respect to the spatial price equilibrium approach have raised a number of questions concerning its adequacy for purposes of policy analysis. Nevertheless, the work represents an extensive test of received spatial equilibrium theory and finds that weaknesses exist in the ability of this theory to fully explain observed agricultural trade. The reasons why such weaknesses may not explain observed trade flows well is that the assumptions underlying spatial equilibrium theory may not always be consistent with the reality of agricultural trade. It is in this area that recent agricultural trade research of all kinds has made the greatest contributions to testing theory.

Some users of trade policy analyses need information on the time paths of adjustment of supply, disappearance, and price. The modeling work to date has provided little in this direction. Takayama and Liu's dynamic world wheat trade model optimized trade simultaneously across regions and through several years by including storage costs as the cost of "moving" wheat from one year to the next. While expensive, due to the large size of the problem, this provided a useful way of studying the optimum reserve stocks issue. A much cheaper and more manageable approach to making a static spatial equilibrium model dynamic is to express current supply as a function of lagged prices and solve the model recursively through time. The only example of this found in the agricultural trade modeling literature is Pieri, Meilke, and MacAulay's (1977) world pork trade model. This is a very straightforward procedure and could make many static, spatial price equilibrium models much more useful for many policy analysis questions.

Another problem with the spatial equilibrium trade models is their assumption that all trading countries behave perfectly competitively. In the world grains market, however, several countries have export marketing boards which exercise a monopoly-like role in export sales. The centrally planned economies and several other countries have import monopolies. The European Community utilizes a variable levy, which according to Carter and Schmitz (1979) in effect, cartelizes its import firms. The grain exports of the United States are largely in the hands of four firms. McCalla (1969) accordingly has argued that the world wheat market behaves like a duopoly; Alaouze, Watson, and Sturgess (1978) as well as Paarlberg and Abbot (1986) suggest a triopoly.

This research implies that the perfectly competitive market assumption of the spatial price equilibrium formulation may not adequately approximate the behaviour of the market intermediaries who transact the world's grain trade.

It is not difficult to alter the objective function of a quadratic programming problem to make every region trade on its marginal import cost or marginal export revenue schedule instead of its export supply or import demand schedule. This approach, however, inadequately reflects the differences in market structure among trading regions. It would be difficult to build in reaction functions that reflect the changes in either the market behaviour or the policy of various regions in response to actions taken by other regions. Market structure is assumed to be competitive, and market behaviour is assumed to be fully described by the export supply and import demand schedules, with exogenously given policies (both tariff and nontariff) and transport costs. The latter are taken as given data by the model, which cannot be altered endogenously in the course of solution for a given year. This represents another disadvantage of the spatial relative to the nonspatial equilibrium formulation.

While many shortcomings of the spatial price equilibrium approach have been outlined above, the greatest deficiencies found in most of the studies surveyed were in empirical content. The deficiencies can be categorized in four areas: (1) data deficiencies, (2) specification error, (3) simultaneous equations bias, and (4) validation. Since the data requirements of a spatial price equilibrium model are the same as those needed for a nonspatial price equilibrium model, the arguments presented above apply here as well and will not be repeated.

The only additional point to be added here with respect to data is that a matrix of transportation costs is a key input into a spatial price equilibrium model. Reliable data on freight rates are, nevertheless, quite difficult to find. Most studies have taken a cavalier attitude toward the importance of these data and have employed very crude approximations. Many assume a constant freight rate per ton-mile on all routes and base their rates solely on distance between ports. Harrer and Binkley (1979) have demonstrated that this assumption is not supported by the data. Other studies have applied an "inflation factor" to a matrix of freight rates used in some previous study. The most commonly cited source is a table of rates for 1964-66 published in Rojko, Urban, and Naive (1971). The problem here is that freight rates have not risen at a uniform rate on all trade routes. Harrer and Binkley thus have recomputed annual average rates for the principal grain trade routes for 1972-76 based on primary data. These are the most recent conveniently available data on freight rates known.

The second empirical problem with most spatial equilibrium models is specification error. Most all of the models surveyed are partial equilibrium models that treat only one commodity in isolation from all others. Most of the models surveyed contained linear export supply and import demand equations for the respective trading regions. A few models included domestic supply and demand equations and derived exports or imports as a residual. It is most common to specify and estimate the export supply quantity or import demand quantity as a function of only its own price. All other arguments of the domestic supply and demand schedules, including all relevant cross-price effects, are usually omitted. As described previously, Paarlberg and Thompson (1980) have demonstrated analytically that even the sign of the effect of a change in trade policy is indeterminate, when there is more than one commodity related in supply and demand. The net effect depends on the relative size of the cross-price terms in the supply and demand equations. This means that omission of related commodities from the model can lead to erroneous policy analysis.

Specification errors can also bias the estimate of the own price parameter and thereby also contribute to erroneous policy analysis. A related problem concerns the failure to include a domestic stock demand equation in almost all of the models surveyed. Without this, a model cannot hope to account for observed price variation. Nevertheless, as described above, a stock demand schedule that is linear also cannot hope to be completely successful at this for moves very far away from the observed price.

The export supply and import demand schedules in most spatial equilibrium models were estimated by ordinary least squares regression procedures (OLS), with quantity a function of only the own price. This procedure is almost certain to produce biased estimates of the price coefficient due to a combination of specification error and simultaneous equations bias from using OLS. The price coefficients are the key parameters in determining the adjustments in response to any shock, such as a policy change. Therefore, if the estimates of the price coefficients are biased, the usefulness of a given model for policy analysis or for any other purpose is highly doubtful. Where the price coefficients or any other parameter estimates in a model are in doubt, sensitivity analysis should be carried out. Such problems with the quality of the empirical content have also limited the contribution that these studies have made to understanding the interrelations among trading countries.

Finally, and closely related to the last point, validation exercises have been neglected in most of the spatial price equilibrium models in the literature. In static equilibrium formulations, some measure of the goodness of fit of the overall model should be calculated, such as the mean absolute deviation or mean squared error of the solution trade flows from the observed based period flows. Alternatively, a Chi-square test could be employed between the observed and predicted trade flow values for the base year of the model. If the model is specified such that it can be run recursively through time, as explained in Chapter 2, the same validation tests, such as the Theil-U statistic, could be applied to the model. In practice, the only difference between the use of this technique for econometric models of world commodity markets and spatial equilibrium models of the same market should be the solution procedure; this should not affect the choice of validation criteria.

The only thoroughly validated spatial equilibrium model found in the literature was Pieri, Meilke, and MacAulay's (1977) Pacific Basin pork market model. That model was solved recursively through the sample time period of the data, and three test statistics for model validation through time were estimated and reported. A similar procedure would be desirable for all spatial equilibrium models, particularly extending the validation tests to some future period of model solution.

Conclusions

The STPA formulation has been one of the most popular approaches to agricultural trade modeling, particularly for purposes of policy analysis. This approach has the apparent advantage of providing information on trade flows and of providing an easy means of introducing nontariff barriers, which are particularly prevalent in agricultural trade. As suggested, however, this approach has problems in explaining observed trade flows well, and nontariff barriers have to be introduced into iterative procedures in order to solve systems of nonlinear equations. As a result, two of the principal justifications for using this approach are undercut. These limitations are reinforced by the fact that most model algorithms except the more recently developed nonlinear spatial equilibrium algorithms have required linear export supply and import demand schedules. This linearity requirement has been a limiting factor in solving QP models, although it no longer is as important. Future work should seriously consider using nonlinear algorithms for model solutions.

The accumulated spatial equilibrium modeling work has extensively tested spatial equilibrium theory and identified a number of its shortcomings. For these reasons, this class of trade models has probably contributed more in terms of confronting a body of theory with data than most other approaches. But the research to date has not lived up to its potential of being able to understand the structure of world commodity markets and the interrelations among the trading regions, mainly because of the weaknesses in the empirical content of the supporting specifications. Much greater attention should be paid in future work to data problems, correct model specification, choice of an appropriate estimator, and model validation. Where problems are unavoidable, sensitivity analysis such as those suggested by Yang and Labys (1982) should be carried out and reported.

Author
Robert L. Thompson
School of Agriculture
Purdue University
Lafayette, IN 47907

References

Alaouze, C.M., A.S. Watson and N.H. Sturgess, (1978). "Oligopoly Pricing in the World Wheat Market," American Journal of Agricultural Economics, 60: 173-185.

Apland, J.D., McCarl, B.A., Thompson, R.L. and J. Santini, (1982). "A Computer Package for Analysis of International Trade in a Single Commodity," Agricultural Experiment Station Bulletin, Purdue University, West Lafayette.

Bates, T.H. and A. Schmitz, (1969). "A Spatial Equilibrium Analysis of the World Sugar Economy," Giannini Foundation Monograph No. 23, University of California at Berkeley.

Bawden, D.L., (1966). "A Spatial Equilibrium Model of International Trade," Journal of Farm Economics, 48: 862-874.

Binkley, J.K. and B. Harrer, (1981). "Major Determinants of Ocean Freight Rates for Grain: An Econometric Analysis," American Journal of Agricultural Economics, 63: 47-57.

Bjarnason, H.F., (1967). "An Economic Analysis of 1980 International Trade in Feed Grains," Ph.D. Thesis, University of Wisconsin, Madison.

Blakeslee, L.L., E.O. Heady and C.F. Framingham, (1973). World Food Production, Demand and Trade, Ames, IA: Iowa State University Press.

Carter, C. and A. Schmitz, (1979). "Import Tariffs and Price Formation in the World Wheat Market," American Journal of Agricultural Economics, 61: 517-522.

Chung, C.H., (1972). "Interregional and International Economic Analysis of the World Feed Grain Economy in 1980 with Emphasis on the U.S. North Central Region," Ph.D. Thesis, University of Wisconsin, Madison.

Dean, G.W. and N.R. Collins, (1967). "World Trade in Fresh Oranges: An Analysis of the Effects of European Economic Community Tariff Policies," Giannini Foundation Monograph No. 18, University of California at Davis.

Duloy, J.H., R.D. Norton, (1975). "Prices and Incomes in Linear Programming Models," American Journal of Agricultural Economics, 57: 591-600.

Edelman, M.A. and W.H. Gardiner, (1979). "Economic Effects of Selected Trade Restrictions on World Sugar Trade," Paper presented at Annual Meeting on the American Agricultural Economics Association, Washington State University, Pullman.

Emerson, P.M., (1972). "An Economic Analysis of World Corn Trade," Ph.D. Thesis, Purdue University, West Lafayette.

Fernandez-Cavada, J.L., (1979). "International Trade in Fresh Oranges and Tangerines: Analysis of Potential Structural Changes Including EC Expansion," Ph.D. Thesis, University of California at Davis.

Furtan, W.H., J.G. Nagy and G.G. Storey, (1979). "The Impact on the Canadian Rapeseed Industry from Changes in Transport and Tariff Rates," American Journal of Agricultural Economics, 61: 238-248.

Gemmil, G.T., (1977). "An Equilibrium Analysis of U.S. Sugar Policy," American Journal of Agricultural Economics, 59: 609-618.

Harrer, B. and J. Binkley, (1979). "International Transport Rates for Grain and Their Determinants," Station Bulletin No. 264, Agricultural Experiment Station, Purdue University, West Lafayette.

Hashimoto, H., (1977). "World Food Projections Models, Projections and Policy Evaluation," Ph.D. Thesis, University of Illinois at Urbana.

Hazell, P.B.R. and P.L. Scandizzo, (1974. "Competitive Demand Structures Under Risk in Agricultural Linear Programming Models," American Journal of Agricultural Economics, 56: 235-244.

Holland, F.D. and J.E. Pratt, (1980). "MESS: A FORTRAN Program for Numerical Solution of Single Commodity Multi-Market Equilibrium Problems with Nonlinear Supply and Demand Functions and Flow Distortions," Agricultural Experiment Station Bulletin No. 296, Purdue University, West Lafayette..

Janjaroen, S., (1979). "An Economic Analysis of Recent Developments in Pacific Basin Corn Trade," Ph.D. Thesis, Purdue University, West Lafayette.

Jellema, B.M., (1972). "Analysis of the World Market for Groundnuts and Groundnut Products," Ph.D. Thesis, North Carolina State University at Raleigh.

King, R.A. and F.S. Ho, (1972). "Reactive Programming, A Market Simulating Spatial Equilibrium Algorithm," Economic Research Report No. 21, North Carolina State University at Raleigh.

Mack, F.G., (1973). "The Impact of Transfer Cost and Trade Policies on International Trade in Beef, 1967-1980," Ph.D Thesis, Texas A & M University, College Station.

MacKinnon, J.G., (1976). "A Technique for the Solution of Spatial Equilibrium Models," Journal of Regional Science, 16: 293-308.

Martin, L. and A.C. Zwart, (1975). "A Spatial and Temporal Model of the North American Pork Sector for the Evaluation of Policy Alternatives," American Journal of Agricultural Economics, 57: 55-66.

McCalla, A., (1966). "A Duopoly Model of World Wheat Pricing," Journal of Farm Economics, 48: 711-727.

Moore, R., S. Elassar and B.V. Lessley, (1972). "Least-Cost World Trade Patterns for Grains and Meats," Agricultural Experiment Station Miscellaneous Publication No. 796, University of Maryland, College Park.

Nguyen, H.D., (1977). "World Food Projection Models and Short-Run World Trade and Reserve Policy Evaluations," Ph.D. Thesis, University of Illinois at Urbana.

Paarlberg, P.L. and P.C. Abbot, (1986). "Oligopolistic Behaviour by Public Agencies in International Trade," American Journal of Agricultural Economics, 68: 528-542.

Paarlberg, P.L. and R.L. Thompson, (1980). "Interrelated Products and the Impact of an Import Tariff," Agricultural Economics Research, 32: 21-32.

Pieri, R.G., K.D. Meilke and T.G. MacAulay, (1977). "North American-Japanese Pork Trade: An Application of Quadratic Programming," Canadian Journal of Agricultural Economics, 25: 61-79.

Polito, J., B.A. McCarl and T.L. Morin, (1980). "Solution of Spatial Equilibrium Problems with Bender's Decomposition," Management Science, 26: 593-605.

Radhi, A.M., (1979). "An Economic Model of the World Nitrogen Fertilizer Market," Ph.D. Thesis, Purdue University, West Lafayette.

Rojko, A.S., F.S. Urban and J.J. Naive, (1971). World Demand Prospects for Grains in 1980 with Emphasis on Trade of Less Developed Countries, FAER-75, Economic Research Service, U.S. Department of Agriculture, Washington, D.C.

Samuelson, P.A., (1952). "Spatial Price Equilibrium and Linear Programming," American Economic Review 42: 283-303.

Schmitz, A., (1968). "An Economic Analysis of the World Wheat Economy in 1980," Ph.D. Thesis, University of Wisconsin, Madison.

Shei, S-Y. and R.L. Thompson, (1977). "The Impact of Trade Restrictions on Price Stability in the World Wheat Market," American Journal of Agricultural Economics, 59: 628-638.

Takayama, T., (1967). "International Trade and Mathematical Programming," Australian Journal of Agricultural Economics, 11: 36-48.

Takayama, T. and H. Hashimoto, (1976). "Dynamic Market-Oriented World Food Projection and Planning Models and Their Empirical Results for the 1970-1974 World Food Situation," World Food Projection Project Report No. 2, Department of Agricultural Economics, University of Illinois, Urbana.

Takayama, T. and H. Hashimoto, (1976). "World Food Projection Models: 1973-74, Policy Evaluations," Illinois Agricultural Economics, 16: 1-8.

Takayama, T and G.G. Judge, (1964). "Equilibrium Among Spatially Separated Markets: A Reformulation," Econometrica 32: 510-524.

Takayama, T. and G.G. Judge, (1971). Spatial and Temporal Price and Allocation Models, Amsterdam: North-Holland.

Takayama, T. and C.L. Liu, (1975). "Projections of International Trade in Farm Products I: Wheat," Illinois Agricultural Economics, 15: 1-7.

Teigen, L.D., (1977). "Testing a Theoretical Model for World Trade Shares," Agricultural Economics Research, 29: 56-59.

Thompson, R.L., (1978). "The Potential Effects of Expanded Corn Exports from Brazil," State Bulletin No. 207, Agricultural Experiment Station, Purdue University, West Lafayette.

Warner, D.L., (1979). "An Econometric Model of the World Wheat Economy," Ph.D. Thesis, Princeton University.

Whitacre, R.C. and S.C. Schmidt, (1980). "Analysis of a World Grain Reserve Plan Under a New International Wheat Agreement," North Central Journal of Agricultural Economics 2: 83-94.

Yang. C.W. and W.C. Labys (1982). "A Sensitivity Analysis of the Stability Property of the QP Commodity Model," Empirical Economics, 7: 93-107.

Zusman, P., A. Melamed and I. Katzer, (1969). "Possible Trade and Welfare Effects of EEC Tariff and Reference Price Policy on the European-Mediterranean Market for Winter Oranges," Giannini Foundation Monograph No. 24, University of California at Berkeley.

PART II
MINERAL AND ENERGY MODELS

4 A sensitivity analysis of the linear complementarity programming model: Appalachian steam coal and natural gas

CHIN-WEI YANG *Clarion University of Pennsylvania*
WALTER C. LABYS *West Viginia University*

Introduction

Central to most spatial equilibrium analysis is a model that optimizes some objective function subject to a system of constraints. However, the treatment of given demand and supply conditions in this class of models has been inadequate, in spite of the effort by Say (1963) in which he restricted the activity levels by the upper and lower bounds in a recursive manner. Despite the quadratic programming (QP) formulation of this model by Takayama and Judge (1964) a major problem still rests in that the model lacks the capability to handle the multi-commodity non-symmetric cross-regression coefficients effectively. In this paper, we overcome the non-symmetry problem by employing Lemke's linear complementarity programming (LCP) Method (Tomlin, 1976). Readers are referred to Cottle, etc. (1979, 1980) for the LCP solution algorithm. Note that Takayama (1971, 1978) first formulated the spatial equilibrium problem in the LCP format and solved a sample problem. However, any practical application was lacking despite the effort by Kennedy (1974). (His use of a symmetric coefficient matrix yielded a standard positive-definite programming problem.)

A Formulation of the LCP Model of the Appalachian Coal-Gas Market

The standard quadratic programming approach suffers a deficiency as a result of the requirement on the symmetry of the regression coefficients. In practical econometric analysis the chance for such a symmetrical relation between each pair of commodities to occur is, to say the least, very remote if not impossible. Of course, linear constraints on the coefficients could be imposed to preserve such a symmetrical property. However, by doing so, an "artificial" instead of a natural spatial equilibrium will be obtained. Note that the LCP model does not maximize the net social payoffs since it basically solves a system of linear inequalities which may be consistent with the Kuhn-Tucker conditions in the standard quadratic programming problem.

The formulation of the present LCP model starts with a set of demand and supply equations of coal and natural gas in linear form as follows:

$$Pd_j^c = a_j^c + b_j^{cc} \; y_j^c + b_j^{cg} \; y_j^g \qquad j = 1, \ldots 7 \qquad (1)$$

$$Pd_j^g = a_j^g + b_j^{gg} \; y_j^g + b_j^{gc} \; y_j^c \qquad (2)$$

$$Ps_i^c = e_i^c + f_i^{cc} \; x_i^c + f_i^{cg} \; x_i^g \qquad i = 1, \ldots 7 \qquad (3)$$

$$Ps_i^g = e_i^g + f_i^{gg} \; x_i^g + f_i^{gc} \; x_i^c \qquad (4)$$

where the superscript g and c denote gas and coal respectively; the subscripts i and j denote supply region i and demand region j; y and x denote consumption and production; and Pd and Ps denote the demand price and the supply price, respectively. For instance, Ps_i^c (supply price of coal in region i) is a linear function of x_i^c (quantity supplied of coal in region i) and x_i^g (quantity supplied of natural gas in region i).

The basic LCP model seeks a nonnegative solution for X, Y, Z, λ, γ subject to the following equilibrium conditions:

$$\gamma \leq Ps\,(X) \qquad (5a) \qquad X^T\,(Ps(X) - \gamma) = 0 \qquad (5b)$$

$$\lambda \geq Pd\,(Y) \qquad (6a) \qquad Y^T\,(\lambda - Pd(Y)) = 0 \qquad (6b)$$

$$G^T\,\binom{\lambda}{\gamma} - T \leq 0 \qquad (7a) \qquad \left(G^T\,\binom{\lambda}{\gamma} - T\right)^T Z = 0 \qquad (7b)$$

$$G^{Z} - \binom{Y}{-X} \geq 0 \qquad (8a) \qquad \left(GZ - \binom{Y}{-X}\right)^{T} \binom{\lambda}{\gamma} = 0 \qquad (8b)$$

where $X \epsilon R^{m.k}$, $Y \epsilon R^{n.k}$, $\gamma \epsilon R^{m.k}$, $\lambda \epsilon R^{n.k}$

$Z \epsilon R^{mn.k}$, $T \epsilon R^{mn.k}$, $G \epsilon R^{k(m+n) X kmn}$

Ps(X) and Pd(Y) are column vectors in $R^{m.k}$ and $R^{n.k}$ denote observed supply and demand prices; m and n denote the number of supply and demand regions, and k denotes the number of commodities. Superscript T denotes the conventional transpose.

With m = 7, n = 7 and k = 2 in our model, the LCP problem takes the following form:

Find X, Y, Z, λ, γ and w such that:

$$w = u + VI \qquad (9)$$

$$w^{T} I = 0 \qquad (10)$$

$$I \geq 0 \text{ and } w \geq 0 \qquad (11)$$

where

$$u = \begin{bmatrix} 0 \\ a_j^k \\ -e_i^k \\ -t_{ij}^k \\ \\ \end{bmatrix} \epsilon R^{154} \qquad 1 = \begin{bmatrix} \lambda_j^k \\ \gamma_i^k \\ y_j^k \\ x_i^k \\ z_{ij}^k \end{bmatrix} \epsilon R^{154} \qquad V = \begin{bmatrix} 0 & H \\ -H^{T} & Q \end{bmatrix} \epsilon R^{154 x 154}$$

$H \epsilon R^{28 x 126}$, $Q \epsilon R^{126 x 126}$, $0 \epsilon R^{28 x 28}$

In addition $w \epsilon R^{154}$ is a slack vector and matrix Q consists of slope coefficients (own and cross) of 28 regression equations.

Description of the Data

Note that signs of the own regression coefficients $b_j^{cc} < 0$, $b_j^{cc} < 0$, $f_i^{cc} > 0$, and $f_i^{gg} > 0$ are actually observed in the estimated regression equations reported in Table 4.1. However, signs of cross-regression coefficients b_j^{gg}, b_j^{cc},

Table 4.1

ESTIMATED REGRESSION COEFFICIENTS

Price Variables	Adjusted Intercept (t value)	Own Regression Coefficient (t value)	Cross Regression Coefficient (t value)	Sample Size	Adjusted R^2
Pd_1^c	50 (1.400)	-1.793 (-2.758)	0.159 (0.124)	10	0.870
Pd_2^c	67.92 (1.591)	-0.511 (-1.931)	0.165 (1.754)	10	0.910
Pd_3^c	60.132 (20.632)	-0.169 (14.953)	-0.136 (-4.212)	5	0.988
Pd_4^c	37.931 (1.183)	-0.349 (-0.818)	0.073 (1.828)	10	0.234
Pd_5^c	61.21 (6.599)	-0.107 (-2.217)	-0.089 (-1.507)	10	0.956
Pd_6^c	52.172 (2.292)	-0.137 (-1.369)	-0.051 (-0.193)	5	0.606
Pd_7^c	76.735 (1.752)	-0.786 (-1.298)	0.193 (0.455)	5	0.708
Pd_1^g	153.045 (19.035)	-2.164 (-5.405)	-0.543 (-2.667)	10	0.982
Pd_2^g	100.78 (2.263)	-0.3 (-2.155)	0.120 (0.305)	10	0.700
Pd_3^g	71.897 (5.631)	-0.113 (-1.109)	-0.007 (-0.121)	10	0.564
Pd_4^g	106.059 (5.616)	-0.353 (-4.121)	0.288 (2.079)	10	0.914
Pd_5^g	101.232 (6.560)	-0.208 (-1.614)	-0.082 (-0.779)	10	0.871
Pd_6^g	67.238 (3.435)	-0.382 (-1.768)	0.222 (1.707)	10	0.859
Pd_7^g	76.998 (6.669)	-0.238 (-1.506)	0.072 (0.659)	10	0.851
Ps_1^c	11.629 (0.293)	0.152 (2.312)	0	5	0.506
Ps_2^c	6.001 (3.771)	0.235 (2.749)	0.07 (0.084)	5	0.994
Ps_3^c	18.312 (0.896)	0.091 (0.928)	0	10	0.383
Ps_4^c	8.213 (1.05)	0.391 (1.552)	0.016 (0.001)	6	0.808

Table 4.1 (cont'd)

Price Variables	Adjusted Intercept (t value)	Own Regression Coefficient (t value)	Cross Regression Coefficient (t value)	Sample Size	Adjusted R^2
Ps_5^c	12.327 (0.450)	0.071 (2.781)	-0.065 (-0.047)	10	0.460
Ps_6^c	27.37 (1.339)	0.234 (0.960)	0	5	0.186
Ps_7^c	15.378 (0.690)	91.781 (1.830)	0.004 (0.478)	10	0.378
Ps_1^g	13.572 (2.602)	5.031 (3.212)	-0.119 (-1.669)	5	0.982
Ps_2^g	28.453 (0.670)	3.152 (4.426)	-0.177 (-0.374)	10	0.761
Ps_3^g	39.965 (11.090)	0.238 (5.906)	0.051 (11.854)	5	0.996
Ps_4^g	44.192 (1.520)	36.328 (5.082)	-0.279 (-1.476)	10	0.898
Ps_5^g	18.559 (1.281)	0.541 (0.753)	0.059 (3.942)	10	0.677
Ps_6^g	32.03 (0.147)	10.599 (4.947)	-0.129 (-0.167)	10	0.902
Ps_7^g	38.112 (0.273)	0.008 (1.029)	0	10	0.219

f_i^{gc}, and f_i^{cg} could be positive, negative or approximately zero. The fact that $b_j^{cg} \neq b_j^{gc}$ and $f_j^{gc} \neq f_i^{cg}$ are estimated using ordinary least squares makes the LCP formulation a computationally efficient model.

The shipping costs for coal and natural gas among regions have been calculated from various sources found in the references. Due to the difficulty of obtaining such shipping costs, in some cases the costs were approximated by taking the difference between average supply value for region i and average demand price for region j. These costs are summarized in Tables 4.2 and 4.3. The production, consumption, and price data appear in the references. Note that sometimes a weighted average price was used to give the major coal or natural gas producing states larger weights. The quantity of coal (in thousand tons) has been converted into Btu's by the state average of Btu per pound whereas the quantity of natural gas (in million cubic feet) is converted into Btu's per cubic feet by the similar state average. This is necessary in order to eliminate the heterogeneous nature of the commodities.

LCP Model Solutions

Our present concern is with the extent to which the Appalachian energy supply market can meet eastern U.S. energy demands. Supply and demand regions are specified in Table 4.4. In each case, coal production represents aggregate supply from both underground and surface mining and natural gas consumption constitutes an aggregate of residential, commercial and industrial demand. While a more detailed disagregation in regions is preferable, it could only be achieved at a much higher cost. In addition, the computational capacity of the LCP package employed was rather limited in carrying out a full-fledged spatial equilibrium model, i.e., see Takayama (1982).

The optimum solutions to the above natural gas-steam coal model are presented in Tables 4.5 and 4.6. It should be pointed out that the optimum steam coal consumption and production levels are reasonably close to the actual performance of the market. The optimum coal flow remains relatively stable as compared to the previous results of Yang and Labys (1980, 1981, 1982). However, the optimal consumption and production levels for major natural gas producing and consuming regions deviate from the actual

Table 4.2

COAL TRANSPORTATION COST

To \ From	1	2	3	4	5	6	7
1	15.47	18.48	15.76	19.61	19.69	12.0	23.59
2	9.57	15.82	11.84	15.69	16.62	16.52	23.32
3	11.69	11.53	10.16	14.45	16.44	16.04	23.50
4	16.23	19.54	17.86	19.23	22.76	14.66	25.00
5	13.23	8.0	7.1	12.21	11.03	13.4	23.80
6	13.31	18.23	17.66	16.13	17.37	5.67	10.50
7	17.01	13.64	16.93	9.35	11.91	13.6	6.50

Table 4.3

NATURAL GAS TRANSPORTATION COST

To \ From	1	2	3	4	5	6	7
1	13.37	16.98	15.91	18.23	19.69	20.2	14.25
2	7.54	15.93	14.13	15.60	17.51	19.52	17.48
3	15.72	15.18	16.02	15.51	17.33	15.05	14.25
4	15.23	16.05	19.11	16.51	16.65	16.11	15.30
5	16.58	9.72	11.05	15.3	17.5	16.89	16.8
6	15.39	16.23	20.79	17.1	8.80	7.02	13.6
7	18.01	17.9	20.23	10.6	15.9	11.57	12.5

Table 4.4

DEMAND AND SUPPLY REGIONS OF THE STEAM COAL AND NATURAL GAS MARKET

Supply Regions

1. Pennsylvania and Maryland
2. Ohio
3. West Virginia
4. Virginia
5. East Kentucky and Tennessee
6. Alabama
7. Arkansas, Texas, Oklahoma, Louisiana, Indiana, Michigan

Demand Regions

1. Connecticut, Maine, Massachusetts, New Hampshire, Rhode Island, Vermont
2. New Jersey, New York, Pennsylvania, Maryland, Delaware and Washington, D.C.
3. Indiana and Michigan
4. Illinois, Wisconsin and Minnesota
5. West Virginia, Ohio and Kentucky
6. Tennessee, Alabama and Mississippi
7. Virginia, North Carolina, South Carolina, Georgia and Florida

Table 4.5

OPTIMAL SOLUTION OF THE LCP MODEL
STEAM COAL (10^{15} Btu)

To \ From	1	2	3	4	5	6	7	Consumption	Demand* Price
1					0.086			**0.086 (0.03)	41.29
2	1.052		0.122					1.175 (1.29)	37.37
3			0.486					0.486 (0.66)	35.69
4				0.145				0.145 (0.03)	43.39
5		0.828	0.185		0.544			1.557 (1.72)	32.63
6					0.458	0.254	0.001	0.713 (0.52)	38.97
7				0.263	0.562			0.825 (0.97)	33.51
Production	1.052 (1.20)	0.828 (0.93)	0.793 (0.80)	0.408 (0.24)	1.650 (1.73)	0.254 (0.32)	0.001 (0.001)		
Supply* Price	27.62	24.63	25.53	24.16	21.60	33.02	28.47		

* U.S. cents per million Btu

** Actual consumption and production level (1978) are in parentheses

Table 4.6

OPTIMAL SOLUTION OF THE LCP MODEL
NATURAL GAS (10^{15} Btu)

To \ From	1	2	3	4	5	6	7	Consumption	Demand* Price
1							0.417	**0.417 (0.28)	58.06
2	0.105						1.682	1.786 (1.59)	61.28
3							1.193	1.193 (1.38)	58.06
4							1.448	1.448 (1.74)	59.11
5		0.118	0.233				0.989	1.339 (1.28)	60.61
6					0.375	0.020	0.276	0.672 (0.61)	57.42
7				0.004			1.115	1.119 (0.94)	56.31
Production	0.105 (0.09)	0.118 (0.13)	0.233 (0.15)	0.004 (0.01)	0.375 (0.18)	0.020 (0.09)	7.120 (7.28)		
Supply* Price	53.74	50.89	49.56	45.71	48.61	50.39	43.81		

* U.S. Cents per million Btu

** Actual consumption and production level (1978) are in parentheses

levels by aproximately 24.5 percent. This can be explained by the substantial amount of price regulation in the natural gas industry. We expect that these results would be much more satisfactory for a model constructed in the post-regulatory period of the natural gas industry.

Sensitivity Analysis of the LCP Model

Based on the optimal results produced in Tables 4.5 and 4.6, we can rewrite (9) as:

$$\bar{w} = \bar{u} + \bar{v}\,\bar{I} = \emptyset \tag{12}$$

where the barred vectors and matrix consist of elements corresponding to positive decision variables, i.e. $\bar{X}_i^k > 0$, $\bar{Y}_j^k > 0$, $\bar{Z}_{ij}^k > 0$, $\lambda_j^k > 0$, and $\gamma_i^k > 0$. Notice that we have in our model $\bar{u} \in R^{82}$, $\bar{I} \in R^{82}$, $\bar{H} \in R^{28x54}$, $\bar{Q} \in R^{54x54}$, $\bar{O} \in R^{28x28}$, $\bar{v} \in R^{82x82}$. The vector of slack variables $\bar{w}$ is a zero vector of R^{82}.

What is offered here is a comprehensive set of spatial equilibrium conditions evaluated at some positive X's Y's, λ's, γ's and $\bar{Z}_{ij}$'s within a given base. For some small changes in $\bar{u}$, the sensitivity of $\bar{I}$ can be measured if $\bar{v}$ is invertible ($\bar{Q}$ is positive semidefinite) or

$$\Delta^{T} = \bar{v}^{-1}\ \Delta\ u \tag{13}$$

To verify such a sensitivity result, we let the demand intercepts of 7 coal regression equations increase by 10 percent. In order to have an unchanged trade pattern, as is frequently done in sensitivity analysis, we keep $\bar{H}$ constant. The Δ^{T} can then be computed, as shown in Table 4.7.

Many times model builders are more interested in the sensitivity of spatial production and consumption levels once the system is perturbed. Under such circumstances, it is simpler to conduct the partial sensitivity analysis by assuming $\bar{\lambda}_j^k = \bar{P}d_j^k$ and $\gamma_i^k = \bar{P}s_i^k$. In other words, one could substitute

$\bar{\lambda}_j^c = a_j^c + b_j^{cc}\ \bar{Y}_j^g + b_j^{cg}\ \bar{Y}_j^g$, $\bar{\lambda}_j^g = a_j^g + b_j^{gg}\ \bar{Y}_j^g + b_j^{gc}\ \bar{Y}_j^c$

$\lambda_i^c = e_i^c + f_i^{cc}\ \bar{X}_i^c + f_i^{cg}\ \bar{X}_i^g$ and $\lambda_i^g = e_i^g + f_i^{gg}\ \bar{X}_1^g + f_i^{gc}\ \bar{X}_i^c$ into

$\lambda_j^c - \bar{\gamma}_i^c = t_{ij}^c$ and $\lambda_j^g - \bar{\gamma}_i^g = t_{ij}$ and (ii) add $\sum_{j=1}^{7} \bar{Y}_j^c = \sum_{i=1}^{7} \bar{X}_i^c$

Table 4.7

SENSITIVITY ANALYSIS OF THE LCP MODEL

i	$\Delta\bar{X}_i^c$	$\Delta\bar{X}_i^c$	$\Delta\bar{\gamma}_i^c$	$\Delta\bar{\gamma}_i^g$	ij	$\Delta\bar{Z}_{ij}^c$	ij	ΔZ_{ij}^g
1	0.171	0.0041	2.6	0.037	1,2	0.171	1,2	-0.004
2	0.113	0.0064	2.6	0.037	2,5	0.113	2,5	0.006
3	0.286	-0.0597	2.6	0.037	3,2	-0.077	3,5	-0.06
4	0.066	0.0005	2.6	0.037	3,3	0.215	4,7	0.0005
5	0.334	-0.0357	2.6	0.037	3,5	0.148	5,6	-0.036
6	0.111	0.0014	2.6	0.037	4,4	0.041	6,6	0.0014
7	0.0003	0.0458	2.6	0.037	4,7	0.026	7,1	-0.003
j	$\Delta\bar{Y}_j^c$	$\Delta\bar{Y}_j^g$	$\Delta\bar{\lambda}_j^c$	$\Delta\bar{\lambda}_j^g$	5,7	0.013	7,2	0.032
1	0.013	-0.003	2.6	0.037	5,5	0.231	7,3	-0.0165
2	0.094	0.036	2.6	0.037	5,6	0.046	7,4	0.032
3	0.215	-0.017	2.6	0.037	5,7	0.044	7,5	-0.142
4	0.041	0.032	2.6	0.037	6,6	0.111	7,6	0.125
5	0.492	-0.196	2.6	0.037	7,6	0.0003	7,7	0.019
6	0.157	0.090	2.6	0.037				
7	0.069	0.019	2.6	0.037				

$\sum_{j=1}^{7} \bar{Y}_j^g = \sum_{i=1}^{7} \bar{X}_i^g$ to the above spatial price equilibrium conditions to form a system of equation as shown below:

$$\underset{28\times28}{\left[\begin{array}{c} 1\ldots1 \ -1\ldots-1 . 0\ldots0 \\ \vdots \\ b_j^{cc} \ - \ f_i^{cc} \ \ldots \ b_j^{cg} \ - \ f_i^{cg} \\ \vdots \\ \hline 0\ \ldots\ 0 \ \ \ldots1.1-1\ldots-1 \\ \vdots \\ b_j^{gc} \ - \ f_i^{gc} \ \ldots \ b_j^{gg} \ - \ f_i^{gg} \\ \vdots \end{array}\right]} \underset{28\times1}{\left[\begin{array}{c} \bar{Y}_1^c \\ \vdots \\ \bar{Y}_7^c \\ \bar{X}_1^c \\ \vdots \\ \bar{X}_7^c \\ \hline \bar{Y}_1^g \\ \vdots \\ \bar{Y}_7^g \\ \bar{X}_1^g \\ \vdots \\ \bar{X}_7^g \end{array}\right]} = \underset{28\times1}{\left[\begin{array}{c} 0 \\ \\ -a_j^c + e_i^c + t_{ij}^c \\ \\ \hline 0 \\ \\ -a_j^g + e_i^g + t_{ij}^g \\ \\ \end{array}\right]} \tag{14}$$

or more compactly as

$$A \ . \ L = N \tag{15}$$

It is now a simple matter to conduct the LCP sensitivity analysis through (14) since it has a much smaller dimension. For instance, the sensitivity of $\bar{X}$ and $\bar{Y}$ due to small changes in all t_{ij}^c and t_{ij}^g can easily be expressed as

$$\Delta L = A^{-1} \begin{bmatrix} 0 \\ \Delta t^c_{ij} \\ 0 \\ \Delta t^g_{ij} \end{bmatrix} \tag{16}$$

Furthermore, a change in the slopes (e.g., $\Delta b^{cc}_j = 1$ for every j) can have the following impact on $\bar{Y}$ and $\bar{X}$ via the differentiating equation system (14) using the chain rule

$$\begin{bmatrix} 1\ldots1\ -1\ldots-1.\ 0\ldots0 \\ \\ b^{cc}_j\ -\ f^{cc}_i \quad b^{cg}_j\ -\ f^{cg}_i \\ \cdot \\ \cdot \\ \hline 0\ \ldots\ 0\ \ \ldots1.1-1\ldots-1 \\ \\ b^{gc}_j\ -\ f^{gc}_i\ \ldots\ b^{gg}_j\ -\ f^{gg}_i \\ \\ \end{bmatrix} \begin{bmatrix} \dfrac{\partial\bar{Y}^c_j}{\partial b^{cc}_j} \\ \cdot \\ \cdot \\ \cdot \\ \dfrac{\partial\bar{X}^c_i}{\partial b^{cc}_j} \\ \hline \dfrac{\partial Y^g_j}{\partial b^g_j} \\ \cdot \\ \cdot \\ \cdot \\ \dfrac{\partial Y^g_j}{\partial b^{cc}_j} \end{bmatrix} = \begin{bmatrix} 0 \\ -\bar{Y}^c_j \\ \\ \\ \\ \hline 0 \\ \\ \\ 0 \end{bmatrix} \tag{17}$$

or more compactly

$$\nabla L^{\sim} = A^{-1} \begin{bmatrix} 0 \\ -Y^c_j\ \ \Delta b^{cc}_j \\ \hline 0 \\ 0 \end{bmatrix} \tag{18}$$

Sensitivity analysis in (17) is immediately verified through solving (18). The result can be of extreme importance especially in the case of the ad valorem tariff and spatial distortion analysis, i.e., see Yang (1983).

Conclusions

We have demonstrated, in this paper, the usefulness of the LCP spatial equilibrium model. The basic distinction between the LCP and the QP is that we are dealing with a set of equilibrium conditions in terms of inequalities. When the cross-regression coefficients are symmetric, the QP is equivalent to the LCP. However, one major problem of the LCP, as experienced here is its limited capability to model the large-scale spatial equilibrium problem. Model-builders must either aggregate economic regions or reduce the number of commodities in order to accommodate the "dimensionality" problem. Of course, an improved algorithm may very well reduce the computational time, i.e., see Irwin (1978) and Irwin and Yang (1982).

A brief sensitivity analysis was conducted with the LCP model. However, this analysis is valid only for a given base or trade pattern. For some small changes in parameters, the sensitivity of the solution vectors is largely dependent on the relative size of characteristic roots of the coefficient matrices ($\bar{v}$ and A), a well known model property. Lastly, changes in the slope and the intercept parameters could have important policy implications, especially in the case of the imposition of an ad valorem tariff.

Authors
Chin-wei Yang
Department of Economics
Clarion University of Pennsylvania
Clarion, PA 16214

Walter C. Labys
Department of Mineral Resource Economics
West Virginia University
Morgantown, WV 26506-6070

Acknowledgment
The chapter originally appeared in Energy Economics, Volume 7, Number 3, July 1985. It is published here with the permission of Butterworth Scientific Ltd.

References

Anderson, D.L. and D.B. Hiatt, (1976). The Transportation of Energy Commodities 1972-1985, Volumes I and II, Cambridge: Transportation System Center.

Bartilson, S., G. Zepp and T. Takayama, (1978). A User's Manual for the LCRAND Mathematical Programming System," Santa Monica: Rand Corporation.

Basic Petroleum Data Book: Petroleum Industry Statistics, (1976-1979). Washington, D.C: American Petroleum Institute.

Cottle, R.W., (1979). "Numerical Methods for Complementarity Problems in Engineering and Applied Science," in Computing Methods in Applied Sciences and Engineering, Lecture Note in Mathematics, 74: Berlin - New York - Heidelberg.

Cottle, R.W. and R.E. Stone, (1980). "On the Uniqueness of Solutions to Linear Complementarity Problems," Technical Report 80-19, Stanford: Stanford University, to appear in Mathematical Programming.

Day, R.H., (1963). Recursive Programming and Production Response, Amsterdam: North-Holland Publishing Company.

Gas Fact: A Statistical Record of the Utility Industry, (1976-1979). Arlington, VA: Department of Statistics, the American Gas Association.

Henderson, J.M., (1958). The Efficiency of the Coal Industry, Cambridge: Harvard University Press.

Historical Statistics of the Gas Utility Industry 1966-1975, Arlington, VA: Department of Statistics, American Gas Association.

Inputs to the Project Independence Evaluation System Integration Model for the Transport of Energy Materials, (1974). Volumes I and II. Federal Energy Administration Project Independence Blueprint Final Task Force Report under Direction of Department of Transportation, Washington, D.C.

Irwin, C.L., (1978). "Analysis of a PIES-Type Algorithm," in Energy Modeling and Net Energy Analysis, Institute of Gas Technology.

Irwin, C.L. and C.W. Yang, (1982). "Iteration and Sensitivity for a Spatial Equilibrium Problem with Linear Supply and Demand Functions," Operations Research, 30: 319-335.

Kennedy, M., (1974). "An Economic Model of the World Oil Market," Bell Journal of Economics and Management Science, 5: 540-577.

Kolstad, C.D. and F.A. Wolak, Jr., (1983). "Competition in Interregional Taxation: The Case of Western Coal," Journal of Political Economy, 91: 443-460.

Labys, W.C. and C.W. Yang, (1980). "A Quadratic Programming Model of the Appalachian Steam Coal Market," Energy Economics, 2: 86-95.

Mineral Year Book, (1974). United States Bureau of Mines, Washington, D.C.: U.S. Government Printing Office.

Mutschler, P.H., R.J. Evans and G.M. Larwood, (1972). Comparative Transportation Costs of Supplying Low-Sulfur Fuels to Midwestern and Eastern Coal Markets, IC 8614, Washington, D.C.: U.S. Bureau of Mines.

Project Independence Evaluation System Documentation, (1976). Washington D.C.: Federal Energy Administration.

Steam-Electric Plant Factors, (1974). Washington, D.C.: National Coal Association.

Takayama, T. and G.G. Judge, (1964). "Equilibrium Among Spatially Separated Markets: A Reformation," Econometrica, 32: 510-524.

Takayama, T. and G.G. Judge, (1971). Spatial and Temporal Price and Allocation Models, Amsterdam: North-Holland Publishing Company.

Takayama, T., (1982). "Frontiers of Interregional Economic Models for Policy and Evaluation," Paper presented at the 29th Annual North American Meetings of the Regional Science Association, Pittsburgh, PA.

Tomlin, J.A., (1976). A Program for Solving Linear Complementarity Problems by Lemke's Method, Stanford: Stanford University.

Uri, N.D., (1975). "A Spatial Equilibrium Model for Electrical Energy," Journal of Regional Science, 15: 323-333.

Yang, C.W. and W.C. Labys, (1981). "Stability of Appalachian Coal Shipment Under Policy Variations," Energy Journal, 2: 111-128.

Yang, C.W. and W.C. Labys, (1982). "A Sensitivity Analysis of the Stability Property of the QP Commodity Model," Journal of Empirical Economics, 7: 93-107.

Yang, C.W., (1983). "A Distortion Analysis of the Spatial Equilibrium Model: The Hickson and Slusky Effect." A Discussion paper.

5 Computing dynamic spatial oligopolistic equilibrium in an exhaustible resource market: the case of coal

CHARLES D. KOLSTAD *University of Illinois*

Introduction

A great deal of model research has been concerned with the computation of economic equilibrium. Probably the most widely applied technique, suggested by Samuelson (1952) and further developed by Takayama and Judge (1971), involves formulating the economic model as a constrained optimization problem for which solution algorithms are widely available. However, this technique cannot usually be applied to general (as opposed to partial) equilibrium problems due principally to an inability to assure that individual budget constraints are satisfied. A variety of other approaches have been developed for computing general competitive equilibria, e.g., see Hansen (1973), Manne et al. (1980), Mathiesen (1985), and Dantzig et al. (1979).

Until recently, all research has focused on the computation of competitive equilibrium; i.e. equilibrium in markets that are perfectly competitive. Yet many markets are not perfectly competitive. Many markets are characterized as monopolistically competitive or oligopolistic. Spence (1976) has shown how the computation of equilibrium in some monopolistically competitive markets can be reduced to the maximization of a single function. Murphy et al. (1982) have proposed an iterative method for computing a Nash equilibrium for an oligopoly by way of a sequence of mathematical programs. It has been known for some time that equilibrium in the case of a pure monopoly (or monopsony) can be determined by maximizing producer (or consumer) surplus (Takayama and Judge, 1971).

The purpose of this chapter is to describe a computational method for determining equilibria in oligopolistic markets. This work permits the empirical analysis of a much richer variety of types of market conduct. Specifically, the technique presented here can be used to compute reaction function equilibria in cases where the conjectural variation is constant (see Friedman, 1982). This includes the familiar Cournot-Nash equilibrium and Bertrand equilibrium but not a consistent conjectures equilibrium (Bresnahan, 1981) nor equilibrium involving limit pricing. The latter two situations involve conjectural variations that are themselves variables and thus endogenous to the problem. The present approach formulates the oligolpoly problem as an n-person game and determines a Nash equilibrium of the game using a nonlinear complementarity algorithm (see Cottle and Dantzig, 1974). The only other known application of complementarity programming to the coal market is that of Yang and Labys (1985).

In the next section we show how reaction function equilibrium conditions can be defined, so that they are amenable to solution using a nonlinear complementarity algorithm. In the third section a static spatial oligopoly model is presented. In the fourth section this static analysis is extended to an intertemporal equilibrium in a spatial market for an exhuaustible resource. The fifth section is concerned with an application of the technique to the interational coal market in which an equilibrium is computed.

Reaction Function Equilibria

Consider the case of i producers of a single commodity. Denote q_i the output of the ith producer and denote by $\pi_i(q)$ the profit of the ith producer. (It is not necessary to explicitly consider demand since each producer's profit function involves the output of all producers.) Each producer (i) has the simple problem of choosing q_i to maximize π_i:

$$\max_{q_i} \pi_i(q) \tag{1a}$$

$$q_i \geq 0 \tag{1b}$$

If π_i is pseudoconvex then necessary and sufficient conditions for q_i^* to solve (1) are:

$$\frac{d\pi_i}{dq_i} + \lambda = 0 \qquad (2a)$$

$$\lambda\, q_i^* \geq 0 \qquad (2c)$$

$$\lambda \geq 0 \qquad (2d)$$

from which λ can be eliminated:

$$\frac{d\pi_i}{dq_i} \leq 0 \qquad (3a)$$

$$q_i^* \left[\frac{d\pi_i}{dq_i}\right] = 0 \quad . \qquad (3b)$$

It is in computing the derivative of profit with respect to output that the conjectural variation enters. Let r_{ij} be the conjectural variation of producer i with respect to producer j; i.e. r_{ij} is producer i's conjecture of how q_j will change when q_i is changed ($r_{ij} = \frac{\partial q_j}{\partial q_i}$, conjectured). Thus (3) can be rewritten as

$$\sum_j \frac{\partial \pi_i}{\partial p_j} r_{ij} \leq 0 \qquad (4a)$$

$$q_i^* \left[\sum_j \frac{\partial \pi_i}{\partial q_j} r_{ij}\right] = 0 \qquad (4b)$$

where of course $r_{ii} = 1$. A Nash equilibrium in this market can be determined by finding a vector q^* which satisfies the pairs of (4) for each producer (I inequalities, I equalities).

In general it would be expected that for a noncooperative oligopoly, $-1 \leq r_{ij} \leq 0$, for $i \neq j$ (e.g., see Cottle and Dantzig 1974). A Cournot-Nash equilibrium corresponds to $r_{ij} = 0$, $i \neq j$ and can be thought of as a maximum market power noncooperative equilibrium in that each producer behaves as if he were a single monopolist facing a residual demand curve. He takes no account of the response of competitors to his actions. A Bertrand equilibrium corresponds to $\sum_{j \neq i} r_{ij} = -1$. This is a minimum market power situation since each producer assumes that any reduction in its own output will be exactly matched by competitors. In the case of constant marginal costs, this results in marginal cost pricing. A conjectural variation greater than zero is consistent with collusion.

The problem of solving the set of equations of the form of (4) is equivalent to finding the vector $q \geq 0$ such that $f(q) \geq 0$ and $< q, f(q) > = 0$, i.e. the inner product of q and f(q) is zero. This problem is known as the complementarity problem or, when f is affine, the linear complementarity problem. The principal algorithm for solving the linear complementarity problem is due to Lemke (1965) and has been implemented by many including Tomlin (1976). A number of algorithms have been proposed for solving the nonlinear complementarity problem. The method of Mathiesen (1985) involves the successive linearization of f, solution of the resulting linear complementarity problem, re-linearization of f, and so on until convergence is attained (if it is attained). It should be noted that in general one is not assured of a unique reaction function equilibrium nor a unique solution to the complementarity problem (see Kolstad and Mathiesen 1987, 1988).

A Static Spatial Model

The model presented here is of a spatial market of a single good at a single point in time. The essence of the spatial aspects of the market is that transportation of goods from producers to consumers is a costly process. The goal of this section is to develop equilibrium conditions in the form of complementarity conditions which can then be solved for a market equilibrium.

Let $i = 1,...,I$ be the index for producers and $j = 1,...,J$ be the index for consumers. In addition let:

q_{ij} denote quantity shipped from producer i to consumer j

P_j denote price of product as delivered to consumer j

τ_{ij} denote the unit transport cost from producer i to consumer j

d_j denote the demand function for consumer j

c_i denote the marginal cost function for producer i.

The first two of these variables are endogenous, to be computed. The transport cost and the supply and demand functions are exogenous. Note that by indexing the shipments by destination, we are allowing producers to price discriminate. The equilibrium conditions in the model consist of two sets of equations: one set for consumers; and one set for producers. A solution is a set of non-negative prices and quantitites which satisfy these equilibrium conditions.

Consumer Optimality Conditions

Each of the j consumers faces a local price for the commodity, p_j. If the price is positive to the jth consumer, demand as a function of price must be equal to the quantity consumed. If the price is zero, then excess demand must be non-positive:

$$u_j \equiv \{\sum_i q_{ij} - d_j(p_j)\} \geq 0, \quad u_j p_j = 0 \quad , \quad \forall_j \tag{5}$$

Here and throughout this chapter, "dummy" variables u_j are used to facilitate writing the complementarity condition.

Producer Profit Maximization Conditions

We will assume there are two types of producers in the market: oligopolists and competitive fringe. Each producer has the same objective, to maximize profits (revenue less costs):

$$\Pi_i = \sum_j (p_j - \tau_{ij}) \, q_{ij} - \int_0^{\Sigma_j q_{ij}} c_i(x)dx \tag{6}$$

The price the producer faces is the consumer price (p_j) less the transport cost (τ_{ij}). Producers maximize profits by choosing output levels, q_{ij}. First order conditions for a maximum of (6) are

$$w_{ij} \equiv \{p_j - \tau_{ij} + q_{ij} \frac{\partial p_j}{\partial q_{ij}} - c_i(\sum_j q_{ij})\} \leq 0 \, , \; w_{ij} q_{ij} = 0 \quad , \; \forall_{i,j} \tag{7}$$

The expression in braces is merely the condition that marginal revenue (the first three terms) equal marginal cost. We have assumed $\partial p_k / \partial q_{ij} = 0$ for $j \neq k$, which means that a consumer's price cannot be affected by changes in shipments to other consumers. The difference between the oligopolists and the competitive fringe is in their perception of how p_j is affected by their choice of q_{ij}.

<u>Oligopolists</u> Denote the set of oligopolists by $M = \{i | i$ is an oligpolist$\}$. Oligopolist i's perception of $\partial p_j / \partial q_{ij}$ depends on (1) the slope of the demand curve for consumer j; and (2) the extent of which competitives will change their sales to consumer j in response to a change in q_{ij}:

$$\frac{\partial p_j}{\partial q_{ij}} = \frac{(1 + r_{ij})}{d_j'(p_j)} \qquad \forall i \epsilon M \tag{8}$$

In (8), r_{ij} is oligopolist i's perception of how sales to consumer j of all competitors combined change with q_{ij}: $r_{ij} = \Delta(\sum_{k \neq i} q_{kj})/\Delta q_{ij}$, conjectured. Note that for simplicity this is an aggregate conjectural variation; individual reactions of competitors are aggregated into r_{ij}. Thus combining (7) and (8), first order conditions for profit maximization for each oligopolist are given by

$$w_{ij} \equiv \{p_j - \tau_{ij} + q_{ij} \frac{(1 + r_{ij})}{d_j'(p_j)} - c_i(\Sigma q_{ij})\} \tag{9}$$

$$\leq 0, \; w_{ij} q_{ij} = 0, \; \forall i \epsilon M$$

This is a standard condition, that for any sales to take place between producer i and consumer j, perceived marginal revenue must be equal to marginal cost. Obviously, with $r_{ij} = -1$ (a Bertrand equilibrium), then (9) reduces to price equals marginal cost (if sales occur).

<u>Competitive Fringe</u> Of course the competitive fringe take a quite different view of the market price p_j; they perceive that they are unable to effect it by changing q_{ij}. Thus first order conditions for profit maximization for the competitive fringe are

$$w_{ij} \equiv \{p_j - \tau_{ij} - c_i(\Sigma q_{ij})\} \leq 0, \; w_{ij} q_{ij} = 0, \quad \forall i \epsilon M \tag{10}$$

In other words price equals marginal cost unless no transaction takes place between producer i and consumer j.

A Model of an Exhaustible Resource Market

In this section we extend the static spatial model just presented to an intertemporal model of an exhaustible resource market. The principal difference between the static and intertemporal formulation is the treatment of the pricing of the exhaustible resource, taking into account the Hotelling (1931) principle of intertemporal pricing.

As before, let $i = 1,\ldots,I$ index producers; $j = 1,\ldots,J$ index consumers; and let $t = 1,\ldots,T$ index time periods. Let

q_{ijt} denote quantity shipped from producer i to consumer j in time period t

p_{jt} denote price of product delivered to consumer j in time period t

ρ denote the discount rate

τ_{ijt} denote the unit transport cost from producer i to consumer j in time period t

d_{jt} denote the demand function for consumer j in time period t

c_i denote the marginal cost function for producer i, assumed to be invariant with time but a function of cumulative production.

As before, the first two variables are endogenous and the remaining parameters and functions are exogenous to the model. For simplicity, we will assume demand at a point in time is a function only of price at that point in time.

Consumer optimality conditions are defined precisely as in the static model given by (5), except that they are to hold at each point in time. Producer profit maximization conditions are somewhat different. The present value of profits for producer i is

$$\pi_i = \sum_{t=1}^{T} (1+\rho)^{-t} [\Sigma (p_{jt} - \tau_{ijt}) q_{ijt} - \int_{a_{t-1}}^{a_t} c_i(x)dx] \qquad (11)$$

where

$$a_t = \begin{cases} 0 & \text{for } t = 0 \\ \sum_{k=1}^{t} q_{ijk} & \text{for } t > 0 \end{cases}$$

Profit is maximized by choosing the appropriate quantity sold at each point in time to each consumer (q_{ijt}). First order conditions for a profit maximum are

$$v_{ijt} \equiv \{p_{jt} - \tau_{ijt} + q_{ijt} \frac{\partial p_{jt}}{\partial q_{ijt}} - c_i(a_t)$$

$$- \sum_{k=t+1}^{T} (1+\rho)^{t-k}[c_i(a_k) - c_i(a_{k-1})]\} \leq 0 \; v_{ijt} \; q_{ijt} = 0 \quad (12)$$

where a_k is defined in (11). As would be expected, when T is finite, potential distortions may enter for time periods close to T (t→T). This horizon effect is often encountered in dynamic planning models. It is less of a problem if T is very large.

The Competitive Fringe

For the competitive fringe, price is given; therefore $\partial p_{jt}/\partial q_{ijt} = 0$. Thus for the fringe, profit maximizing conditions are

$$v_{ijt} \equiv p_{jt} - \tau_{ijt} - c_i(a_t) - \sum_{k=t+1}^{T} (1+\rho)^{t-k}[c_i(a_k) \quad (13)$$

$$- c_i(a_{k-1})] \leq 0, \; v_{ijt}q_{ijt} = 0 \text{ for } i \notin M$$

where a_k is defined in (11).

The interpretation of (13) is that for production to occur at any point in time, price must be equal to the marginal production cost $[c_i(a_t)]$ plus the opportunity cost of producing a unit of output at that point of time. This opportunity cost is the summation in (13) and represents the present value of the increased costs (and thus decreased revenues) from producing a unit of output at time t rather than foregoing production. Since marginal costs are a function of cumulative production, producing a unit now causes all subsequent costs to be slightly higher.

Oligopolists

The situation of an oligopolist is not much more complicated than that of the competitive fringe, particularly if we assume that (1) current final demand is only a function of current prices; and (2) competitors are not conjectured to change output in one time period in response to a change in own output in a different time period. First order conditions for a profit maximum are

$$v_{ijt} = \{p_{jt} - \tau_{ijt} + q_{ijt} \frac{(1+r_{ijt})}{d'_{jt}(p_{jt})} - c_i(a_t) \tag{14}$$

$$- \sum_{k=t+1}^{T} (1+\rho)^{t-k}[c_i(a_k)-c_i(a_{k-1})]\} \leq 0 \quad v_{ijt}\, q_{ijt} = 0$$

for $i \epsilon M$

where a_k is defined in (11).

This condition is very similar to the profit-maximizing conditions for the competitive fringe except that marginal revenue has been changed to reflect the slope of the demand curve the oligopolist faces. Marginal revenue at time t must be equal to the marginal cost of production at time t plus the opportunity cost of producing now rather than deferring production to a later point in time.

A Model of International Coal Trade

In the last two sections, spatial models of oligpolistic markets were developed. In this section we apply the exhaustible resource model to an actual market: the international steam coal market.

The Steam Coal Market

Given the rise in the real prices of oil and natural gas over recent years, coal has come to be regarded as a principal alternative source of energy. The use of coal has been encouraged in countries with plentiful domestic resources (such as the United States) and in countries with negligible domestic resources (such as Japan). This has led to modest international trade in steam coal and expectations of more significant trade over the coming decades.

Until the late 1970s, metallurgical coal dominated international coal trade to the virtual exclusion of steam coal. This situation is changing due in large part to the oil price rises of recent years. Table 5.1 lists steam coal exports by country for 1979 and 1980 and U.S. Department of Energy (DOE) projections (made in 1982) for 1990. As can be seen trade grew by a third from 1979 to 1980. Although the 1990 DOE forecast may be optimistic, it was generally consistent with other U.S. Government forecasts (Interagency Coal Export Task Force, 1981), and Australian forecasts

Table 5.1

STEAM COAL EXPORTS
(10^{a} TONS)

Country	1979	1980	1990[c]
Australia	5.9	9.4	83.9
Canada	1.0	1.2	3.6
Republic of South Africa	15.9	21.4	63.2
United States to Canada	11.0	10.3	10.9
United States excluding Canada	2.4	15.2	61.8
Poland[a]	19.5	15.8	20.0
China	0.3	0.6	9.1
United Kingdom[b]	2.3	3.8	7.0
USSR	N/A	N/A	0.9
Other	N/A	N/A	25.6
Total	58.3	77.8	286.1

[a]Exports to West only.

[b]Total exports, principally steam coal.

[c]Projections from DOE (1982).

Source: Abbey (1983).

(Australian Department of Trade and Resources, 1981). One can conclude from these data that the international market is likely to undergo limited growth over time.

A basic problem in understanding the development of the international steam coal market can be appreciated by examining the role of the United States in that market. Table 5.1 indicates that the U.S. share of the steam coal market has been and was projected to remain at around 25 percent. The 1980 share is higher than the 1979 share, although this may be due at least in part to reduced 1980 exports from Australia and Poland and the inability of South Africa to take up this slack by quickly increasing exports. It appears that only the United States has surge capacity sufficient to meet these unexpected increases in world demand. The problem is that these high current and anticipated U.S. shares of the steam coal market would appear to be inconsistent with production cost information. Cost studies, such as the Interagency Coal Export Task Force (1981), have shown that U.S. coal is not particularly cost competitive with South African or Australian coal in either Europe or Japan (by far the dominant importers of coal). Indications are that this situation will persist even after significant resource depletion. This cost information would suggest that the United States would have a fairly small role to play in a competitive world coal market.

Thus the fundamental problem is that the past and future trade data presented in Table 5.1 coupled with high U.S. production costs appear to be inconsistent with perfect competition, at least as viewed from the early 1980s. The structure of the coal market suggests that a more realistic market conduct assumption may be that of a duopoly with a competitive fringe, with the duopolists being South Africa and Australia, i.e. see Abbey and Kolstad (1983) and Kolstad and Abbey (1984). This market conduct hypothesis is examined further in the duopoly model described below.

A Duopoly Model

The model described here corresponds to the exhaustible resource model of the previous section. Four time periods were considered, from 1985 through 2000 in 5-year intervals. A real discount rate of 10 percent per annum was used for the intertemporal pricing decision. Twenty-one consuming regions, principally in the developed, non-centrally-planned world, are considered. Demand in each of these regions at each time period is characterized by a constant elasticity demand function. Ten producing regions are considered. In the six major producing regions, costs are characterized by linear marginal cost curves (as a function of cumulative production) for up to four different grades of coal. In the four other producing regions, inelastic estimates of supply are used. Producing and consuming regions are connected by a time-varying matrix of per-unit transport costs. The data and analysis reported here were performed in the early 1980s and represent perceptions, at that time. The market has changed somewhat since then although is qualitatively similar. See Kolstad and Abbey (1984) and Kolstad et al. (1983) for more detail.

The entire model is formulated as a single nonlinear complementarity problem. Thus the equilibrium prices and quantitites are determined simultaneously. The model consists of 1136 variables and an equal number of equations /constraints. Using a sequential version of Tomlin's (1976) algorithm for solving the linear complementarity problem, solution CPU time was typically 25-30 minutes time on a DEC VAX-11/780 computer.

Results

As mentioned earlier, the market conduct assumption examined here is that of a duopoly (South Africa and Australia) with a competitive fringe of all other producers. The behavioural model used was that of reaction function equilibrium with one parameter, given by the assumed conjectural variation. Letting the conjectural variation r_{ijt} in (14) be the same for both duopolists and all time periods, Table 5.2 shows equilibrium trade shares (as a fraction of total internationally traded steam coal) for the second time period (the year 1990) as a function of the conjectural variation. Also shown in Table 5.2 is the DOE (1982) forecast of 1990 trade shares. Obviously, the DOE forecast may not be accurate but it represents an "expert" baseline with which to compare model output.

As discussed earlier, when the conjectural variation is -1, trade is the same as under competitive market conditions, as in (14). Note from the Table that in this case, South Africa and Australia truly dominate the market. This is in significant disagreement with the data in Table 5.1 which show a much smaller market share for these two countries. Moving away from this conduct assumption towards that of Cournot equilibrium ($r_{ijt} = 0$), note the extent to which other producers, particularly Canada, displace the two

Table 5.2

1990 FORECAST TRADE SHARES UNDER DUOPOLY MARKET STRUCTURE[a]

From	To	"Actual"[b]	Conjectural Variation				
			0	- .25	- .5	- .75	- 1.0
U.S.A.	Europe[c]	0.19	0.10	0.07	0.04	--	--
Canada	Europe[c]	--	--	--	--	--	--
South Africa	Europe[c]	0.22	0.27	0.33	0.38	0.46	0.53
Australia	Europe[c]	0.02	0.08	0.08	0.08	0.05	--
Other	Europe[c]	0.17	0.13	0.13	0.12	0.12	0.11
U.S.A.	East Asia	0.02	0.01	0.01	--	--	--
Canada	East Asia	0.01	0.24	0.20	0.15	0.08	--
South Africa	East Asia	--	0.03	0.03	0.03	0.03	--
Australia	East Asia	0.27	0.10	0.13	0.17	0.24	--
Other	East Asia	0.04	--	--	--	--	--

[a]Units are fraction to total overseas trade. Entries may not add to unity because a number of minor producers and some consumers are not included.

[b]"Actual" trade shares are as forecast by DOE (1982).

[c]Includes North Africa and Middle East.

duopolists. The total market shares of the two duopolists for the Cournot model is in fair agreement with the "actual" share.

Unfortunately, none of the duopoly models gives trade shares that, at a detailed level are in particularly good agreement with "actual" trade shares. Focusing on the case of $r_{ijt} = 0$, the Canadian share of the East Asian market is far in excess of the "actual" share, principally at the expense of Australia. In Europe, Australia has a more significant share that it occurs principally at the expense of the U.S.

Turning now to the market shares of the duopolists, trade shares and monopoly rent for 1990 can be expressed as a function of the conjectural variation. Recall from Table 5.1 that in 1980, South Africa and Australian market shares were 28 percent and 12 percent respectively, and that the DOE expects these shares in 1990 to be 22 percent and 29 percent respectively.

Rents are likely to go to zero as r_{ijt} goes to - 1, corresponding to a marginal cost pricing situation. The market shares for the two duopolists approach 90 percent in this case. As the conjectural variation moves away from - 1 towards 0 (the Cournot equilibrium), the shares of the two duopolists combined shrink considerably, reaching just under 50% for the Cournot equilibrium. However, in the model, South Africa dominates Australia which is the reverse of the DOE projections. Further tests of this model appear in Kolstad and Abbey (1983). Although the Cournot equilibrium ($r_{ijt}=0$) corresponds to maximum market power, in that prices are highest and market shares lowest for the duopolists, monopoly rents peak in the vicinity of $r_{ijt} = -.5$. Furthermore, rents are relatively constant over the range in conjectural variations from 0 to - .5, only dropping to zero as one moves fairly close to $r_{ijt} = -1$.

Conclusions

This chapter has served to demonstrate how conventional spatial equilibrium theory can be extended to non-competitive markets, specifically reaction-function type oligopolies. In developing the mathematics of computing such market equilibria, we have shown that it is quite straightforward to formulate oligopolistic spatial equilibrium models. In fact, the complementarity approach presented here could be considered an alternative to optimization methods for solving competitive spatial equilibrium models.

To demonstrate the applicability of the methodology, an example of the international steam coal market was presented. Although the model of the coal market was quite large, it was relatively easy from a computational point of view to find equilibrium solutions. Unfortunately, it did not appear that for this market, the duopoly market conduct assumptions gave totally satisfactory results, at least given the assumptions underlying the model. Nevertheless, we did demonstrate the potential applicability of spatial models of imperfect competition. It is hoped the methods presented here can find applications in other imperfect market situations.

Author
Charles D. Kolstad
Department of Economics
University of Illinois
Champaign, Illinois 61821

References

Abbey, S.D., (1983). "Trends in International Coal Markets," Los Alamos National Laboratory Report.

Abbey, S.D. and C.D. Kolstad, (1983). "The Structure of International Steam Coal Markets," Natural Resources Journal 23: 859-891.

Bresnahan, T.F., (1981). "Duopoly Models with Consistent Conjectures," American Economic Review, 71: 934-945.

Cottle, R.W. and G.B. Dantzig, (1974). "Complementary Pivot Theory of Mathematical Programming," in G.B. Dantzig and B.C. Eaves (eds.) Studies in Optimization, New York: Mathematical Association of America, pp. 27-51.

Dantiz, G.B., B.C. Eaves and D. Gale, (1979). "An Algorithm for a Piecewise Linear Model of Trade with Negative Prices and Bankruptcy," Mathematical Programming, 16: 190-209.

Friedman, J., (1982). "Oligopoly Theory," in K.J. Arrow and M.D. Intriligator (eds.) Handbook of Mathematical Economics: Amsterdam: North-Holland Publishing Company, pp. 491-534.

Hotelling, H., (1931). "The Economics of Exhaustible Resources," Journal of Policy Economics, 39: 137-175.

Kolstad, C.D., D.S. Abbey and R. Bivens, (1983). "Modeling International Steam Coal Trade," Los Alamos National Laboratory Report LA-9461-MS, Los Alamos, NM.

Kolstad, C.D. and D.S. Abbey, (1984). "The Effect of Market Conduct on International Steam Coal Trade," European Economic Review, 24: 39-59.

Kolstad, C.D. and A.E. Burris, (1986) "Imperfectly Competitive Equilibria in International Commodity Markets," American Journal of Agricultural Economics, 68: 27-36.

Kolstad, C.D. and L. Mathiesen, (1987). "Necessary and Sufficient Conditions of Uniqueness of a Cournot Equilibrium," Review of Economic Studies, 54: 681-690.

Kolstad, C.D. and L. Mathiesen, (1988). "Computing Cournot-Nash Equilibria," University of Illinois, BEBR Working Paper, Champaign, IL.

Lemke, C.E., (1965). "Bimatrix Equilibrium Points and Mathematical Programming," Management Science, 11: 681-689.

Manne, A.S., H. Chao and R. Wilson, (1980). "Computation of Competitive Equilibria by a Sequence of Linear Programs," Econometrica, 48: 1595-1615.

Mathiesen, L., (1985). "Computational Experience in Solving Equilibrium Models by a Sequence of Linear Complementarity Problems," Operations Research, 33: 1225-1250.

Murphy, F.H., H.D. Sherali and A.L. Soyster, (1982). "A Mathematical Programming Approach for Determining Oligopolistic Market Equilibrium," Mathematical Programming, 24: 92-106.

Scarf, H. and T. Hansen, (1973). The Computation of Economic Equilibria, New Haven: Yale University Press.

Spence, M., (1976). "The Implicit Maximization of a Function in Monopolistically Competitive Markets," Harvard Institute of Economic Research Discussion Paper 461, Cambridge, MA.

Takayama, T. and G.G. Judge, (1971). Spatial and Temporal Price and Allocation Models, Amsterdam: North-Holland Publishing Company.

Tomlin, J.A., (1976). "Robust Implementation of Lemke's Method for the Linear Compementarity Problem," Systems Optimization Laboratory Report SOL 76-24, Department of Operations Research, Stanford University, Stanford, CA.

U.S. Department of Energy, (1982). "U.S. Coal Exports: Projections and Documentation," Report DOE/EIA-0317.

Yang. C.W. and W.C. Labys, (1985). "A Sensitivity Analyses of the Linear Complementarity Programming Model: Appalachian Steam Coal and the Natural Gas Market," Energy Economics, 7: 145-152.

6 Air quality standards, coal conversion and the steam-electric coal market

ALAN SCHLOTTMAN AND ROBIN A. WATSON
University of Tennessee

Introduction

In the United States coal-fired electric power plants generate the major portion of sulfur emissions, accounting for most of the approximately 50 percent of emissions attributable to electric utilities. Historical figures for electric utilities' share of sulfur emissions are available in U.S. Environmental Protection Agency (1973). Current statistics on electric generation and coal use are available from the Office of Coal, Nuclear, Electric and Alternate Fuels, Energy Information Administration. Natural gas is essentially a sulfur-free fuel, since the technology to remove its sulfur compounds during routine preparation prior to shipment is well advanced. Oil is generally low sulfur due to alternative blending and refining techniques. Monthly sulfur content of oil deliveries to electric utilities is approximately 0.9 percent to 1.0 percent (based on Federal Power Commission Form 423).

Certain standards for sulfur emissions to be imposed either at the stack or directly on the fuel being burned have been proposed for air quality controls. Most states now have plans to reduce sulfur emissions in the near term in conventional steam electric generation through regulations on emitted sulfur from coal use. These sulfur standards can provide incentives to develop techniques, such as stack gas scrubbing, for controlling sulfur emissions. However, a major effect of sulfur emissions standards is to promote the substitution of lower sulfur coals for those facing difficulties in complying with the standards.

In recent years, serious concern has been expressed over the United States' continued reliance on imported oil as a major energy source. Recent demand for energy in the United States has slowed from increasing at an annual average rate of 3.5 percent per year to 1.0 percent. Nevertheless, much of this increase is being met by petroleum, mostly imported petroleum products. This trend had been particularly noticeable in the early seventies. For example, imports of foreign oil products, both crude and refined, increased by 82 percent from 1970 to 1973 while output of domestic petroleum products decreased by approximately two percent; i.e., see Energy Information Agency (1982). The implications of this increasing reliance on foreign sources were clarified by the 1973 Arab oil embargo. As a result, current proposals have been made to prohibit conventional power plants from using oil or natural gas as their primary generating fuel, with the explicit purpose of increasing the utilizatin of domestic coal resources. Given the concern over sulfur emissions from electric power plants, there has been serious debate on the impacts on air quality of reconversion to coal.

Since the coal used in electric generation, often termed steam-coal, provides not only the major market for coal but the only one which has not declined in recent years, national coal and sulfur emissions policies and their related effects would have a major impact on the coal industry. In this chapter we first investigate the possible impacts that such standards for existing power plants would have on coals with different sulfur contents and, consequently, the regional effects on the entire coal industry. As shown, public policy towards alternative energy-environmental issues can have important interactions. Air quality policies which decrease sulfur emissions can stimulate surface mining and regional land use controversies. The feasibility of placing sulfur limits directly on coal use is then considered. With these results, a final purpose of our analysis will be to investigate the implications for public policy emphasizing power plant conversions to coal. The regional impacts of sulfur-reducing technology, which would permit current high sulfur coal production, are analyzed for their interaction with coal conversion and air quality.

Table 6.1 shows by supply district for 1981 the level of shipments, the average sulfur content of steam electric coal, and the percent surface mined. Using the standard classification by supply district, Districts One and Two, for example, are both in Pennsylvania. The coal fields of District Two supply the industrial centers of southern Pennsylvania, while District One is the primary source of shipments to electric utilities in the northeast. Similarly, Districts Eight and Nine split Kentucky into eastern and western coal fields. The western fields of Kentucky are a major source of surface mined, high sulfur coal, while the eastern fields are an important area for lower sulfur underground coal. The districts which have the highest average sulfur are the major producers in total tonnage of steam electric coal. Further, these districts produce almost entirely for electric utilities, because their coals have no coking or related properties suitable for steel production and other uses.

The Regional Model

Coal resources are nonrenewable stocks with fixed locations. The study of a resource which has a spatial dimension fixed by the nature of its available deposits must consider the regional implications of the analysis. Because of the impact of coal extraction on land use, these regional considerations are relatively more important for coal resources than for other fossil fuels.

We have attempted to model these fundamental structural characteristics of regional production capabilities and electric utility demand for coal in power plant generation in a spatial programming model of steam-electric coal production, distribution and use, i.e. see the Appendix as well as Schlottmann and Abrams (1977), Labys and Yang (1980), and Watson (1979). The model's basic activity is the delivery and utilization in a demand region of coal which has been extracted and shipped from one of the coal supply districts. The programming model consists of 52 electric power producing demand regions and the 23 coal supply districts. Coal shipments from any one supply district are differentiated by type of mining (surface and underground) and by source (new or existing mines). This is an important distinction because surface mining has grown dramatically in recent years, as indicated by Mining Information Services (1982, p. 729). In 1950, 24 percent of production was from surface mines. By 1981, surface mines accounted for 60 percent of total production. The relative importance of

Table 6.1

SHIPMENTS AND AVERAGE SULFUR CONTENT OF STEAM ELECTRIC COAL BY SUPPLY DISTRICTS, 1981

District of Origin	Average Sulfur Content	Quantity Shipped	Percent Surface
1 Eastern Pennsylvania	1.9	40,777	62.1
2 Western Pennsylvania	2.1	8,534	73.7
3 Northern West Virginia	2.3	19,765	47.4
4 Ohio	3.4	31,453	64.8
5 West Virginia (Panhandle)	3.8	5,561	0.4
6 Southern Numbered 1	1.1	2,031	41.2
7 Southern Numbered 2	1.1	116,613	50.9
8 West Kentucky	3.3	35,849	53.7
9 Illinois	2.7	43,877	45.4
10 Indiana	2.6	21,848	98.8
11 Iowa	2.5	323	63.4
12 Southeastern	1.4	13,619	68.5
13 Arkansas-Oklahoma	1.4	7	100.0
14 Southwestern	1.5	36,146	100.0
15 Northern-Colorado	0.6	1,024	86.3
16 Southern-Colorado	0.4	13,628	77.4
17 New Mexico	0.6	27,967	100.0
18 Wyoming	0.4	101,229	98.8
19 Utah	0.5	7,450	0.4
20 North-South Dakota	0.6	15,782	100.0
21 Montana	0.6	29,973	98.0
22 Washington	0.7	4,400	100.0

Sources: Data from Bituminous Coal Research, Inc. of the National Coal Association and Energy Information Administration [5].

these two mining methods varies across coal supply districts. Surface mining is predominant in Western states. With the exception of the Eastern Kentucky fields, which are a center for underground mining, the two methods are used almost equally in the majority of Appalachian districts. Surface mining is more important in the Midwest than underground operations. Missouri, for example, has only surface production. Approximately three-fourths of total surface mine production is delivered to steam-electric plants, which is 72 percent of coal delivered to utilities.

The utilization of any coal in steam-electric generation is dependent on its energy value, measured in Btu's. These energy values can differ by extraction method and by sulfur level. The average heat content by supply district of underground coal, for example, is about eight percent higher than that for surface mined coal. This different is greater n the lower sulfur coals, generally from 12 to 14 percent more, based on data reported on Federal Power Commission Form 423, "Cost and Quality of Fuels for Steam Electric Plants." On a price per million Btu basis, this helps to offset the initial disadvantage of underground mining where the extraction cost per ton is greater than surface production.

The sulfur content of coal can differ from one region to another. As we have seen, sulfur is the chief chemical property of coal which is subject to air pollution regulations. By most classifications of coal reserves by sulfur content, the West has the most low sulfur coal. The Midwest has relatively small low sulfur deposits. The Appalachian area, contrary to popular belief, does contain a significant amount of low sulfur reserves. The programming model differentiates coal shipments by five levels of sulfur, ranging from those emitting 0-.6 pounds of sulfur per million Btu to those emitting 3 pounds or more of sulfur per million Btu. Thus, differences by method of extraction, sulfur content and Btu value for each supply district are considered separately.

Solutions are characterized as determining the most efficient (minimum cost) network of productuion, distribution and use for coal in steam-electric generating plants. A convex programming model, which results from nonlinearities in the cost estimates, is used to attain this solution. Regional air quality standards which limit average sulfur emissions from coal-fired power plants can have important interactions with the spatial location of production activities, if a premium is placed on low sulfur emissions.

As public policy alters the delivered price of steam-electric coal to a demand region, two types of substitution can occur. First, since there are nonuniform impacts on coal supply regions, particularly from the simulation of various sulfur emissions policies, substitution between shipments from alternative domestic coal producing regions can be made, resulting in significant interregional production shifts. Second, substitution of alternative fuel sources, particularly lower sulfur oil, can be analyzed in the model by interfacing demand equations for coal use and their elasticities with the convex programming model. A similar programming procedure is described in F.E.A. (1977). This results in a heuristic programming procedure to approximate the spatial equilibrium values for coal production and use as an alternative solution technique to the classical nonlinear models. Such a procedure was utilized in the model of Schlottmann and Spore (1976).

As we have discussed, our main purpose here is to consider the feasibility and implications of possible interregional domestic coal substitution rather than the increased use of alternative fossil fuels to coal.

Air Quality Standards and Regional Surface Mining Issues

The regional impacts on coal shipments of presently proposed sulfur emission standards at coal-fired power plants for 1990 are shown in Table 6.2. Sulfur standards for existing coal-fired facilities are assumed to meet each state's respective old source performance standards as outlined in the state implementation plans. Recent proposals for new facilities would require a 90 percent removal of sulfur (regardless of the sulfur content of the coal burned) with associated state ceilings on sulfur emissions. This strategy attempts to take advantage of the "best available control technology" associated with stack gas scrubbing (desulfurization) at coal-fired steam electric plants. Our analysis assumes the availability of this technology at moderate cost (37 to 47 cents per million Btu).

As shown in Table 6.2 (when compared to production figures noted in Table 6.1), there is a marked expansion in coal shipments from the West to every coal-generating region of the country. The implicit average growth rate in Western coal production over the period exceeds ten percent. However, this projected growth appears sustainable in light of recent (and planned) expansion. See, for example, the annual statistics on the capacity of new coal mines and major

Table 6.2

REGIONAL SHIPMENTS WITH "BEST AVAILABLE TECHNOLOGY" SULFUR EMISSIONS STANDARDS
(Millions of Tons)

From	To				
	East	South	Midwest	West	Total
Northern Appalachia	100.85	1.37	0.00	0.00	102.22
Central Appalachia	7.43	102.51	0.00	0.00	109.94
Southern Appalachia	0.00	5.80	0.00	0.00	5.80
Midwest	70.08	77.17	71.35	0.00	218.60
West	319.31	102.84	167.29	93.59	683.03
United States	497.67	289.69	238.64	93.59	1,119.59

[a]The regions are identified as: Northern Appalachia - Districts 1, 2, 3, 4, 5, 6; Central Appalachia - Districts 7, 8; Southern Appalachia - District 13; Midwest - Districts 9, 10, 11, 12, 14, 15; West - Districts 16, 17, 18, 19, 20, 22, 23.

expansions planned by region in Mining Information Services (1982). Although coal production is expected to expand throughout most of the coal supply districts, the West is projected to increase its share of the steam-electric coal market to over 60 percent of total tons shipped. The increase in Western production is a definite result of public policy which attempts to restrict total sulfur emissions.

The generally accepted hypothesis that Eastern coal producers would be hurt most severely is not supported by our results. Central Appalachia, for example, is a major source of coal which can meet proposed air quality standards. In this respect, shipments to electric utilities by Appalachian producers do not decline from current levels except for Southern Appalachia (where older coal-fired generation should be retired). Assuming moderate costs for stack gas scrubbing, significant utilization of Midwestern coal could be expected. With a location central to major utility markets, our results suggest a signficant expansion in the producing areas of the Midwest.

The increases in Western surface production indicated in the results bring into focus the debate over surface mine reclamation in the West. The environmental issues for surface mining in the West differ from other producing regions. Adequate reclamation to insure solid stability particularly on steep slopes in the mountainous coal fields, has been the primary cause of concern in the producing areas of Appalachia. In the Midwest the environmental issues in strip mining deal mainly with the elimination of unreclaimed land from alternative uses in the future and the disruption of wildlife habitats. The coal industry often points out the potential of reclaimed Midwestern surface mined lands for grazing, farming, orchards, and possibly new wildlife and lake areas. Interested readers can consult Mined Land Conservation Committee (1964).

In the relatively dry areas of the West, however, there is some question of whether proper revegetation is possible as a method of reclamation. Soil conditions in the West are extremely fragile, and direct rainfall and other sources of water are limited. A study undertaken by the National Academy of Sciences (1974) concludes that reclamation does not appear feasible where the rainfall is less than 10 inches annually and where soils have difficulty in retaining the moisture. A similar conclusion has been reached in the analysis of the Northern Great Plains coal study (1975). At current levels of production, these minimum conditions are met in the West's two most heavily mined areas, the Northern Great Plains and the Rockies, which also contain 60 percent of the region's surface mine reserves of coal. However, these studies generally conclude that, although water requirements for mining and reclamation in these areas can be met, "there is not enough water available there for large scale operations like gasifying and liquefying coal or generating electric power," (Box et al., 1974). The implication of the reports for reclamation in other Western areas is not clear, however, since revegetation issues are emphasized where substantial original ground cover exists.

The remaining area of significant surface production in the West is found in the generally contiguous fields of northeastern Arizona and northwestern New Mexico. This area supplies mostly Western utilties, particularly those in Arizona. In parts of these states, annual rainfall can be less than five inches and the surface soil is gnerally alkaline. By contrast, average rainfall in Appalachia can be up to 45 inches and in other Western areas, 14 to 16 inches, as reported in Council on Envrinomental Quality (1973). As a result, little or no vegetation exists under normal circumstances. Since most of the deposits currently under extraction are on Navajo or Hopi Indian lands, the effort at present is to determine which vegetation will produce the best grazing crop for sheep and cattle.

The highest reclamation costs occur in the eastern fields, with the lowest in the producing areas of the West. Based upon updating the estimates in Schlottmann and Spore (1976), average reclamation costs per ton in Appalachia are $4.11 (1981 dollars). Reclamation of area mining in the Midwest has a value of $2.19 a ton, with the average value in the West at $0.59 a ton.

The results of imposing a reclamation policy on the western coal industry as currently developed leads to the conclusion that the use of western coal is relatively unaffected by additional production costs associated with reclamation. In the West, coal normally is a least-cost generation source, relative to the costs of natural gas and oil. Its use outside of the West is determined as a consequence of sulfur emission issues, not by a relative cost comparison to alternative production, which is so marginal that slightly raising the lowest production costs in the United States would make its use noncompetitive.

This is also an important result for the effects of reclamation on the future patterns of surface mining development in Appalachia. Since reclamation costs increase with increasing slope angles of production, one might expect an increased use of lower slope strippable reserves. The sulfur content of Central Appalachian coal reserves, however, is inversely correlated with increasing slope angle. Lower sulfur reserves are mined on steep slopes, most on slopes exceeding 20⁰. This contour surface mining on steep slopes in Appalachia has been the most controversial environmental issue for the land use impacts of surface mining. In particular, the problem of soil stability after mining is generally considered to be difficult to deal with. Thus there is no reason to expect a decline in the intensity of the use of higher slope surface reserves as long as public policy results in a premium to low sulfur coal.

A Ban on the Highest Sulfur Coals

A major effect of sulfur emissions standards is to reduce the use of the highest sulfur coals. We define the highest sulfur coals as those emitting three pounds of sulfur or more per million Btu. It has been suggested that one way to reduce the use of such coal as a generating fuel is simply to ban it. These proposals generally suggest that alternative coals, rather than oil, be substituted. This has occurred in some urban situations. For example, in recent years Chicago utilities have used (some) Western coal instead of relying solely on Illinois production.

But what would be the effect of such a policy as an overall regulation? The shortage of lower sulfur coals and the variances granted for utilities to burn high sulfur coal even in urban areas would lead us to believe that such a policy over the near term would be costly. The basic solution in our model shows that the highest sulfur coals comprise 11 percent of all coal used. One might ask if this figure is perhaps too high, that actual use is so much less than in the basic model (123.0 million tons) that we overestimate the importance of high sulfur output. If we aggregate the data available from the F.P.C., which lists all coal deliveries to utilities by sulfur content, we find that, during 1981, high sulfur coal comprised approximately 14 percent of total steam-electric coal shipments, i.e. see F.P.C. (1982).

Table 6.3 shows the simulated increases in local production required to replace high sulfur coal in the basic solution without changing the relative regional production levels.

Table 6.3

RELATIVE REGIONAL INCREASES IN COAL PRODUCTION TO COMPENSATE FOR THE HIGHEST SULFUR COAL LOSSES

Region	Percentage Increase in Other Capacity	Required Additional Tonnage (millions of tons)
Appalachia	15.8	34.5
Midwest	40.6	88.7
West[a]	--	--
United States	10.98	123.2

[a]No increase required.

The greatest expansion would be required in the Midwest, where failure by Midwestern producers to supply this additional tonnage would require the use of Western coal. This would add approximately 36 to 44 cents per million btu to the average delivered costs of coal in the Midwest utility market. However, new sources for 123 million tons of coal would have to be found, a difficult task considering the current time lag for expanding existing underground and surface mining or for establishing new mines, i.e. see O.T.A. (1979). Particularly with the assumed availability of scrubbing technology to reduce emissions, such a policy seems somewhat costly.

Coal Conversion

The main public policy tool to increase coal use in conventional power generation lies in the original Energy Supply and Environmental Coordination Act of 1974, which allows the Department of Energy to prohibit power plants with a capability to use coal from relying on natural gas or oil as their main generating fuel. (The main reference for the data used here is an unpublished report by F.E.A. (1975). Further details are available on coal conversion from the Office of Fuels Conversion, Energy Information Administration). The regional distribution of the maximum feasible power plant capacity conversions of existing and planned units is shown in Table 6.4. The majority of the additional demands for coal would be in the Western states as a substitute for natural gas and in the East to replace oil. Significant reductions in oil use particularly would result.

The Environmental Protection Agency, which is required to certify the conversion actions and essentially is given a veto power, has been less than enthusiastic about coal conversion. This has resulted because of difficulties in existing coal-fired power plants as well as additional conversions to meet the suggested primary air quality standards of 1.2 pounds of sulfur oxide per million Btu in the amended Clean Air Act of 1971. Stack gas scrubbing, which removes sulfur from the fuel gases after combustion, could affect the use of higher sulfur coals and allow low sulfur emissions standards to be met, e.g., see Gordon (1975, pp. 109-125). Efforts to reduce the sulfur level of coal before shipment and combusion have not had much success. The sulfur is found in coal in two forms, organic and pyrite. Pyrite sulfur, which varies among coal fields from four percent to 60 percent of total sulfur, can be reduced by mechanical cleaning and crushing. At present, around 50

Table 6.4

REGIONAL POWER PLANT CONVERSION POTENTIAL

Region[a]	Conversion Capacity (megawatts)	Decreased: Oil Use (million barrels)	Decreased: Natural Gas (billion CF)	Additional Coal (millions of tons)[b]
Northeast	10,862	84.67	30.76	24.9
East Central	2,366	5.95	69.76	4.9
Southeast	3,948	28.50	25.62	9.1
West Central	730	5.04	.93	1.4
South Central	3,067	27.65	2.11	7.8
West	3,418	29.22	10.18	8.6
Total, United States	24,392	181.04	139.38	56.6

[a]Regions correspond to the EIA National Power Regions.

[b]Additional demand based on a uniform coal ton equivalent of 22.2 million Btu per ton as described in Federal Energy Administration (1975); actual coal shipments by region from the model in Table 6.5 differ as a result.

percent of all coal produced is cleaned, but, since organic compounds are unaffected by cleaning, these operations usually remove less than half of the sulfur, i.e., see O.T.A. (1979). The only possibility of eliminating sulfur from coal appears to be through the development of a method of producing synthetic fuels from coal, particularly synthetic gas.

In the metallurgical coal market, cleaning is a routine step in preparing high grade coal for coking and related uses. Other cleaning operations are undertaken explicitly to reduce the sulfur levels in coal for the electric utility market. In Illinois, Indiana, and Western Kentucky, for example, practically all coal produced is for electric utilties. The average sulfur content in 1981, shown in Table 6.1 was 2.6-3.3 percent, a high level. Yet production records indicate that almost all of this coal had been first mechanically cleaned at the mines. Thus, the removal of pyrite sulfur alone, while it improves the quality of coal somewhat, cannot reduce the sulfur content to a sufficient degree.

Table 6.5 shows the increases in regional shipments required to satisfy the demands resulting from coal conversion as well as to meet low primary air quality emission standards at alternative levels of stack gas scrubbing costs. These results clearly indicate that Western coal use would be competitive in Midwestern and Appalachian markets given the current levels of stack gas scrubbing costs. It is important to consider what level of surface mining public opinion will allow in the West, before local and state action hinder its development. Most surface mining reserves occur in remote areas, where the alternative value of grazing is relatively low. Yet the controversy over surface mine reclamation shows that public opinion can be an important variable in the West. It could significantly affect the Midwestern utilities' use of Western coal for meeting sulfur emissions standards. Sulfur emission policies have boosted the competitive position of Western coal over local coal production in Midwestern markets. Whether Western producers could expand production into new reserve areas might well depend on local response.

It is true that the large scale installation of stack gas scrubbers will minimize the need for heavily increased low sulfur coal producing capacity. Our analysis shows, however, that this could be expected only if the current costs of

Table 6.5

REGIONAL SHIPMENT INCREASES IN COAL PRODUCTION TO MEET COAL CONVERSION DEMANDS (1980)

	Stack Gas Scrubbing Costs (cents per million Btu)	
Region	37-47 cents[a]	128-146 cents[b]
Appalachia	34.17	24.84
Midwest	13.30	5.20
West	12.03	36.50
United States	59.50	66.54

[a]The figures here represent a mid-range estimate for possible scrubbing costs as utilized in the model.

[b]These figures represent the higher end of the range for possible scrubbing costs.

scrubbing technology are moderate or if large scale development of Western surface mining is prohibited.

A similar conclusion occurs when considering coal gasification, i.e. see F.E.A. (1977). Coal gasification could make these higher sulfur coals almost sulfur free. Unfortunately, it is difficult to use the high coking coals of the Eastern fields in the most advanced technique presently available for gasification -- the Lurgi process. The cost estimates for gasification range from $2.60 to $3.09 per million Btu. Any changes in the price of coal utilized for gasification are significant because the efficiency of conversion of only 67 percent magnifies any rise in coal prices. In terms of domestic energy independence, this conversion factor means that any long-term reliance on gasification would deplete coal reserves at a faster rate than if they were mined and used directly.

Conclusions

The use of Western coal in particular has been shown to be significantly affected by sulfur emissions policies. The issue of adequate surface mine reclamation in the West would receive new emphasis, if public policies were seriously undertaken to lower current levels of sulfur emissions at coal-fired power plants. These results would only be intensified with coal conversion policies at power plants currently using oil and natural gas as their main fossil fuel. Midwestern high sulfur coal can compete with Western coal only if operating costs for sulfur reducing technologies are moderate.

Perhaps the main point to be learned through this analysis is that public policies were seriously undertaken to lower current levels of sulfur emissions at coal-fired power plants. These results would only be intensified with coal conversion policies at power plants currently using oil and natural gas as their main fossil fuel. Midwestern high sulfur coal can compete with Western coal only if operating costs for sulfur reducing technologies are moderate.

Perhaps the main point to be learned through this analysis is that public policy towards alternative energy-environmental issues can have important interactions. Air quality policies which decrease sulfur emissions can stimulate surface mining and regional land use controversies. Simply banning the use of highest sulfur coal may be difficult given current regional production capabilities;

coal conversion at power plants does reduce oil use but overall cannot easily meet low sulfur emission standards; pressure by government agencies for clean coal burning technology to be installed at power plants without consideration for the prices of substitute fuels may aggrevate the surface mining controversy even further. In short, the interrelationships among energy policies in the United States concerning coal use and its environment are sensitive and worthy of further investigation.

Appendix

The Model and Parametric Procedures

The basic activity in the model is denoted as X_{ijklm}, that is, the coal extracted in the ith coal supply district by the jth mining method (with the kth sulfur level) in new or existing mines (mth) and delivered to the lth demand region, measured in 1,000 ton units.

The main behavioural assumption of the model is contained in the objective function

$$\text{Minimize } \Sigma_i \Sigma_j \Sigma_k \Sigma_l \Sigma_m (C_{ijm} + t_{il}) X_{ijklm} \qquad (A.1)$$

where C_{ijm} represents the per unit extraction costs of the respective activities and t_{il} represents the per unit transportation costs. The optimal solution to (A.1) minimized the total cost of the production, delivery, and utilization of steam electric coal subject to the constraint system. If a supply district can provide the requirements of a demand area at a lower delivered price than a competing district, either because of an extraction cost advantage or a transport cost advantage, the model attempts by the specification in (A.1) to ship from that district. Utilities in each state are seen as attempting to minimize the costs of their fuel input deliveries, and producing districts as shipping where they have the greatest relative cost advantage.

Given the increased demands resulting from coal conversion, the impacts of stack gas scrubbing were analyzed by modifying the objective function to:

$$\Sigma_i \Sigma_j \Sigma_k \Sigma_l \Sigma_m \Sigma_s [C_{ijm} + t_{il}) X_{ijklm} + \Phi(b_{ijkms}) X_{ijklms}] \qquad (A.2)$$

where Φ is the level of the stack gas scrubbing costs. The terms X_{ijklms} represent the scrubbing of coal in the model. This technology alters the user cost of a ton of coal from any region by the emitted pounds of sulfur per million Btu's in that ton times the appropriate scrubbing costs. The coal supply curves by district, such as shown in Figure A-1, are entered in the model with linear approximations. These supply curves are discussed in more detail in Watson (1979).

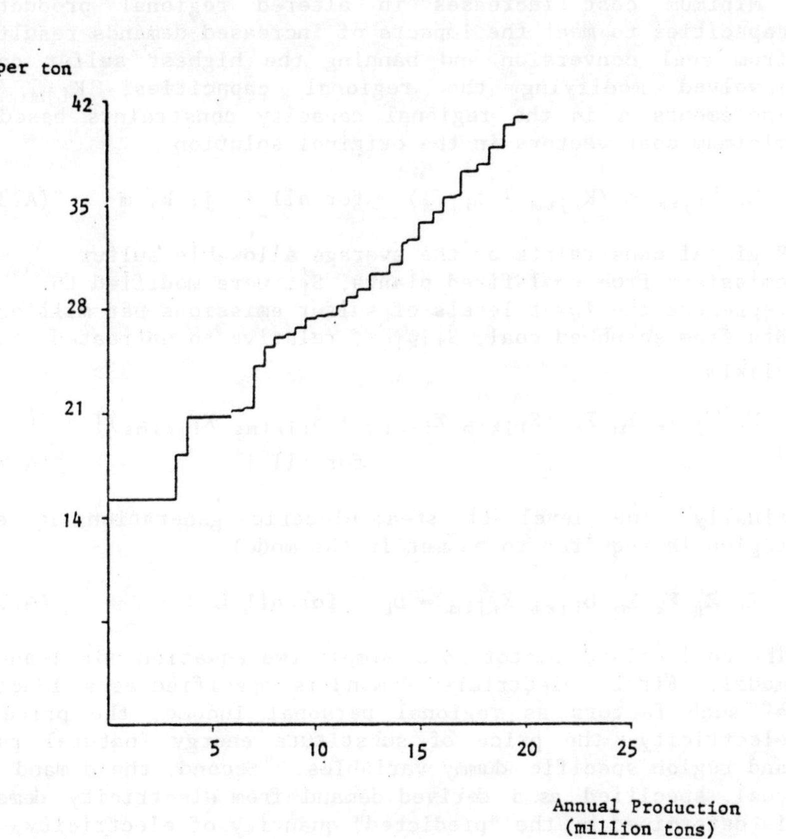

Figure 6.A.1

COAL SUPPLY-SOUTHERN APPALACHIA
(District 13, 1981 dollars)

Minimum cost increases in altered regional production capacities to meet the impacts of increased demands resulting from coal conversion and banning the highest sulfur coals involved modifying the regional capacities, K_{ijm}, by increments Δ in the regional capacity constraints based on minimum cost vectors in the original solution

$$\Sigma_i X_{ijkm} \leq (K_{ijkm} + \Delta_{ijkm}) \quad \text{for all } i, j, k, m \qquad (A.3)$$

Regional constraints on the average allowable sulfur emissions from coal-fired plants, S_1', were modified to represent the lower levels of sulfur emissions per million Btu from scrubbed coal, $\bar{S}_{ijklms}$, relative to untreated coal, S_{ijklm}

$$\Sigma_i \Sigma_j \Sigma_k \Sigma_m \Sigma_s [S_{ijklm} X_{ijklm} + \bar{S}_{ijklms} X_{ijklms})] \leq S_1' \quad \text{for all } i \qquad (A.4)$$

Finally, the level of steam-electric generation in each region is required to be met in the model

$$\Sigma_i \Sigma_j \Sigma_k \Sigma_m b_{ijkm} X_{ijkm} = D_L \quad \text{for all } L \qquad (A.5)$$

The coal demand sector is a simple two equation simultaneous model. First, electricity demand is specified as a function of such factors as regional personal income, the price of electricity, the price of substitute energy (natural gas), and region specific dummy variables. Second, the demand for coal, specified as a derived demand from electricity demand, is determined by the "predicted" quantity of electricity, the price of coal, the price of substitute energy (oil), and regional specific dummy variables. The demand model is also discussed in detail in Watson (1979).

Authors
Alan Schlottman
Department of Economics
University of Tennessee
Knoxville, TN 37916

Robin A. Watson
Department of Economics
University of Tennessee
Knoxville, TN 37916

References

Box, T. et al., (1974). Rehabilitation Potential of Western Coal Lands, National Academy of Sciences, Cambridge: Ballinger.

Coal Age, (1982). Mining Informational Services, "Surface Mining Law," New York, NY.

Council on Environmental Quality, (1973). Surface Mining and Reclamation, Washington, D.C.: U.S. Government Printing Office.

Energy Information Administration, (1982). U.S. Department of Energy, Annual Report, Washington, D.C.: U.S. Government Printing Office.

Energy Information Administration, (1982). U.S. Department of Energy, Cost and Quality of Fuels for Electric Utility Plants, Washington, D.C.: U.S. Government Printing Office.

Federal Energy Administration, (1975). "Coal Conversion Program," unpublished draft environment statement, Office of Coal.

Federal Energy Administration, (1977). "Documentation of the Project Independence Assessment Model," unpublished.

Federal Power Commission, (1982). "Monthly Report of Cost and Quality of Fuels at Steam Electric Generating Plants." Washington, D.C.

Gordon, R., (1975). Coal and the U.S. Electric Power Industry, Baltimore: Johns Hopkins Press.

Henderson, J., (1958). The Efficiency of the Coal Industry: An Application of Linear Programing, Cambridge, MA: Harvard University Press.

Labys, W.C. and C.W. Yang, (1980). "A Quadratic Programming Model of the Appalachian Steam Coal Market," Energy Economics, 2: 86-95.

M.I.T. Energy Policy Study Group, (1974). "Energy Self Sufficiency: An Economic Evaluation," Technology Review, 76: 22-58.

Mined Land Conservation Conference, (1964). What About Strip Mining, Washington, D.C.: Mined Land Conservation Committee.

Mining Information Services, (1982). Keystone Coal Industry Manual, New York: McGraw-Hill.

National Petroleum Council, Task Force, (1973). U.S. Energy Outlook, Washington, D.C.: National Petroleum Council.

Northern Great Plains Coal Study Group, (1975). Northern Great Plains Coal, Minneapolis: Upper Midwest Council.

Office of Emergency Preparedness, Executive Office of the President, (1973). The Potential for Energy Conservation, Substitution for Scarce Fuels, Washington, D.C.: U.S. Government Printing Office.

Office of Technology Assessment, Congress of the United States, (1979). The Direct Use of Coal, Washington, D.C.: U.S. Government Printing Office.

Schlottmann, A. and L. Abrams, (1977). "Sulfur Emissions Taxes and Coal Resources," Review of Economics and Statistics, 59: 50-55.

Schlottmann, A. and R. Spore, (1976). "Economic Impacts of Surface Mine Reclamation," Land Economics, 52: 265-277.

U.S. Department of Energy, Office of Analytical Services, (1979). National Energy Plan II, Appendix B: U.S. Energy Projections, Washington, D.C.: U.S. Government Printing Office.

U.S. Environmental Protection Agency, (1973). Nationwide Air Pollutant Emission Trends 1940-1970, Research Triangle Park, N.C.: Environmental Protection Agency.

Watson, R.A., (1979). "Uncertainty and the Regional Allocation of Steam Electric Coal in the United States," unpublished Ph.D. dissertation, University of Tennessee.

7 A comparative study of linear complementarity programming models and linear programming models in multi-region investment analysis: aluminium and bauxite

TAKASHI TAKAYAMA *University of Western Australia*
HIDEO HASHIMOTO *The World Bank*

Introduction

Since the linear programming (LP) method was developed at the end of the 1940s by Dantzig (1951), it has been successfully applied to a large number of fields in business and industrial management as well as to military logistic operation. This method has also been used in the areas of regional, interregional, and international economic planning as well as project evaulation. In the field of economic planning, the LP spatial and temporal optimization approach was further extended to include investment models in which the optimal determination of both the location of productive activities and the time of capacity investment can be attained by minimizing total cost (the sum of capital, operating and transport cost) (Massé and Gibrat 1964, and Stevens, 1959). Note that a comprehensive survey of LP investment models appears in Turvey and Anderson (1977). Later, to encompass economies of scale with respect to investments in production capacity, the cost minimization approach was applied to the mixed-integer programming model (Kendrick and Stoutjesdijk, 1978). The mixed-integer programming investment model has been applied to the fertilizer industry (Choksi, Meeraus and Stoutjesdijk, 1980) and the aluminum industry (Brown, et al. 1983).

Takayama and Judge (1971) developed a series of spatial and temporal equilibrium, market-oriented models. Under certain conditons for demand and/or supply functions, the models can be solved in a finite number of iterations (like the LP simplex method) by a quadratic programming (QP) method (the simplex method modified by Wolfe (1959)), or other finite termination methods such as the Lemke method (Lemke, 1965, and Tomlin, 1976), or by the linear complementarity programming (LCP) method (Cottle and Dantzig, 1968). These models were extended to include investment in production capacity in the QP form (Uri, 1975), and in the LCP form (Hashimoto, 1981a, 1981b, and 1983b). The fundamental logic behind the QP and the LCP investment models is the optimality condition of capital theory (under certainty). In this theory, investment takes place up to the point where the sum of the discounted future stream of cash flows expected from the investment is exactly equal to the cost of the investment.

In this paper, the differences in the performance of the LCP and LP investment models are examined, using the bauxite-alumina-aluminum industry as an example. (A similar comparison appears in Hashimoto (1983a)). The differences in performance are examined with respect to two different criteria: (1) the stability of solutions given pertubations in parameters; and (2) the ability to handle constraints on the supply of inputs. For the former case three parameter changes are tested: (1) changes in electricity costs, (2) changes in transport costs, and (3) changes in the tax on bauxite supply. For the latter case, two examples are used: first, where policy decisions constrain the quantity of bauxite production, and second, where the supply of electricity for smelting within a region is limited by existing generation capacity (electricity supply is determined outside the models).

The Models

Outline of the Models of the Bauxite-Alumina-Aluminum Industry

Both LCP and LP investment models of the bauxite-alumina-aluminum industry encompass three regions, three processing stages, and two periods. The models deal only with the market economies, which are decomposed into three regions. The market economies are defined as the world minus centrally planned economies. China is included in the centrally planned economies. Region 1 roughly corresponds to industrial countries, including Southern Europe; Region 2 is the developing countries; Region 3 is Australia. Australia is dealt with separately from other industrial countries because it is a focal country for new processing activities, given its endowments of low-cost electricity and abundant bauxite.

The models specify three stages of processing: bauxite mining, alumina refining and aluminum smelting. It is assumed that bauxite, alumina and aluminum can be produced in all three regions through the only mining, refining or smelting process specific to each region in each period. The markets for bauxite, alumina and aluminum in 1980, denoted as Period 0, are used as the initial conditions of the model. (The actual statisitics in 1980 have been adjusted somewhat to smooth out year-specific effects.) Periods 1 and 2 represent 1985 and 1990. The intertemporal linkages are made by investments in production capacity.

Besides the constraint on production capacity, within each region determined endogenously by the intitial capacity plus investments implemented the succeeding periods, maximum limits on bauxite extraction and use of electricity for aluminum smelting have been assumed for each region in each period to simulate physical resource endowment conditions or producing countries' supply policies. The Lagrangean multiplier of these constraints can be interpreted as the rent accruing to those suppliers. The differences among regions in perceptions of future risks are captured by the use of differential rates of discount of future earnings.

The LCP model has three kinds of linear equations. Demand for aluminum is assumed to be a function of its price. The unit cost of operating goods and services and the unit cost of investment in production capacity are assumed to increase linearly as the amount consumed or the scale of investment increases. In the LP model, a minimum fixed demand for aluminum is assumed for each region in each period of time. The two types of costs mentioned above are fixed for each region in each period of time. The parameters used were derived partly by econometric estimation methods and partly from industry sources. The relative position of each region with respect to costs of bauxite production, electricity for aluminum smelting and investments in production capacity, as well as relative risk factors is shown in Table 7.1.

To illustrate the differences between the LCP and LP models, an illustrative programming tableau is shown for each

Table 7.1

RELATIVE COST AND RISK POSITIONS

	Region 1	Region 2	Region 3
Bauxite Mining Cost	High	Low	Medium
Electricity Cost	High	High	Low
Investment Cost	Low	High	Medium
Risk Factor	Low	High	Medium

type of model (Tables 7.2 and 7.3). Notation for the variables employed in the model are summarized in Table 7.4.

Market Equilibrium Conditions of the LCP Model The market equilibrium conditions of the model are presented in three groups. All the endongenous and counterpart variables are non-negative. We consider the following functions as linear.

Demand Function for Aluminum The following linear demand function is specified for aluminum:

$$WDM_{it} = PDM_{it} - \lambda_{it} + \omega_{it}\ DM_{it} \geq 0 \text{ and}$$

$$WDM_{it} \cdot DM_{it} = 0 \qquad (3)$$

Function of Costs of Operating Goods and Services The unit cost of operating goods and services (excluding the major inputs) is assumed to vary as the total quantity of those items changes.

$$WS'Q_{it} = -\ PS'Q_{it} + \delta_{Qit} + \epsilon_{Qit}\ S'Q_{it} \geq 0 \text{ and}$$

$$WS'Q_{it} \cdot S'Q_{it} = 0 \qquad (4)$$

Investment Cost Function As stated before, the unit cost of investment in production capacity varies as the scale of investment changes.

$$WIQ_{i(t-1)t} = -\ PIQ_{i(t-1)t} + \alpha_{Qit} + \beta_{Qit}\quad {}_{(t-1)t} \geq 0 \text{ and}$$

$$WIQ_{i(t-1)t} \cdot IQ_{i(t-1)t} = 0 \qquad (5)$$

Demand and Supply Equilibrium Conditions

The following conditions are usual pairs for regulating demand- and supply-flows. The first pair states that each region's total inshipment quantity of Q must be large enough to satisfy the region's demand for Q and the demand price can be positive if the demand is exactly met by the total inshipment. The second pair states that the supply of Q must be large enough to meet the outshipment (including self-supply) requirements of Q and the supply price can be positive if there is no excess supply. As electricity is not transmitted outside each region in this model, its demand and supply can be connected directly by eliminating the term for shipment $TQ_{jit}t$. In such a case, some modifications in (6), (7), (8) and (15) are needed. (See Table 7.1).

Table 7.2 TRUNCATED TABLEAU OF THE BAUXITE-ALUMINA-ALUMINUM MODEL (LCP VERSION)

	DM11	S'M11	S'X11	IM101	IX101	JM101	SM11	TM111	D'M11	CM11	JX101	DX11	SX11	TX111	D'X11	CX11	DE11	SE11	PDM11	PSM11	PD'M11	PS'M11	PIM101	PCM11	PKM11	PMX11	PDX11	PSX11	PD'X11	PS'X11	PIX101	PCX11	PKX11	PRX11	PDE11	PSE11	PRE11	
WDM11	ω																		1																			$-\lambda$
WS'M11		ε																				−1																δ
WS'X11			ε																											−1								δ
WIM101				β																			−1															α
WIX101					β																										−1							α
WJM101																							1		$-\sigma$													
WSM11																				−1	1			1		μ									μ			
WTM111																			−1	1																		$\overline{PTM111}$
WD'M11																					−1	1																
WCM11																								$-\gamma$	1													
WJX101																															1		$-\sigma$					
WDX11																										−1	1											
WSX11																												−1	1			1		1				
WTX111																											−1	1										$\overline{PTX111}$
WD'X11																													−1	1								
WCX11																																$-\gamma$	1					
WDE11																																			−1	1		
WSE11																																				−1	1	$\overline{PGE11}$
WPDM11	−1							1																														
WPSM11							1	−1																														
WPD'M11							−1		1																													
WPS'M11		1							−1																													
WPIM101				1		−1																																
WPCM11							−1			γ																												
WPKM11						σ'				−1																												$\sigma'\overline{CM10}$
WPMX11							$-\mu$					1																										
WPDX11												−1		1																								
WPSX11													1	−1																								
WPD'X11													−1		1																							
WPS'X11			1												−1																							
WPIX101					1						−1																											
WPCX11													−1			γ																						
WPKX11											σ'					−1																						$\sigma'\overline{CX10}$
WPRX11													−1																									$\overline{UX11}$
WPDE11							$-\mu$										1																					
WPSE11																	−1	1																				
WPRE11																		−1																				$\overline{UE11}$

Table 7.3 TRUNCATED TABLEAU OF THE BAUXITE-ALUMINA-ALUMINIUM MODEL (LP VERSION)

	JM101	SM11	TM111	D'M11	CM11	JX101	DX11	SX11	TX111	D'X11	CX11	DE11	SE11	PDM11	PSM11	PD'M11	PCM11	PKM11	PMX11	PDX11	PSX11	PD'X11	PCX11	PKX11	PRX11	PDE11	PSE11	PRE11	
WJM101																		$-\sigma$											$\overline{PIM101}$
WSM11															-1	1	1		μ							μ			
WTM111														-1	1														$\overline{PTM111}$
WD'M11																-1													$\overline{PD'M11}$
WCM11																	$-\gamma$	1											
WJX101																								$-\sigma$					$\overline{PIX101}$
WDX11																			-1	1									
WSX11																					-1	1	1		1				
WTX111																				-1	1								$\overline{PTX111}$
WD'X11																						-1							$\overline{PD'X11}$
WCX11																							$-\gamma$	1					
WDE11																										-1	1		
WSE11																											-1	1	$\overline{PGE11}$
WPDM11			1																										$\overline{DM11}$
WPSM11		1	-1																										
WPD'M11		-1		1																									
WPCM11		-1			γ																								
WPKM11	σ				-1																								$\sigma\,\overline{CM10}$
WPMX11		$-\mu$					1																						
WPDX11							-1		1																				
WPSX11								1	-1																				
WPD'X11								-1		1																			
WPCX11								-1			γ																		
WPKX11						σ					-1																		$\sigma\,\overline{CX10}$
WPRX11								-1																					$\overline{UX11}$
WPDE11		$-\mu$										1																	
WPSE11												-1	1																
WPRE11													-1																$\overline{UE11}$

Table 7.4

DEFINITION OF MODEL VARIABLES[a]

Indices

Q, Q'	-	Output or input which can be aluminum (M), alumina (N), bauxite (X) or electricity (E).
i, j	-	Region. (To save space, Region i is expressed as Ri in the Tables and in Appendix 2.)
t, r	-	Period: 1980 - 0, 1985 - 1, 1990 - 2.

Endogenous Variables

DQ_{it}	-	Demand for Q.
SQ_{it}	-	Supply of Q.
TQ_{ijt}	-	Shipment of Q from Region i to Region j.
$D'Q_{it}$	-	Demand for operating goods and services used for production Q.
$S'Q_{it}$	-	Supply of the above.
CQ_{it}	-	Capacity of Production of Q.
$IQ_{(t-1)t}$	-	Supply of net increase in capacity for production of Q resulting from investment in production capacity implemented between Periods t-1 and t.
$JQ_{(t-1)t}$	-	Demand for net increase in the above-mentioned capacity.
PDQ_{it}	-	Demand price of Q.
PSQ_{it}	-	Supply price of Q.
$PD'Q_{it}$	-	Demand price of operating goods and services.
$PS'Q_{it}$	-	Supply price of the above.
PQQ'_{it}	-	Charge of Q' as a part of production costs of Q that can be claimed by producers of Q.
PRQ_{it}	-	Rent accruing to a limited supply of Q.
PCQ_{it}	-	Demand rental fee of the use of capacity of production of Q.

Table 7.4 cont'd.

PKQ_{it}	-	Supply rental fee of the use of capacity mentioned above.
$PIM_{(t-1)t}$	-	Cost of investment in production capacity of Q implemented between Periods t-1 and t.

Counterpart Variables

Each of the above variables has a counterpart slack variable, denoted by the initial letter W.

Exogenous Variables and Parameters[b]

$\overline{CQ}_{i0}$	-	Capacity of production of Q.
$\overline{UQ}_{it}$	-	Upper bound on supply of Q.
$\overline{PTQ}_{ijt}$	-	Transportation costs of Q from Region i to Region j.
$\overline{PGE}_{it}$	-	Generating and transmitting costs of electricity.
$\overline{DM}_{it}$	-	Fixed minimum demand for aluminum (used in the LP model).
$\overline{PD'Q}_{it}$	-	Fixed price of operating goods and services for production of Q (used in the LP model).
$\overline{PIQ}_{i(t-1)t}$	-	Fixed cost of investment in production capacity in Q (used in the LP model).
$\mu_{QQ'it}$	-	Requirement of Q' to product a unit of Q.
γ_{Qit}	-	Upper limit of capacity utilization rate of production of Q.
$\sigma_{Qi\tau t}$	-	Discount rate applied to earnings in year τ which result from investments in capacity of production of Q implemented between Periods t-1 and t.
$\sigma'_{Qi\tau t}$	-	Discount rate in year τ, applied to the production capacity of Q incremented by the investment implemented between Periods t-1 and t.
--	-	Interest or normal rate of return, used as a basis for the calculation of the discount rate applied to earnings.
$-'_{i}$	-	Depreciaton rate, as a basis for the calculation of actual production capacity.

[a]In the explanation of variables and parameters below, "in Region i in Period t" is implied.
[b]The parameters used in the demand function for aluminum, in the cost function are not listed, because they are self-explanatory.

$$WPDQ_{it} = DQ_{it} + \sum_{j=1}^{3} TQ_{jit} \geq 0 \text{ and}$$

$$WPDQ_{it} \cdot PDQ_{it} = 0 \qquad (6)$$

$$WPSQ_{it} = SQ_{it} - \sum_{j=1}^{3} TQ_{ijt} \geq 0 \text{ and}$$

$$WPSQ_{it} \cdot PSQ_{it} = 0 \qquad (7)$$

Input-Output Relationships The requirement of the input to produce one unit of a specified output is determined by a given coefficient. The following input-output relationships specify the requirements of alumina and electricity in production of aluminum and that of bauxite in alumina production:

$$WPQQ'_{it} = -\mu_{QQ'it}\, SQ_{it} + DQ'_{it} \geq 0$$

$$WPQQ'_{it} \cdot PQQ'_{it} = 0 \qquad (8)$$

Operating Goods and Services For simplicity let us assume that one unit of operating goods and services is associated with one unit of output of any Q. The quantity balances of those goods and services are regulated as follows:

$$WPD'Q_{it} = D'Q_{it} - SQ_{it} \geq 0 \text{ and}$$

$$WPD'Q_{it} \cdot PD'Q_{it} = 0 \qquad (9)$$

$$WPS'Q_{it} = S'Q_{it} - D'Q_{it} \geq 0 \text{ and}$$

$$WPS'Q_{it} \cdot PS'Q_{it} = 0 \qquad (10)$$

Supply, Production Capacity and Investment The supply of Q is limited by the existing capacity times an upper limit of the capacity utilization rate.

$$WPCQ_{it} = -SQ_{it} + \gamma_{Qit} CQ_{it} \geq 0 \text{ and}$$

$$WPCQ_{it} \cdot PCQ_{it} = 0 \qquad (11)$$

The demand for an increase in production capacity is related to its supply, which is determined by the investment cost function (5). Then the production capacity in period t is determined in such a way that it cannot exceed the sum of the initial-period capacity plus the increase in capacity resulting from investments implemented in the successive years until period t. (In this calculation, production capacity is depreciated properly). If the equality holds, the rental fee for the use of the production capacity can be positive.

$$WPIQ_{i(t-1)t} = IQ_{i(t-1)} - JQ_{i(t-1)t} \geq 0 \text{ and}$$

$$WPIQ_{i(t-1)t} \cdot PIQ_{i(t-1)t} = 0 \qquad (12)$$

$$WPKQ_{it} = - CQ_{it} + \sum_{\tau=1}^{t} \sigma Q_{it(\tau-1)} JQ_{i(\tau-1)\tau}$$

$$+ \sigma_{Qit0} \cdot \overline{CQ}_{i0} \geq 0 \text{ and}$$

$$WPKQ_{it} \cdot PKQ_{it} = 0 \qquad (13)$$

where

$$\sigma_{Qi\tau t} = (1 + r_i)^{-(\tau - t - 1/2)}$$

Upper Limit on Supply The supply of electricity for aluminum smelting can be limited, and the extraction of bauxite can also be limited. A positive rent can arise if the constraint is bound.

$$WPRQ_{it} = - SQ_{it} + \overline{UQ}_{it} \geq 0$$

$$WPQ_{it} \cdot PRQ_{it} = 0 \qquad (14)$$

Price Equilibrium Conditions

The following is the usual pair of conditions regulating the transport activity between any pair of regions, given a fixed transportation cost per unit of Q. If the flow is positive (shipment takes place), the demand price must be exactly equal to the sum of the supply price and the transport cost; and if the latter is larger than the former, there should not be any shipment.

$$WTQ_{ijt} = - PDQ_{jt} + PSQ_{it} + \overline{PTQ}_{ijt} \geq 0 \text{ and}$$

$$WTQ_{ijt} \cdot TQ_{ijt} = 0 \qquad (15)$$

Supply Price, Production Costs and Economic Rent The supply price of any product cannot exceed the sum of its total production cost and the economic rent, if applicable, and the equality must hold if the supply of that product is positive.

$$WSQ_{it} = PSQ_{it} + PD'Q_{it} + \mu_{QQ'it}PQQ'_{it} + PCQ_{it}$$

$$+ \mu_{QEit}PDE_{it} \geq 0 \text{ and}$$

$$WSQ_{it} \cdot SQ_{it} = 0 \qquad (16)$$

A similar relationship must hold for suppliers of electricity:

$$WSE_{it} = - PSE_{it} + PRE_{it} + \overline{PGE}_{it} \geq 0 \text{ and}$$

$$WSE_{it} \cdot SE_{it} = 0 \qquad (17)$$

The material charge of a specified raw material Q' as a part of the production cost of its product Q is equated to the demand price of Q', as long as Q' is consumed.

$$WDQ''_{it} = - PQQ'_{it} + PDQ''_{it} \geq 0 \text{ and}$$

$$WD'Q_{it} \cdot D'Q_{it} = 0 \qquad (18)$$

Because no trade is assumed for operating goods and services, their demand price is directly linked to the supply price.

$$WD'Q_{it} = - PD'Q_{it} + PS'Q_{it} \geq 0 \text{ and}$$

$$WD'Q_{it} \cdot D'Q_{it} = 0 \qquad (19)$$

Demand and Supply Rental Fees and Investment Cost The demand rental fee for the use of capacity of production of Q cannot exceed its supply rental fee and the equality must hold as long as the capacity exists.

$$WCQ_{it} = - \gamma_{Mit}PCQ_{it} + PKQ_{it} \geq 0 \text{ and}$$

$$WCQ_{it} \cdot CQ_{it} = 0 \qquad (20)$$

The following pair is the core of the LCP investment model, which states that the expected present value of investment cannot exceed its investment cost, and that investment must be zero if the former is less than the latter.

$$WJQ_{i(t-1)t} = - \sum_{\tau=t}^{2} \sigma_{Qi\tau t} PKQ_{i\tau} + PIQ_{i(t-1)t} \geq 0 \text{ and}$$

$$WJQ_{i(t-1)t} \cdot JQ_{i(t-1)t} + 0 \qquad (21)$$

where

$$\sigma_{Qi\tau t} = (1 + r_i)^{-(\tau - t - 1/2)}$$

PKQ_{i3}, PKQ_{i4}, ..., $PKQ_{it'}$ are assumed to be predetermined, where t' stands for the last period of the lifetime of the production capacity concerned.

Market Equilibrium Conditions of the LP Model

All the conditions specified in the LCP model, except for those expressed in functional-form equations, are maintained in the LP model. As in the LCP model, all the endogenous and counterpart variables are non-negative. The linear equations are now replaced by fixed demand and prices (or costs). A minimum demand for aluminum $\overline{DM}_{it}$, given in each region at each point of time, is integrated into the demand-flow equation, as follows:

$$WPDM_{it} = - \overline{DM}_{it} + \sum_{j=1}^{3} TQ_{jit} \geq 0 \text{ and}$$

$$WPD'M_{it} \cdot PD'M_{it} = 0 \qquad (22)$$

The cost of operating goods and services and the investment cost are now fixed; thus, $PD'Q_{it}$ in (16) and $PIQ_{i(t-1)t}$ in (21) are replaced by $\overline{PD'Q}_{it}$ and $\overline{PIQ}_{i(i(t-1)t}$ respectively. Furthermore, because the coefficient matrix in (1) must be symmetric in the LP model, the discount rate used in (13) is identical to the one in (21). In the LCP model, differentiated parameters for input-output coefficients may be also used in (8) and (16); however, they must be identical in the LP model.

Comparison of LCP and LP Solutions of the Bauxite-Alumina-Aluminum Model

Base Case and Five Scenarios

In order to facilitate the comparison between the LCP and LP models, we first constructed a base-case model for each which is numerically as similar and consistent as possible.

For example, the LCP solution value of each region's demand for aluminum is used as that region's demand quantity in the LP model. The comparison was then made on the basis of the solutions in each model resulting from the perturbations of the parameters, as stipulated by the following five scenarios.

Scenario 1: Change electricity cost in Region 1 from 40 mills/kWh (a mill equals one-tenth of a cent) to 30 mills/kWh in 1985; and from 50 mills/kWh to 40 mills/kWh in 1990.

Scenario 2: Increase the unit transport cost by 50 percent in both 1985 and 1990.

Scenario 3: Charge a 20 percent tax on the bauxite supply price in Region 2.

Scenario 4: Restrict the bauxite production in each region to 103 percent of the 1980 level; the upper bounds assumed for both 1985 and 1990 are $\overline{UX}_{1t} = 7.90$, $\overline{UX}_{2t} = 33.2$, $\overline{UX}_{3t} = 20.8$.

Scenario 5: Set an upper bound on electricity availability in Region 3 at 45,000 million kWhs in 1985 and 1990.

Scenarios 1 through 3 test the stability of solutions with respect to the perturbations of parameters, while Scenarios 4 and 5 test the LP and LCP models' capacity to handle constraints on the supply of inputs. In Scenario 4 it is assumed that policy (either industry or government) decisions constrain the quantity of bauxite produced in each region. This is essentially an assumption of cartel-like behaviour. A summary of the results for the base-case and five scenarios are presented in Tables 7.5 and 7.6 for the LCP model and in Tables 7.7 and 7.8 for the LP model.

Comparison of LCP and LP Scenario Results

Scenario 1 includes a 5 mill decrease in the per kWh cost of electricity in Region 1 in both periods -- from 35 to 30 mills in 1985 and from 45 to 40 mills in 1990. With an I/O coefficient to 14,000 kWh/ton of aluminum in Region 1, the 5 mill/kWh reduction translates to a decrease in the production cost of aluminum of \$70/ton. By comparison, the base-case electricity cost advantage of Region 3 over Region 1 is \$265/ton in 1985 and \$420/ton in 1990.

Table 7.5

PRICE, DEMAND, SUPPLY AND INVESTMENT OF ALUMINUM, ALUMINA AND BAUXITE (LCP SOLUTIONS)

Economic Variable	Commodity	Region	Actual	Base Case		Scenario 1		Scenario 2		Scenario 3		Scenario 4		Scenario 5	
			Period 0	Period 1	Period 2	Period 1	Period 2	Period 1	Period 2	Period 1	Period 2	Period 1	Period 2	Period 1	Period 2
Price ($/ton)	Aluminum	R1	1531	1868	1962	1838	1926	1875	1970	1877	1974	2027	2430	1870	2039
		R2	1524	1868	1962	1838	1926	1875	1970	1877	1974	2027	2430	1870	2039
		R3	1501	1838	1927	1808	1891	1830	1917	1847	1939	1887	2395	1740	2004
	Alumina	R1	237	318	301	323	307	325	303	324	308	412	578	321	315
		R2	230	311	293	316	299	314	291	317	300	405	570	314	307
		R3	207	288	328	293	322	240	330	294	332	382	605	291	280
	Bauxite	R1	32.0	47.0	43.4	47.5	44.3	49.6	13.1	51.1	47.4	93.9	166	47.3	45.3
		R2	25.0	40.0	35.4	40.5	36.3	39.1	3.06	44.1	39.4	86.9	158	40.3	37.3
		R3	25.0	30.0	35.5	30.5	35.0	29.4	.560	30.6	35.9	63.9	158	30.1	30.7
Demand (mt)	Aluminum	R1	10.3	11.5	13.2	11.7	13.5	11.4	10.2	11.4	13.1	10.2	9.43	11.4	12 6
		R2	1.47	2.08	3.06	2.12	3.11	2.07	.997	2.07	3.05	1.89	2.50	2.08	2.97
		R3	.220	.345	.557	.352	.566	.347	5.56	.343	.554	.308	.447	.345	.539
Supply (mt)	Aluminum	R1	10.1	9.77	10.2	10.4	11.1	9.68	10.2	9.71	10.0	8.63	7.07	10.1	11.7
		R2	1.59	.954	.948	.869	.700	.964	.997	.945	.930	.869	.538	.989	.117
		R3	.284	3.15	5.70	2.90	5.38	3.17	5.56	3.14	5.73	2.88	4.77	2.81	3.21
	Alumina	R1	13.3	14.5	15.5	14.8	16.2	14.4	15.1	14.2	15.1	12.7	11.6	14.8	16 1
		R2	4.83	5.79	6.99	5.96	7.33	5.98	7.22	5.64	6.77	4.79	4.83	5.99	7.67
		R3	5.90	7.50	11.1	7.61	10.8	7.28	11.1	7.75	11.5	7.30	8.32	6.92	7.67
	Bauxite	R1	7.64	8.66	8.44	9.04	9.25	10.2	11.0	11.1	12.5	7.90	7.90	9.09	10.16
		R2	32.2	42.0	47.9	42.8	49.5	40.7	44.9	38.5	42.3	33.2	33.2	42.9	51.1
		R3	20.2	18.8	27.7	19.0	26.9	18.2	27.8	19.4	28.6	20.8	20.8	17.3	19.7
Investment In Production Capacity /a (equivalent of mtpy)	Aluminum	R1	5.30	4.28	4.72	5.11	5.37	4.15	4.84	4.19	4.61	2.74	1.61	4.67	6.51
		R2	1.44	.125	.600	0	.306	.140	.664	.111	.582	0	.0655	.177	.897
		R3	.207	4.20	5.28	3.85	5.05	4.23	5.06	4.19	5.33	3.82	4.21	3.72	2.08
	Alumina	R1	9.67	6.01	7.67	6.42	8.25	5.90	7.19	5.66	7.37	3.62	3.99	6.51	9.02
		R2	3.18	4.07	5.46	4.33	5.83	4.34	5.65	3.84	5.27	2.59	3.13	4.36	6.32
		R3	5.13	4.87	9.03	5.01	8.52	4.56	9.30	5.22	9.37	4.58	5.35	4.04	4.77
	Bauxite	R1	4.37	4.42	3.43	4.94	4.17	6.47	5.43	7.67	6.71	3.40	3.39	5.01	5.21
		R2	28.0	34.2	35.5	35.3	37.2	32.3	32.2	29.1	30.1	21.2	21.1	35.6	39.4
		R3	18.3	8.30	22.5	8.66	21.2	7.52	23.2	8.18	23.3	11.2	11.1	6.24	11.9

/a : The figures in the "actual" column are referred to as those in the years between 1975 and 1980. The figures in the first columns of Base and Scenario cases are referred to as those in the years between Periods 0 and 1 and the figures in the second columns as those in the years between Periods 1 and 2.

Table 7.6

LCP SOLUTIONS:
TRADE OF ALUMINUM, ALUMINA AND BAUXITE
(Metric Tons)

		Aluminum			Alumina			Bauxite		
From	To	R1	R2	R3	R1	R2	R3	R1	R2	R3
					Base Case					
R1	Period 0	--	0	0	--	0	0	--	0	0
	Period 1	--	0	0	--	0	0	--	0	0
	Period 2		0	0	--	0	0	--	0	0
R2	Period 0	.176	--	0	1.65	--	0	20.1	--	0
	Period 1	0	--	0	3.88	--	0	27.5	--	0
	Period 2	0	--	0	4.76	--	.330	30.4	--	0
R3	Period 0	.170	0	--	5.33	0	--	5.42	0	--
	Period 1	1.68	1.12	--	1.21	0	--	0	0	--
	Period 2	3.02	2.12	--	0	0	--	0	0	--
					Scenario 1					
R1	Period 1	--	0	0	--	0	0	--	0	0
	Period 2	--	0	0	--	0	0	--	0	0
R2	Period 1	0	--	0	4.23	--	0	27.8	--	0
	Period 2	0	--	0	5.93	--	0	31.2	--	0
R3	Period 1	1.30	1.25	--	1.81	0	--	0	0	--
	Period 2	2.41	2.41	--	0	0	--	0	0	--
					Scenario 2					
R1	Period 1	--	0	0	--	0	0	--	0	0
	Period 2	--	0	0	--	0	0	--	0	0
R2	Period 1	0	--	0	4.05	--	0	25.8	--	0
	Period 2	0	--	0	5.23	--	0	26.9	--	0
R3	Period 1	1.72	1.11	--	.941	0	--	0	0	--
	Period 2	2.94	2.06	--	0	0	--	0	0	--
					Scenario 3					
R1	Period 1	--	0	0	--	0	0	--	0	0
	Period 2	--	0	0	--	0	0	--	0	0
R2	Period 1	0	--	0	0	--	0	24.4	--	0
	Period 2	0	--	0	0	--	0	25.3	--	0

Table 7.6 cont'd

R3	Period 1	1.67	1.12	--	1.47	3.75	--	0	0	--
	Period 2	3.05	2.12	--	0	4.91	--	0	0	--
					Scenario 4					
R1	Period 1	--	0	0	--	0	0	--	0	0
	Period 2	--	0	0	--	0	0	--	0	0
R2	Period 1	0	--	0	3.05	--	0	21.2	--	0
	Period 2	0	--	0	2.54	--	1.22	21.1	--	0
R3	Period 1	1.55	1.02	--	1.53	0	--	2.56	0	--
	Period 2	2.36	1.97	--	0	0	--	0	0	--
					Scenario 5					
R1	Period 1	--	0	0	--	0	0	--	0	0
	Period 2	--	0	0	--	0	0	--	0	0
R2	Period 1	0	--	0	4.01	--	0	28.0	--	0
	Period 2	0	--	0	5.34	--	0	31.9	--	0
R3	Period 1	1.37	1.09	--	1.30	0	--	0	0	--
	Period 2	.87	1.80	--	1.24	0	--	0	0	--

Table 7.7

PRICE, DEMAND, SUPPLY AND INVESTMENT OF ALUMINUM, ALUMINA AND BAUXITE (LP SOLUTIONS)

Economic Variable	Commodity	Region	Actual	Base Case		Scenario 1		Scenario 2		Scenario 3		Scenario 4		Scenario 5	
			Period 0	Period 1	Period 2	Period 1	Period 2	Period 1	Period 2	Period 1	Period 2	Period 1	Period 2	Period 1	Period 2
Price ($/ton)	Aluminum	R1	1531	1856	1904	1746	1893	1852	1921	1864	1904			1816	1963
		R2	1524	1856	1904	1753	1901	1852	1921	1864	1904			1816	1963
		R3	1501	1826	1869	1768	1866	1807	1869	1834	1869			1786	1928
	Alumina	R1	237	300	304	300	304	304	305	304	305			300	304
		R2	230	293	296	293	296	293	293	297	297			293	296
		R3	207	300	328	270	327	290	328	303	328			279	328
	Bauxite	R1	32.0	38.2	39.2	38.2	39.2	39.4	39.5	39.4	39.5	Infeasible		38.2	39.2
		R2	25.0	31.2	31.2	31.2	31.2	28.9	27.5	32.4	31.5			31.2	31.2
		R3	25.0	22.9	34.0	15.0	33.6	19.0	34.0	24.4	34.0			15.0	34.0
Demand (mt)	Aluminum	R1	10.3	11.5	13.2	11.5	13.2	11.5	13.2	11.5	13.2			11.5	13.2
		R2	1.47	2.08	3.06	2.08	3.06	2.08	3.06	2.08	3.06			2.08	3.06
		R3	.220	.345	.557	.345	.597	.345	.557	.345	.557			.345	.557
Supply (mt)	Aluminum	R1	10.1	10.4	7.10	12.7	14.7	10.4	7.10	10.4	7.10			11.0	13.1
		R2	1.59	.869	.493	.869	.493	.869	.493	.869	.493			.869	.493
		R3	.284	2.57	9.20	.345	1.60	2.57	9.20	2.57	9.20			2.03	3.21
	Alumina	R1	13.3	19.6	13.5	20.7	28.7	19.6	13.5	19.6	13.5			20.7	25.4
		R2	4.83	3.03	1.72	3.03	1.72	3.03	1.72	3.03	1.72			3.03	1.72
		R3	5.90	5.15	18.4	4.05	3.21	5.15	18.4	5.15	18.4			4.05	6.43
	Bauxite	R1	7.64	5.37	3.66	5.37	3.66	37.7	27.2	37.7	27.2			5.37	3.66
		R2	32.2	51.1	34.3	53.9	72.3	18.8	10.7	18.8	10.7			53.9	64.2
		R3	20.2	12.9	46.0	10.1	8.02	12.9	46.0	12.9	46.0			10.1	16.1
Investment In Production Capacity /a (equivalent of mtpy)	Aluminum	R1	5.30	5.17	0	8.17	8.19	5.17	0	5.17	0			5.91	7.56
		R2	1.44	0	0	0	0	0	0	0	0			0	0
		R3	.207	3.39	10.7	.247	1.96	3.39	10.7	3.39	10.7			2.62	2.76
	Alumina	R1	9.67	12.9	.186	14.4	19.7	12.9	.186	12.9	.186			14.4	15.3
		R2	3.18	0	0	0	0	0	0	0	0			0	0
		R3	5.13	1.55	21.5	0	.982	1.55	21.5	1.55	21.5			0	5.52
	Bauxite	R1	4.37	0	0	0	0	43.5	2.16	43.5	2.16			0	0
		R2	28.0	47.7	7.76	51.8	61.5	0	0	0	0			51.8	49.6
		R3	18.3	0	53.6	0	0	0	53.6	0	53.6			0	11.4

/a : The figures in the "actual" column are referred to as those in the years between 1975 and 1980. The figures in the first columns of Base and Scenario cases

Table 7.8

LP SOLUTIONS:
TRADE OF ALUMINUM, ALUMINA AND BAUXITE
(Metric Tons)

From	To	Aluminum			Alumina			Bauxite		
		R1	R2	R3	R1	R2	R3	R1	R2	R3
					Base Case					
R1	Period 0	--	0	0	--	0	0	--	0	0
	Period 1	--	0	0	--	0	0	--	0	0
	Period 2		0	0	--	0	0	--	0	0
R2	Period 0	.176	--	0	1.65	--	0	20.1	--	0
	Period 1	0	--	0	1.29	--	0	43.6	--	0
	Period 2	0	--	0	.733	--	0	30.0	--	0
R3	Period 0	.170	0	--	5.33	0	--	5.42	0	--
	Period 1	1.02	1.21	--	0	0	--	0	0	--
	Period 2	63.07	2.57	--	0	0	--	0	0	-
					Scenario 1					
R1	Period 1	--	1.21	0	--	0	0	--	0	0
	Period 2	--	1.52	0	--	0	0	--	0	0
R2	Period 1	0	--	0	1.29	--	0	46.3	--	0
	Period 2	0	--	0	.733	--	0	68.0	--	0
R3	Period 1	0	0	--	3.36	0	--	0	0	--
	Period 2	1.05	0	--	0	0	--	0	0	--
					Scenario 2					
R1	Period 1	--	0	0	--	0	0	--	0	0
	Period 2	--	0	0	--	0	0	--	0	0
R2	Period 1	0	--	0	1.29	--	0	11.2	--	0
	Period 2	0	--	0	.733	--	0	6.41	--	0
R3	Period 1	1.02	1.21	--	0	0	--	0	0	--
	Period 2	6.07	2.51	--	0	0	--	0	0	--
					Scenario 3					
R1	Period 1	--	0	0	--	0	0	--	0	0
	Period 2	--	0	0	--	0	0	--	0	0

Table 7.8 cont'd.

R2	Period 1	0	--	0	1.29	--	0	11.2	--	0
	Period 2	0	--	0	.733	--	0	6.41	--	0
R3	Period 1	1.02	1.21	--	0	0	--	0	0	--
	Period 2	6.07	2.57	--	0	0	--	0	0	--
					Scenario 4					
					Infeasible					
					Scenario 5					
R1	Period 1	--	0	0	--	0	0	--	0	0
	Period 2	--	0	0	--	0	0	--	0	0
R2	Period 1	0	--	0	1.29	--	0	46.3	--	0
	Period 2	0	--	0	.733	--	0	59.9	--	0
R3	Period 1	.475	1.21	--	0	0	--	0	0	--
	Period 2	.090	2.57	--	0	0	--	0	0	--

As can be seen from the tables, the results of this electricity cost change are very different in the two models. Tables 7.5 and 7.7 show that the impact of the change on the LCP projections, while significant, is much smaller than in the LP case; for example, in the LCP model, aluminum investment in Region 1 goes from 4.28 mtpy to 5.11 mtpy in 1985, and from 4.72 mtpy to 5.37 mtpy in 1990; while in the LP model those same responses are from 5.17 mtpy to 8.17 mtpy in 1985 and from zero to 8.19 mtpy in 1990. Furthermore, while the LCP case shows that Region 1's increased advantage in aluminum processing leads to modest shifts in the distribution of investment and production in bauxite mining and alumina refining, the swings are much more extreme in the LP version; for instance, Region 3, which was the dominant supplier of both bauxite and alumina in 1990, loses all of its 1990 bauxite investment to Region 2, and 95 percent of its alumina investment to Region 1. As can be seen from Tables 7.6 and 7.8 the trade pattern projections are similarly more volatile in the LP case. Note also that the shadow price of the aluminum price in the LP model falls further than the price in the LCP case. This is to be expected, since in the latter model, falling prices are partially compensated for by increased demand.

Both Scenario 2, in which all transportation costs are increased by 50 percent, that is, by $3.50 ($4.00)/ton between Regions 1 and 2 in 1985 (1990) and by $15.0 ($17.5)/ton to or from Region 3 in 1985 (1990), and Scenario 3, which is defined by a 20 percent tax on bauxite supply price in Region 2, have precisely the same effects on investment, production and trade in the LP model. Simulation of the LP model results in changes that are large enough to move all of Region 2's bauxite investment into Region 1; however, none of the aluminum or alumina quantity variables are affected at all. By contrast, the LCP model results give impacts on bauxite that are much less drastic in both scenarios and the changes in transportation cost. To some extent even the application of the bauxite tax, has smaller but noticeable effects on the aluminum and alumina variables. A significant difference between the LP and LCP solutions is also seen in the trade results. In the LP model with a shift-out of Region 2's investment in bauxite, its bauxite export decreased by 74 percent in 1985 and by 79 percent in 1990, in comparison with the base-case solution. By contrast, the decrease is modest in the LCP model; ranging from only 6 percent to 17 percent.

Scenario 4 illustrates an important difference in the capabilities of the LCP and LOP models. In this scenario, which simulates the actions of a hypothetical global bauxite cartel, bauxite extraction in each region is limited to 103 percent of its production level in 1980. Without price-sensitive demands the LP model cannot produce a feasible solution to this problem. The LCP model, on the other hand, allows for a decrease in aluminum demand in each region to accommodate the decrase in the total supply of bauxite. The model also projects a doubling of bauxite prices in 1985 and a quadrupling of 1990 prices. These lead to alumunim price hikes of about $160/ ton in 1985 and $470/ton in 1990, and to an increasing tilt in aluminum investment toward Region 3.

In Scenario 5, a limit is placed on the use of electricity in aluminum smelting in Region 3, allowing production of 3mt in 1985. Due to an assumed increase in the electricity use (from 15,000 kWh to 14,000 kWh per ton of aluminum) efficiency, production of 3.21 mt in 1990. Tables 7.7 and 7.8 show the by-now familiar pattern of much larger changes in the LP model. As the result of the imposed halt of Region 3's explosive growth in aluminum production, that region's investment in the latter half of the 1980s is significantly lower in both models in comparison with the base case solutions, these decreases are 74 percent in the LP model and 62 percent in the LCP model. A significant difference between these two models is seen in Region 1's investment in aluminum smelting in the latter half of the 1980s. In the LP model, it increases from zero to 7.56 mtpy, while the projected increase in the LCP model is modest from 4.72 mtpy to 6.51 mtpy.

In summary, the perturbations of parameters create smooth changes in both price and quantity solutions in the LCP model, while the LP counterpart shows sudden changes, which are due to the so-called "upper-semi-continuity" or "point-to-set" mapping characteristics of the LP. In particular in the LP solutions, drastic changes occur in investment which sift from zero to a large quantity and vice-versa. This characteristic of the technique presently limits the applicability of LP models for investment planning.

Conclusions

The comparative analysis of the previous sections has revealed the following differential characteristics of the LCP and LP models:

(1) The LCP model possesses a mechanism to solve for regional market demand quantitites which are consistent with market prices, while this mechanism is missing in the LP model. The implication of this difference is straightforward. If the regional market demand functions can be approximated by the linear form, LCP modelling enables analysts to project the market clearing prices as well as the corresponding quantitites consumed. In LP modelling, however, the dual LP solutions (that is, the shadow prices) may not be consistent with market clearing prices. Because such a market (Marshallian) operates in reality in many free market economies, socially sub-optimal pricing and allocation policy decisions may be made if policy decisions are taken on the basis of LP methods. To overcome the deficiency of no regional solutions for LP models, various solution algorithms have been developed to solve non-linear programming problems through LP methods. Typical of those models are Duloy and Norton (1975) and Hazell (1979).

(2) Due to the representation in functional form of regional demands for final products, operating costs and investment costs in the LCP model, quantity and price variables respond continuously ("piecewise continuously") to continuous parameter perturbations. In the LP model, parameter perturbations result in some discrete jumps in the quantity solutions ("upper-semi-continuity"). In particular, drastic changes occur in investment, which often shifts from zero to a large quantity and vice-versa. This characteristic limits the applicability of the LP model for investment planning. Also note that whereas transportation costs are assumed to be constant in the present LCP model, the shipment directions may switch discontinuously due to changes in transportation costs, i.e., see Table 7.6 and Yang (1980).

(3) The LCP approach is useful for solving prices of primary commodities and their downstream (or final) products, particularly when the supplies of primary commodities are globally tight or are fixed by the producers. This is because the Lagrangean multipliers of the given constraints in the LCP approach can be interpreted as economic rents, which can be passed on in prices of both primary and final products. However, in such a situation, the LP approach may prove to be either infeasible, as shown in this

chapter, or some ingenious calibration of the regional demand specifications is required to derive feasible solutions.

In summary, although the basic structure of the LCP and LP investment models are very similar, the LCP model is capable of dealing with a wider range of policy questions. The LCP model as developed in this paper can be effectively applied to the evaluation of such national or regional economic policy issues as the pricing or taxing (subsidizing) of commodities, or the determination of future refining (or smelting) capacity expansion. In practical application, various challenges such as indivisibility (integer constraint) and economies of scale problems of plant investment have been taken up in the LP investment modelling framework. To date such problems have not been solved within the LCP algorithmic framework, but the authors believe they can be.

Before concluding, one remark on the LCP (or QP) software may be worthwhile. By comparison with the phenomenal development of LP software packages such as MPSX, APEX, MPS III, GAM, etc., along with that of matrix generators and report writers to go with them, the operational drawback of the LCP (or QP) methods is that software development for these methods has been almost ignored for about two decades. At this stage two packages are available: (1) the LCPL (Tomlin, 1976) which can handle a matrix with rows up to 500 and (2) the LCRAND (Bartilson, Zepp and Takayama, 1978) which can handle a matrix with rows up to 2,500 (the lack of personal computer software is even more severe). To solve some important classes of national or international political economic problems, the mentioned dimensionality is obviously too restrictive. Therefore, in the absence of effective software, many of those commodity-related policy and investment problems will be relegated to a less effective tool, resulting perhaps in nationally or internationally sub-optimal policies. Thus, it is highly desirable that some effort be made to develop an LCP software capable of handling a matrix with 5,000 rows to 8,000 rows.

Appendix 1

Fundamental Relationships Among LCP, QP and LP

The following <u>Fundamental Problem</u> (Cottle and Dantzig, 1968) defines the basic common structure of the three mathematical programming problems, LCP, QP and LP:

(FP) Find vectors w and z that satisfy the following conditions

$$w = q + Mz \tag{A.1}$$

$$z'w = 0; \text{ and } w \geq 0; \ z \geq 0 \tag{A.2}$$

where q is a real (p x 1) vector, M is a real (p x p) matrix, and w and z are (p x 1) vectors.

This is exactly the form in which the bimatrix (two-person nonzero-sum) games are defined (Lemke, 1965, and which is called LCP by Cottle and Dantzig, 1968). In this paper, this problem is defined as FP, because our use of LCP, defined later, is a special case of FP.

QP in its general form can be defined as follows:
(QP) Find an (n x 1) vector x that maximizes

$$c'x - 1/2\ x'Qx \tag{A.3}$$

subject to

$$Ax \geq b \tag{A.4}$$

$$x \geq 0 \tag{A.5}$$

where c is an (n x 1) real vector, Q and (n x n) real matrix, A an (m x n) real matrix, and b an (m x 1) real vector.

This QP problem can be written in the following Kuhn-Tucker form following Kuhn and Tucker (1950):
(QP′) Find [u′ v′] and [x′ λ′] that satisfy the following conditions:

$$\begin{bmatrix} u \\ \\ v \end{bmatrix} = \begin{bmatrix} -c \\ \\ b \end{bmatrix} + \begin{bmatrix} 1/2\ (Q+Q') & A' \\ \\ -A & 0 \end{bmatrix} \begin{bmatrix} x \\ \\ \lambda \end{bmatrix} \tag{A.6}$$

$$\begin{bmatrix} u \\ \\ v \end{bmatrix} \begin{bmatrix} x \\ \\ \lambda \end{bmatrix} = 0, \text{ and} \begin{bmatrix} u \\ \\ v \end{bmatrix} \geq 0, \begin{bmatrix} x \\ \\ \lambda \end{bmatrix} \geq 0 \tag{A.7}$$

Clearly (QP) is equivalent to (QP′), which is equivalent to (FP), where M takes a specific form stipulated by (1.6).

In many applied problems (Chapters 12 and 14 of Takayama and Judge, 1971 and Chapter 3 of Hashimoto, 1977, M does not have to take this special (A.6) form, but can be

$$\begin{bmatrix} Q & B \\ \\ -A & 0 \end{bmatrix} \tag{A.8}$$

where B is an (n x m) real matrix, which can be either B ≠ A′ or B = A′, and Q does not have to be symmetric like 1/2 (Q + Q′) in (A.6). With this modification, let us define the LCP as follows:

(LCP) Find [u′ v′] and [x′ λ′] that satisfy

$$\begin{bmatrix} u \\ \\ v \end{bmatrix} = \begin{bmatrix} -c \\ \\ b \end{bmatrix} + \begin{bmatrix} Q & A' \\ \\ -A & 0 \end{bmatrix} \begin{bmatrix} x \\ \\ \lambda \end{bmatrix} \tag{A.9}$$

$$\begin{bmatrix} u \\ \\ v \end{bmatrix}, \begin{bmatrix} x \\ \\ \lambda \end{bmatrix} = 0, \text{ and} \begin{bmatrix} u \\ \\ v \end{bmatrix} \geq 0, \begin{bmatrix} x \\ \\ \lambda \end{bmatrix} \geq 0 \tag{A.10}$$

The problem defined by (A.9) and (a.10) contains that satisfying (A.6) and (A.7) as a special case. Therefore, it is clear that the following inclusion relationships hold:

$$(FP) \supset (LCP) \supset (QP) \qquad (A.11)$$

If LP is shown to a special case of QP, the hierarchical relationships of these problems will be clearly established, pointing to the inclusion relationships that would prevail in judging the capabilities and flexibility of each tool dealing with policy decision issues in application.

The LP problem can be defined as:

(LP) Find x that maximizes

$$r'x \qquad (A.12)$$

subject to

$$Dx \geq g \qquad (A.13)$$

$$x \geq 0 \qquad (A.14)$$

Following the Kuhn-Tucker equivalence, this LP can be written in the following form:

(LP') Find [u' v'] and [x' λ'] that satisfy the following conditions:

$$\begin{bmatrix} u \\ v \end{bmatrix} = \begin{bmatrix} -r \\ g \end{bmatrix} + \begin{bmatrix} Q & D' \\ -D & 0 \end{bmatrix} \begin{bmatrix} x \\ \lambda \end{bmatrix} \qquad (A.15)$$

$$\begin{bmatrix} u \\ v \end{bmatrix}, \begin{bmatrix} x \\ \lambda \end{bmatrix} = 0, \text{ and} \begin{bmatrix} u \\ v \end{bmatrix} \geq 0, \begin{bmatrix} x \\ \lambda \end{bmatrix} \geq 0 \qquad (A.16)$$

LP proves to be a special case of QP' where Q = 0, and thus a subset of QP', and along with (A.11) the following inclusion relationships are established:

$$(FP) \supset (LCP) \supset (QP) \supset (LP) \qquad (A.17)$$

Logically, we can now state that FP can handle a wider range of issues than LCP, which can deal with a wider range of issues than QP, which in turn can handle a wider range of issues than LP.

The solution algorithm for the standard linear programming problems, known as the Simplex method is also a powerful engine in solving FP, LCP and QP, given minor modifications (Cottle and Dantzig, 1968). The proof of the finite termination of the so-called "principal pivoting method" depends on the following qualifications on M:

M is <u>copositive plus</u> (A.18)

M being copositive plus is equivalent to the statement that M satisfies the following two conditions:

$$u'M\,u \geq 0 \text{ for all } u \geq 0 \qquad (A.19)$$

$$(M + M')u = 0 \text{ if } u'Mu = 0 \text{ and } u \geq 0 \qquad (A.20)$$

The matrix in (A.6) satisfies (A.18) if Q is a positive semi-definite matrix. Thus, a concave or strictly concave quadratic programming problem satisfies this qualification. However, the matrix in (A.9) requires a more careful scrutiny. It is extremely laborious and difficult to check the presence of requirement (A.18), and in many cases problems in LCP formulation have been satisfactorily solved even thought he ex-post numerical investigations proved that M did not satisfy copositive plusness, i.e. see Hashimoto (1977).

Appendix 2

Parameters and Exogenous Variables Used for Both LCP and LP Versions

$\overline{PTQ}_{ijt}$ Transportation costs ($/ton) are assumed to be the same for all three products for each time period:

		1985			1990		
From	To	R1	R2	R3	R1	R2	R3
R1		0	7	30	0	8	35
R2		7	0	30	8	0	35
R3		30	30	0	35	35	0

$\overline{PGE}_{it}$ Electricity costs (mills/kWh) are fixed at the following levels

1985			1990		
R1	R2	R3	R1	R2	R3
35	35	15	45	40	15

$\overline{CQ}_{i0}$ Initial production capacities (mtpy) are as follows:

	R1	R2	R3
M	10.772	1.703	.304
N	16.339	5.937	7.247
X	8.776	36.864	23.101

Also note that

$\overline{UX}_{it}$ Each region's maximum availability of bauxite (mt) are assumed to be unbounded (+ ∞)

$\overline{UE}_{it}$ Each region's maximum availability of electricity (million kwh) are assumed to be unbounded (+ ∞)

μ_{MNit} Alumina requirements (ton) per ton of aluminum production is a fixed constant of 2.

μ_{NXit} Bauxite requirements (ton) per ton of alumina production is also assumed to be a fixed constant, 2.5.

μ_{MEit} Electricity requirements (kwh) per ton of aluminum production are as follows:

1985			1990		
R1	R2	R3	R1	R2	R3
14,000	15,000	15,000	14,000	15,000	14,000

γ_{Qit} Capacity utilization rate is common to each region, processing stage and time; $\gamma = 0.9$.

τ_{it} Discount rates and τ_{it} the depreciation rate are assumed to be the same in our models for convenience; they are also assumed to be invariant between 1980-1985 and 1985-1990:

R1	R2	R3
8%	12%	10%

Parameters and Exogenous Variables Used for the LCP Version

λ_{it} Aluminum demand function intercept parameters are:

1985			1990		
R1	R2	R3	R1	R2	R3
3,300	3,600	3,300	3,609	4,515	4,286

ω_{it} Aluminum demand function slope parameters are assumed to be the same between 1985 and 1990:

R1	R2	R3
125	833	4,234

δ_{Qit} Operating cost function intercept values are assumed to be as follows and unchanged between 1985 and 1990:

	R1	R2	R3
M	300	400	300
N	30.0	33.3	30.0
X	22.5	6.67	10.0

Σ_{Qit} Operating cost function slope parameters are:

	1985			1990		
	R1	R2	R3	R1	R2	R3
M	10.6	92.6	104	10.2	71.9	59.6
N	.80	2.19	3.39	.83	1.54	2.44
X	.701	.100	.355	.536	.089	.272

Q_{it} Investment cost function intercept parameters are:

	1980-1985			1985-1990		
	R1	R2	R3	R1	R2	R3
M	304	260	308	181	166	190
N	121	108	140	72.3	69.1	86.3
X	18.2	11.3	14.6	10.8	7.19	8.98

β_{Qit} Investment cost function slope parameters are:

	1980-1985			1985-1990		
	R1	R2	R3	R1	R2	R3
M	26.5	136	40.3	13.21	72.4	20.8
N	12.0	16.0	10.3	5.01	7.19	4.49
X	.843	.522	.337	.401	.265	.166

Parameters and Exogenous Variables Used for the LP Version

$\overline{DM}_{it}$ Regional demands for aluminum are the same as in Table 7.6 solution values of the LCP base case model.

$\overline{PDQ}_{it}$ Operating costs ($/ton of output) are assumed to be the same for 1985 and 1990:

	R1	R2	R3
M	400	600	600
N	50	55	60
X	20	10	15

$\overline{PIQ}_{it}$ Investment costs ($/ton of output) actually fed into the farthest right column of the coefficient matrix were derived as follows. First absed on the industry information, the following set of unit investment costs for each processing stage in each region was established. (The unit investment costs were assumed the same for 1980-1985 and 1985-1990.)

	R1	R2	R3
M	2,500	3,000	2,800
N	1,200	1,250	1,250
X	150	130	130

Then, $\overline{PIQ}_{it}$, which must match the sum of earnings in all the benchmark years within the model period, was derived on the basis of the assumed discount rate τ_{it}. The PIQ_{it} derived in this matter was as follows:

	1980-1985			1985-1990		
	R1	R2	R3	R1	R2	R3
M	405	520	462	241	332	285
N	194	217	210	116	138	130
X	24.3	22.5	21.8	14.5	14.4	13.6

Authors
Takashi Takayama
Department of Economics
University of Western Australia
Perth, Australia 6009

Hideo Hashimoto
Commodity Studies and Projections Division
The World Bank
Washington, D.C. 20433

Acknowledgement
The authors would like to acknowledge the contribution of Mr. Perry Beider, who skillfully handled the tasks of executing a series of the computer models contained in this paper. The authors are grateful to Professor Roger Norton of the University of New Mexico and Mr. Ronald Duncan of the World Bank for their valuable comments.

References

Bartilson, S., G.A. Zepp and T. Takayama, (1978). A User's Manual for the LCRABD Mathematical Programming System, Economics Report 91, Gainesville: Food and Resources Economics Department, University of Florida.

Brown, M., A. Dammert, A. Meeraus and A. Stoutjesdijk, (1983). Worldwide Investment Analysis, the Case of Aluminum, World Bank Staff Working Paper No. 603, Washington, D.C.: The World Bank.

Choksi, A.M., A. Meeraus and E.J. Stoutjesdijk, (1980). The Planning of Investment Programs in the Fertilizer Industry, Baltimore: Johns Hopkins University Press.

Cottle, R.W. and G.B. Dantzig, (1968). "Complementary Pivot Theory of Mathematical Programming," Linear Algebra and Its Applications, 1: 103-125.

Dantzig, G.B., (1951). "Maximization of a Linear Function of Variables Subject to Linear Inequalities," in T.C. Koopmans (ed.), Activity Analysis of Production and Allocation, New York: John Wiley & Sons, pp. 339-347.

Duloy, J.H. and R.D. Norton, (1975). "Prices and Incomes in Linear Programming Models," American Journal of Agricultural Economics, 57: 591-600.

Hashimoto, H., (1977). World Food Projection Models, Projections, and Policy Evaluations, unpublished Ph.D. thesis, Urbana-Champaign, IL: Department of Economics, University of Illinois.

Hashimoto, H., (1981a). "A World Iron and Steel Economy Model: The WISE Model," in World Bank Commodity Models, Vol. 1, World Bank Staff Commodity Working Paper, Washington, D.C.: The World Bank.

Hashimoto, H., (1981b). "A Tin Economy Model for Decision-Making About Investment in Production Capacity," a paper presented at the Fifth World Conference on Tin, held at Kuala Lumpur, Malaysia.

Hashimoto, H., (1983a). A Positive Use of Linear Complementarity Programming to Analyze Commodity and Sector-Related Issues -- A Global Investment Model, Commodities Division Working Paper, Washington, D.C.: The World Bank.

Hashimoto, H., (1983b). "A World Iron and Steel Economy Model: A Projection for 1980-95," Journal of Policy Modeling, 5: 379-396.

Hazell, P.B.R., (1979). "Endogenous Input Prices in Linear Programming Models," American Journal of Agricultural Economics, 61: 476-481.

Kendrick, D. and E.J. Stoutjesdijk, (1978). The Planning of Industrial Investment Programs, A Methodology, Baltimore: Johns Hopkins University Press.

Kuhn, H.W. and A.W. Tucker, (1950). "Nonlinear Programming," in J. Neyman (ed.) Proceedings of the Second Berkeley Symposium on Mathematical Statistics and Probability, Berkeley, CA: The University of California Press, pp. 481-492.

Lemke, C.E., (1965). "Biamatrix Equilibrium Points and Mathematical Programming, Management Science, 11: 681-689.

Massé, P. and R. Gibrat, (1964). "Application of Linear Programming to Investments in the Electrical Power Industry," in J.R. Nelson (ed.) Marginal Cost Pricing in Practice, Englewood Cliffs, NJ: Prentice-Hall.

Stevens, B.H., (1959). "An Interregional Linear Programming," Journal of Regional Science, 1: 60-98.

Takayama, T. and G.G. Judge, (1971). Spatial and Temporal Price and Allocation Models, Amsterdam: North-Holland Publishing Co.

Tomlin, J.A., (1976). Programming Guide to LCPL, A Program Solving Linear Complementarity Problems by Lemke's Method, Stanford, CA: Department of Operations Research, Stanford University.

Turvey, R. and D. Anderson, (1977). Electricity Economics, Essays and Case Studies, Baltimore: Johns Hopkins University Press.

Uri, N., (1975). Towards Efficient Allocation of Electric Energy, Lexington, D.C. Heath and Co.

Wolfe, P., (1959). "The Simplex Method for Quadratic Programming," Econometrica, 27: 382-398.

Yang, C.W., (1980). "The Stability of Interregional Trade Model: The Case of the Takayama-Judge Model," in W.G. Vogt, et al. (ed.) Modeling and Simulation, Instrument Society of America.

8 Linear complementarity programming: electrical energy as a case study

NOEL D. URI *U.S. Department of Agriculture*

Introduction

The elements of investment planning continue to play an important role in the operation of electric utilities. The formulation of suitable policies to carry out the activities of generation, transmission and distribution, and consumption over time are crucial. Considerable attention has focused on these concerns over the past decade. A variety of approaches have been suggested to provide a suitable planning structure to assist in examining the relevant issues. For example, Baughman, Joskow, and Kamas (1979) suggest a least cost selection procedure based on an ad hoc selection for generation capacity. Turvey and Anderson (1977) suggest the use of linear programming as does the CERES approach of the National Regulatory Research Institute (1981). Other approaches have been advocated by the U.S. Department of Energy.

One of the major shortcomings of these considerations is that demand is not truly integrated with the generation and capacity expansion considerations. In particular demand is exogenously given. (Note that the assumed underlying demand structure might be appropriate.) The point estimate of demand is then used in determining the optimal configuration of generating capacity in the dynamic environment. This de facto is not appropriate. It has been well established that the quantity demanded of electrical energy is dependent on the price of electrical energy, i.e., see Taylor (1976). Moreover, given the regulated nature of the industry in the United States, the price of electrical energy is a function of, among other things, generating costs and capacity costs. The result then is that most of the previous formulations are problematic at best. What is proposed in this Chapter is the development of a planning model devoid of this inherent limitation. That is, a model will be presented and implemented which will yield an economically efficient solution with regard to generation, consumption, and pricing over time. A by-product of this will be the applicability of the model to determine whether the electric utility industry in the United States is operating efficiently.

Background

The issue of economic efficiency between markets that are spatially separated can be formulated in terms of descriptive price behaviour and then converted to a problem whose objective is the maximization of net social payoff (NSP). One defines net social payoff in terms of the underlying demand and cost relations for all spatially diffuse markets as the sum of the areas under the demand functions less the sum of the reas under the marginal cost functions at the equilibrium prices. Moreover, this notion of spatial equilibrium can be adapted to include the temporal domain as well as to allow for the analysis of equilibrium pricing and allocation over time. This form of spatial price and temporal allocation model (STPA) has been theoretically defined in Chapter 2.

Combining the spatial and temporal aspects of the problem, the notion of net social payoff will be used in the following to delineate the requisite conditions for spatial and intertemporal equilibrium and hence economic efficiency. The institutional peculiarities of the electrical energy industry together with some simplifying assumptions are then incorporated into the resultant linear complementarity programming (LCP) model that can be solved for the equilibrium. The introduction of the time dimension permits the consideration of the difficult question of determining the optimal rate of investment in plant and equipment in the industry.

There is one additional issue of concern in the current analysis. Recent years have witnessed a growing concern for the quality of the environment. Since the late 1960s a variety of environmental quality standards have been actively discussed and implemented. (Culminating in the Clean Air Amendments of 1970 and Federal Water Pollution Control Amendments of 1972 and the New Source Performance Standards of the Clean Air Amendments of 1978.) One of the important questions that has remained only partially answered about these options is the effect of their implementation on the pricing and allocation of electrical energy.

Existing regulations, as well as those adopted in the future, directly affect consumption through price increases resulting from the regulation of the emission of air pollutants from burning fossil fuels, thermal pollution, and the creation of noise. Thus, for example, all coal and oil fired generating plants of less than 200 megawatt capacity and those with a 30 percent or less utilization factor were required to burn low sulfur coal by 1976 (Council on Environmental Quality). Because low sulfur fuel is more expensive, the increase in fuel costs will reduce demand. Other types of controls will similarly affect cost. It is the effects of these regulations on the pricing and allocation of electrical energy that also need to be included in the considerations.

Coincident with these consideration has been legislation specifically mandating the Department of Energy to prohibit the use of oil and natural gas in the generation of electrical energy (unless exempted). Specifically, the Power Plant and Industrial Fuel Use Act of 1978 (PIFUA) prohibits new generating plants from using oil or natural gas as primary fuel sources and existing generating facilities cannot burn natural gas after January 1, 1990 (unless exempted). The impact of this legislation will also be discussed in the context of environment/energy consumption by electric utilities.

The Economic Environment

Consider a multiregion, multiconsuming sector economy for electrical energy. To better understand the development of the model, the following notation is introduced:

i, j (= 1, 2, ..., N) denotes the regions;

k (= 1, 2, ..., M) denotes the consuming sectors;

s (= 1, 2, ..., S) denotes individual environmental/ energy consumption requirements;

p (= 1, 2, ..., L) denotes the capital stock (plant) type used to produce the electrical energy;

t (= 1, 2, ..., T) denotes the discrete time periods;

y_{kjt} (all j, k, t) denotes the quantity of electrical energy demanded by consuming sector k in region j and time period t;

x_{jit} (all i, j, t) denotes the quantity of electrical energy transmitted and distributed from region i to region i in period t;

x^p_{jt} (all p, j, t) denotes the net quantity of electrical energy generated in region j by plant type p in period t;

I^p_{jt} (for all p, j, t) denotes the investment in capacity of each plant type p in region j and period t;

$\hat{I}^p_{jt}$ (for all p, j, t) denotes the maximum feasible plant capacity addition of type p in region j and period t:· (this is the result of the institutional structure within the industry);

K^p_{j1} (for all p, j) denotes the existing capacity (i.e., t=1) in region j of type p;

$\hat{X}^p_{jst}$ (for all p, j, s, t) denotes the generation restriction on plant type p in region j and period t as the result of a specific environmental or energy consumption standard;

a^p_{jt} (all j, j, t) denotes the marginal operating and maintenance cost (including fuel cost) of one unit of output from plant type p in region j and period t;

b^p_{jt} (all p, j, t) denotes the marginal cost of adding one unit of capacity of plant type p in region j and period t;

c^p_{jst} (all p, j, s, t) denotes the cost of installing and maintaining envrionmental control equipment designed to meet the environmental quality standard s on plant type p in region j and period t;

d_{jit} (all i, j, t) denotes the cost of transmitting electrical energy from region j to region i plus (implicitly) the cost of distributing it within region j and period t;

r_s denotes the social rate of discount;

σ^{t-1} equals $1/(1+r_s)^{t-1}$ and denotes the discount factor for the net social payoff in period t.

A fundamental assumption of the economic environment for electrical energy is that the demand and cost functions for each consuming sector, each region and each time period are known with certainty or are available in the certainty equivalence sense. With this assumption, as explained by Mohring, the demand functions are given as:

$$p_{kjt} = f_{kjt}(y_{kjt}) \tag{1}$$

where p_{kjt} is the price of electrical energy to the consuming sector k in region j and period t.

Two implications of this assumption are that the division into periods of equal duration presents no problem and that the demand curves are not stochastic. The combination of fluctuations in weather together with a significant use of electrical energy for either space heating or air conditioning introduces an important stochastic element into electrical energy demand, since in addition to the regular daily and seasonal variations of these loads, there are also variations due to short-term weather changes. Prices should be varied to meet short-run fluctuations in demand induced by weather changes.

Consumers however, may prefer a simpler rate schedule which covers the cost of meeting stochastically fluctuating demand. What they desire is both electrical energy and the right to use more of it as the weather changes for the worse. Consequently, utilities provide a margin of spare capacity to meet this occasional demand. This means that expected demand is less than available capacity. The magnitude of this margin depends on how much consumers value its availability. It will be assumed here that this margin is constant across all plants for all time periods.

The search for optimal demands, prices, and operating schedules is subject to several constraints:

(1) For all consuming sectors in each region and each time period, the total quantity of electrical energy demanded is less than or equal to the quantity supplied by all regions:

$$\sum_k y_{kjt} \leq \sum_i x_{ijt} \tag{2}$$

(2) For each region and each time period, the total generation of electrical energy is less than or equal to the generation from all plants within that region:

$$\sum_i x_{jit} \leq \sum_p x^p_{jt} \tag{3}$$

(3) For each plant in a region, generation is less than or equal to the generation from the generating capacity existing in the first period plus the generation from capacity additions in the first and subsequent periods:

$$x^p_{jt} \leq K^p_{j1} + \sum_{\tau=1}^{t} I^p_{j\tau}. \tag{4}$$

There is a temptation to include a term accounting for the rate of decline of output over time due to "age". Since it is not significant for well maintained plants, however, the concept is not included. Further, if capacity is not added in period t or that plant does not exist in the initial period I^p_{jt} or K^p_{jl} will be zero.

(4) For each region, investment in generating capacity is constrained by physical, institutional, and technological limitations:

$$I^p_{jt} \leq \hat{I}^p_{jt}. \tag{5}$$

For example, it is well known that there is a maximum feasible expansion in, say, nuclear power development because of the following kinds of constraints: licensing, development of additional uranium supplies, technical and construction manpower limitations, difficulties with new and extrapolated equipment, and so on, i.e., see Joint Committee on Atomic Research.

Further, proposed locations for new generating plants are held up to environmental scrutiny and sites optimal in all respects may still be deemed environmentally unacceptable, because they violate laws such as the nonsignificant deterioration of the environment clause in the Clean Air Act. The cancellation of the new coal fired plant proposed for the Kaiparowits Plateau in Southern Utah in 1978 is an example of the limitations of capacity additions arriving from environmental considerations.

Additionally, given that the problem is marked at an initial point (i.e., t=1), capacity additions in this period are non-existent:

$$I_{j1}^{p} = 0 \tag{5a}$$

Note that this constraint is subsumed in constraint (5).

(5) For any plant in a region in a specific period, output might be limited to control for environmental effects or the consumption of a specific type of energy:

$$x_{jt}^{p} \leq \hat{X}_{jst}^{p} \tag{6}$$

This constraint needs elaboration. It is potentially desirable during a specific period during the year to control the volume of atmospheric pollutants coming from a given plant. By limiting output, the pollutants can be controlled. Thus, sulfur emissions from fossil plants might be severely restricted during the periods when air pollution is at its maximum, i.e., during the summer. Alternatively, complaints of nuisance type noise from residents near the boundaries of generating plants have been problems which electric utilities have faced for years. The noise level can be controlled by controlling output, as explained by the Federal Energy Regulatory Commission. Finally, the limitation of fuel consumption of a specific type due to PIFUA is introduced via this constraint.

Before proceeding, a number of points need to be clarified concerning the economic environment:

(1) Additions to capacity are looked upon as an average. To include a margin of spare capacity required to meet demands above the mean expection I_{jt}^{p} can be inflated by the appropriate margin.

(2) There is no discussion of terminal conditions. This does not preclude such discussions in a variant of the model.

(3) The formulation is deterministic. Accounting for uncertainties in demand, plant availability, and so forth can be included in the margin of the spare capacity factor.

(4) Attention is focused on the basic economic aspects of the problem with no attention being paid to all sorts of practical engineering aspects. It must be recognized that the use of this model is the first of several stages of the investment decision process. The search for a solution that satisfies economic and social criteria is an iterative process.

Mathematical Formulation

If future social welfare is looked at as commensurable with present social welfare through a common time discount factor σ, the the following discounting convention can be employed:

$$NSP = NSP(1) + \sigma NSP(2) +, \ldots ,+ \sigma^{T-1} NSP(T) \tag{7}$$

where NSP and NSP (t), for all t, denote the total discounted net social payoff and the undiscounted net social payoff in period t, respectively. One can now form the total discounted net quasi-welfare function as

$$NSP = \sum_t \sigma^{t-1} \{ \int \sum_k \sum_j f_{kjt} (y_{kjt}) dy_{kjt} \tag{8}$$

$$- \sum_j \sum_p a^p_{jt} x^p_{jt} - \sum_j \sum_p \sum_s c^p_{jst} x^p_{jt}$$

$$- b^p_{jt} I^p_{jt} - \sum_j \sum_i d_{jit} x_{jit} \}$$

Providing the demand functions are downward sloping, the objective function is concave and the Kuhn-Tucker conditions will give the necessary and sufficient conditions for optimality. Associating the dual variables

$$\sigma^{t-1} \lambda_{1kjt}, \sigma^{t-1} \lambda_{2jt}, \sigma^{t-1} \mu_{pjt}, \sigma^{t-1} \rho_{pjt}, \sigma^{t-1} \lambda^p_{jst}$$

with constraints (2) through (6) respectively and multiplying throughout by σ^{t-1} where appropriate, the Kuhn-Tucker conditions are:

$$y_{kjt} \leq \sum x_{jt} \qquad \lambda_{1kjt} \geq 0 \tag{9}$$

$$\sum_i x_{jit} \le \sum_p x^p_{jt} \qquad \lambda_{2jt} \ge 0 \tag{10}$$

$$x^p_{jt} \le K^p_{j1} + \sum_{\tau=1}^{t} I^p_{j\tau} \qquad \mu_{pjt} \ge 0 \tag{11}$$

$$I^p_{jt} \le \hat{I}^p_{jt} \qquad \rho_{pjt} \ge 0 \tag{12}$$

$$x^p_{jt} \le \hat{x}^p_{jst} \qquad \lambda^p_{jst} \ge 0 \tag{13}$$

$$f_{kjt}(y_{kjt}) \le \lambda_{1kjt} \qquad y_{kjt} \ge 0 \tag{14}$$

$$\lambda_{1kjt} \le d_{jit} + \lambda_{2jt} \qquad x_{jkt} \ge 0 \tag{15}$$

$$\lambda_{2jt} \le a^p_{jt} + \sum c^p_{jst} + \quad x^p_{jt} \quad \mu_{pjt} + \lambda^p_{js*t} \quad x^p_{jt} \ge 0 \tag{16}$$

$$\sum_{t' \ge t} \sigma^{t'-t} \mu_{pjt'} \le b^p_{jt} + \rho_{pjt} \quad I^p_{jt} \ge 0 \tag{17}$$

The variable μ_{pjt} can be interpreted as the quasi-rent of plant p in region j in period t and, if that plant is utilized, is equal to the supply price minus the marginal operation and maintenance cost (hereafter, operating cost), the sum of the explicit costs of each of the environmental quality standards $\sum_s c^p_{jst}$, and the implicit cost of the environmental quality standards λ^p_{js*t}. Thus, if

$$x^p_{jt} > 0, \text{ then } \mu_{pjt} = \lambda_{2jt} - (a^p_{jt} + \sum_s c^p_{jst} + \lambda^p_{js*t}). \tag{16a}$$

Note that at most one of the capacity constraints arising from environmental quality standards (resulting in an implicit cost) is binding at any particular time in a given region. The binding constraint is denoted by s^*. Supposing in addition $y_{kit} > 0$ and $x_{ijt} > 0$, the quasi-rent will be exactly equal to the market demand price λ_{1kjt} less the sum of the marginal costs.

To minimize total cost, generation will be scheduled on equipment in increasing order of operating cost plus the explicit costs of the environmental quality standards plus transmission cost. Therefore, the demand price to any consuming sector in any period t in region j equals the sum of these costs on the least efficient plant in any region j, denoted by ϕ, being used to general electrical energy. Thus if

$$0 < x^{\phi}_{jt} < k^{\phi}_{j1} + \sum_{\tau=1}^{t} I^{\phi}_{jt}, \qquad (11a)$$

then

$$f_{kjt}(y_{kjt}) = a^{\phi}_{jt} + \sum + c^{\phi}_{jst} + d_{ijt}$$

provided $x^{p}_{kt} < \hat{x}^{p}_{jst}$ for all s.

The quasi-rent of any plant is equal to the difference between the sum of its operating and maintenance cost, implicit and explicit environmental quality costs and delivery cost and those of the least efficient plant. Thus, if

$x^{\phi}_{jt} > 0$, then

$$\mu_{\phi jt} = a^{\phi}_{jt} + \sum_{s} c^{\phi}_{jst} + d^{\phi}_{jit} - (a^{p}_{jt} + \sum_{s} c^{p}_{jst} + d_{jit}). \qquad (18)$$

where d^{ϕ}_{jit} denotes the delivery cost from the least efficient plant. Observe that it is possible to use a plant to generate electrical energy that does not have the lowest operating cost. If the transmission (as well as distribution) cost is sufficiently large then it might be optimal to use a plant with higher combined operating and environmental quality costs while shutting down a more efficient one.

The relationships (11a) and 16a) indicate effects on price of the imposition of environmental quality standards. The price of electrical energy to the consumer j in period t inregion j will increase by the explicit cost of the environmental
quality standards $\sum_{s} c^{p}_{jst}$ plus the implicit cost λ^{p}_{js*t}.
This assumes, of course, that plant p is being used to generate electrical energy and that it is the least efficient one in operation in period t. The value of the explicit cost can be computed simply from the knowledge of, say, the operating cost of cooling towers per kilowatt-hour (about .05 mills/kWh) or the operating cost for the limestone scrubbing (about .34 mills/kWh), i.e., see the Council on Environmental Quality. The implicit cost, the cost of electrical energy

due to the restriction of generation from a particular plant, cannot a priori be calculated. It is dependent on the level of the capacity constraint for the particular plant, total system demand for electrical energy, and generation constraints on other plants. Thus, for example, if a given plant is the most efficient in all respects (based on an operating cost and explicit environmental quality cost criterion), but it is required to forego all generation during a particular period, the implicit cost in this period for this plant would equal the difference between its operating cost plus explicit environmental cost and these costs for the next most efficient plant.

Additions to capacity are undertaken on the basis of a least-cost criterion. New capacity (either an additional plant or an expansion of an existing plant) should be added in any period up the point where the discounted sum of its quasi-rents equals the purchase price plus the marginal value of a particular plant addition (or quasi-rent because the capacity expansion is limited either by technological or environmental considerations). Thus,

If $I^p_{jt} > 0$, then (17a)

$$\sum_{t'>t} \sigma^{t'-t} \mu_{pjt'} = b^p_{jt} + \rho_{pjt}.$$

The pricing implications of prohibiting capacity expansion in a particular region can be seen by focusing on, say, period t, when it would have been optimal to build a plant in region j but it must be built in region i because of environmental prohibitions. The increase in the price of electrical energy, measured by the quasi-rent ρ_{pjt} will equal the difference between: (1) total costs including capital cost, operating cost, explicit and implicit environmental costs and delivery cost on the plant that is built, and (2) these costs for the plant that was prohibited.

The quasi-rent of a plant in any period can be regarded as that part of the supply price set aside to cover depreciation and interest on capital. This is what Turvey (1969) calls amortization. If new capacity is added in any period, and if the maximum capacity addition is not reached, demand price in that period is equal to the operating cost plus amortization on the new plant plus explicit and implicit environmental costs plus transmission cost. Thus, denoting the new plant by n,

If $x^n_{jt} > 0$ and $y_{kjt} > 0$, then (19)

$$f_{kjt}(y_{kjt}) = a^n_{jt} + \mu_{njt} + \sum_s c^n_{jst} + \lambda^n_{js*t} + d_{jit}$$

A plant should begin to be retired when its operating cost and environmental quality costs rise above the level of the operating cost plus amortization plus environmental quality costs of the new plant (given transmission cost is the same). Thus

$$\text{If } a^m_{jt} + \sum_s c^m_{jst} + \lambda^m_{js*t} > a^n_{jt} + \mu_{njt} + \sum_s c_{jst} + \lambda^n_{js*t}, \quad (20)$$

then

$x^m_{jt} = 0.$

The implications of this are that a sufficiently high combination of costs to meet environmental quality standards will force the retirement of existing generating capacity before what otherwise would have been optimal.

Equation (17a) can be interpreted to mean that the present value of amortization equals the purchase price of new capacity plus the quasi-rent of the capacity limitation. Consequently, the present value of total profit is zero. The issue to be emphasized is that the amount set aside for amortization varies from period to period depending on demand and perhaps is equal to zero in some periods. With demand varying, a constant proportion of capacity cost each period should not necessarily be recouped. Rather, price should be set to just fully utilize capacity (conditional upon price not being below marginal production cost and the cost of meeting environmental quality standards), and capacity should be selected so that over the life of the plant, capacity cost is just recouped.

Analysis of the Model

By casting the problem in a spatial dimension as well as the temporal dimension, the way has been opened to handle many of the difficult problems with investment in generating capacity as well as the problems involved with price adjustment and allocation over time on such things as stricter environmental quality standards in conjunction with technological change, permitting the cheaper transmission of electrical energy over long distances, becomes realistic.

The general principles of optimal pricing from this model can be summarized as follows:

(1) Set prices by time of day (or seasons of the year) in accordance with the pattern of demand. This means that any consumer or class of consumers in a particular hour be treated the same regardless of how much is consumed.

(2) Charge high prices when the quantity demanded rises above the level of capacity. Thus, a utility can obtain a quasi-rent in the short-run by charging a price in excess of the operating, capital, environmental and transmission costs. This ignores the longer run consideration of imposing a penalty on the utility due to inadequate capacity to meet future requirements.

(3) Vary prices spatially depending on how far the consumer is from the generating plant.

(4) Capital costs are imputed to consumers only to the extent their demand presses on the capacity of a generating plant. Thus, any increase in demand during a peak period requiring a utility to expand its generating capacity will result in a charge for electrical energy, just sufficient to compensate for the increased cost associated with satisfying demand.

(5) Require consumers to bear the implicit and explicit costs of implementing environmental quality standards.

The impact of environmental quality standards will vary from one time period to another and from one region to another depending upon the plants used and the standards imposed in any particular region during the time interval of interest. With an increase in the price of electrical energy resulting as the consumer is required to bear these costs, the aggregate effect will be dependent on the reduction in output which in turn is dependent on the demand elasticities in each time period.

The Economic Setting

Now with the objective of empirically implementing the model developed in the preceeding section, it is necessary to delineate the regional classification, consuming sectors, plant types, time period, and so on. The regional delineation used is that defined for the contiguous United States by the Department of Commerce. This is given in Table 8.1. Three consuming sectors - residential, commercial and industrial - will be considered in each region. Each of these sectors exhibits an identifiable, distinguishable demand for electrical energy. There is a fourth sector (nominally referred to as other) consisting of transportation use, government use, street and highway lighting, agricultural use, etc., that on average across all regions accounted for only 3.9 percent of total electrical energy consumption in 1982. Because of its small proportion and heterogeneous composition, consideration of this other sector will be deferred, assuming that all the desired electrical energy can be purchased at the prevailing market price. This will of necessity tend to slightly understate net social payoff.

On the supply side, five alternative methods of generating electrical energy will be considered. The structure of the generating system rests on the mix of hydroelectric schemes, three conventional fossil fuel steam electric plant types (coal oil (primarily residual fuel oil), and natural gas), and nuclear steam reactors. There are some alternative methods of generating electrical energy (e.g., internal combustion, geothermal, and gas turbine). In 1982 these accounted for only 0.94 percent of the total electrical energy generated in the United States. Given the relative unimportance of these alternative technologies for electrical energy generation and based on the presumption that they will continue to play only a minor role in the overall generation configuration, they are excluded from explicit consideration.

In order to make the empirical solution to the problem manageable, the period 1980 to 1990 will be focused upon at 5 year intervals.

Model Parameter Estimates

Up to now, the equilibrium model hypothesizes a general demand relationship. The solution of the problem necessitates an exact functional specification. Because it is mathematically tractible, a linear demand relationship is presumed. This converts the problem at hand into an LCP problem, i.e., see Chapter 2 and Takayama and Uri. Because of well known econometric problems, linear demand functions in terms of price and quantity are not directly estimable. Instead, the estimates of the demand curve coefficients are obtained first by estimating the price elasticity and then

Table 8.1

REGIONAL CLASSIFICATION

Region	Composition
1. New England	Maine, New Hampshire, Vermont, Massachusetts, Rhode Island, Connecticut
2. Middle Atlantic	New York, New Jersey, Pennsylvania
3. East North Central	Ohio, Indiana, Illinois, Michigan, Wisconsin
4. West North Central	Minnesota, Iowa, Missouri, North Dakota, South Dakota, Nebraska, Kansas
5. South Atlantic	Delaware, Maryland, District of Columbia, Virginia, West Virginia, North Carolina, South Carolina, Georgia, Florida
6. East South Central	Kentucky, Tennessee, Alabama, Mississippi
7. West South Central	Arkansas, Louisiana, Oklahoma, Texas
8. Mountain	Montana, Idaho, Wyoming, Colorado, New Mexico, Arizona, Utah, Nevada
9. Pacific	Washington, Oregon, California

translating these elasticities into point estimates of the requesite demand functions. To estimate regional-consuming sector price elasticities, the method used in Uri is employed. In particular, for each consuming sector, a translog price possibility frontier is specified whereby expenditure shares are hypothesized to be a function of the prices of the various types of energy. Upon pooling cross section and time series data across all nine regions and for the period 1947 through 1980, the price elasticity estimates for 1980 were found to range between -0.96 and -0.45 for the residential sector, between -1.02 and -0.50 for the commercial sector, and between -1.05 and -0.52 for the industrial sector.

Given the temporal nature of the problem, it is necessary a priori to forecast demand over the planning horizon to provide estimates of the demand functions. This is accomplished by using the estimated price possibility frontiers and the price changes in the various energy sources as provided by the U.S. Department of Energy. With expected price and expected quantity demanded values available for each consuming sector, each region and each time period (except for 1980 where actual values are used), linear approximations of the relevant demand functions are obtained.

Turning to cost considerations, transmission and distribution costs are computed using the approach of Baughman, Joskow, and Kamat (1979). In particular transmission and distribution demand changes are related to the characteristics of utility service areas and electrical energy consumption patterns. Capital expenditures for transmission and distribution are computed for two classes of customers: (1) residential and commercial as one class, and (2) industrial as the other. Captial expenditures are converted to an annual charge using an annual capital charge rate of 13.5 percent. Based on the annual capital rate and the cost for each equipment item, the average costs per kilowatt-hour proportional to the customer and energy related explanatory variables are then obtained. For residential and commercial customers the average transmission and distribution costs for 1980 range from 1.9 to 3.6 cents per kilowatt-hour. For the industrial sector, the costs vary between 1.0 and 2.3 cents per kilowatt-hour. Marginal operating and maintenance costs including fuel costs for each of the plant types are computed for 1980 using the monthly power plant report (for EIA-759) of the Department of Energy (formerly Form 4 of the Federal Energy Reulatory Commission). To project these costs over the planning horizon, the forecast fuel price increases of the 1982 Annual Energy Outlook published by the U.S. Department of Energy were used.

Capital cost, the fixed cost component of the total cost of supplying electrical energy is estimated using a series of programs developed at Oak Ridge National Laboratory. Based on the assumption that any central station power plant of the same type involves approximately the same major cost components regardless of location or data of intitial operation, the programs establish trends in these cost components as a function of time, location and plant type to estimate costs for any particular case.

Estimates of the limitations on investment in new generating capacity were taken from the Data Resources, Inc. (1980). These estimates are looked upon as the likely additions to generating capacity. Moreover, capacity factors for existing and new generation are computed as averages for the 1971-1980 period.

The choice of an appropriate rate of social discount is surrounded by a considerable literature, i.e., see Beaumont (1968). From relationship (17a), it is clear that the rate selected will affect the amortization of new generating capacity which in turn will impact the optimal solution. The rate currently used by the U.S. government is 10 percent. This, as shown by Bradford (1975), is excessive. Instead, a value of 4 percent suggested by Gramlich (1981) is selected as being consistent with the real social optimum rate of discount.

With regard to the environmental costs associated with the initial solution of the model, these costs are all assumed to equal zero. Limitations on the use of specific energy types are extracted from the analysis underlying the 1980 Annual Report to Congress prepared by the U.S. Department of Energy.

As a final comment before turning to a solution of the model, all of the values of the primal variables in the linear complementarity formulation are in net terms. Consequently to obtain values for total generation, for example, it would be necessary to inflate the net generation figures by the amount lost upon transmission.

The Optimal Solution

Assuming that competitive conditions prevail across all consuming sectors, producing sectors, regions, and time periods (i.e., 1980, 1985, and 1990) and using the data previously discussed, the solution to the linear complementarity program can be obtained. Since there is a voluminous amount of output, only a small portion can be examined here for 1980 and 1990. The values for 1985 shed little light on the issues at hand. The solution values can be found in Table 8.2 through Table 8.4.

The values reported here reveal a number of interesting facts. The growth in the demand for electrical energy from Table 8.2 of about 3 percent over the 1980 to 1990 period is consistent with the post-Arab oil embargo growth rate and considerably less than the 7 percent rate of the 1950 through 1972 period. One surmizes that higher electrical energy prices, a sustained energy consciousness, various energy conservation activities and an aging of a more stable population all will contribute to the anticipated lower expected rate of growth in electrical energy demand. Of course, these values would differ, given changes in the world oil market.

The overall price profile that results is a revealing aspect of the model. Note that the price differential will arise because of the differences in transmission and distribution costs. They, as it will be recalled, were computed to be the same for both the residential and commercial sectors and somewhat less for the industrial sector. If one de facto believes that electrical energy should be regulated in such a way as to approximate the competitive norm, then the State regulatory commissions are slightly remiss in setting the rate structure. As we noted above, the residential and commercial sectors should be charged the same price for the homogeneous good which currently is not the practice. In fact in 1982, the average price of electrical energy to the average residential consumer was 6.86 cents per kilowatt-hour (in current year dollars). Moreover, given the differences in transmission and distribution costs between the residential and commercial consumers and the industrial consumers, the established price differential is approximately correct.

As has been implicitly and explicitly observed in the foregoing pages, costs are a most significant consideration in the analysis of determining the least-cost investment in electrical energy generation. Because of their lower costs, coal and nuclear capacity are expected to exhibit the largest increases. Oil generating capacity is expected to decline due to the requirements of the Power Plant and Industrial

Table 8.2

OPTIMAL DEMAND FOR ELECTRICAL ENERGY BY SECTOR AND REGION
(Billions of kWh)

Region	Years[a]	Residential Sector	Commercial Sector	Industrial Sector
1. New England	1980	31.055	24.381	21.299
	1990	43.861	30.031	31.059
2. Middle Atlantic	1980	85.069	78.067	89.919
	1990	115.924	96.215	115.392
3. East North Central	1980	122.141	92.118	164.297
	1990	150.369	108.202	229.374
4. West North Central	1980	59.139	45.106	47.807
	1990	78.663	60.308	65.902
5. South Atlantic	1980	146.534	89.330	104.463
	1990	206.592	132.545	146.501
6. East South Central	1980	73.024	28.634	109.400
	1990	90.520	35.612	159.362
7. West South Central	1980	99.028	69.347	113.301
	1990	132.651	109.766	169.548
8. Mountain	1980	33.079	39.436	36.781
	1990	53.860	58.313	53.696
9. Pacific	1980	89.549	92.903	95.528
	1990	135.438	136.574	124.125

[a] 1980 values represent actual figures.

Table 8.3

OPTIMAL DEMAND PRICE IN CENTS PER kWh
(Constant 1980 Dollars)

Region	Sector	1980	1990
1. New England	Residential and Commercial	6.40 (5.53)	14.81
	Industrial	5.03 (4.17)	13.82
2. Middle Atlantic	Residential and Commercial	6.62 (5.99)	13.65
	Industrial	4.52 (3.51)	11.54
3. East North Central	Residential and Commercial	5.06 (4.69)	10.65
	Industrial	3.40 (3.00)	8.68
4. West North Central	Residential and Commercial	4.51 (4.19)	10.36
	Industrial	3.76 (3.67)	9.37
5. South Atlantic	Residential and Commercial	4.75 (4.39)	12.03
	Industrial	3.54 (2.93)	10.78
6. East South Central	Residential and Commercial	3.95 (3.54)	10.51
	Industrial	3.28 (2.74)	9.32
7. West South Central	Residential and Commerical	4.62 (3.99)	15.43
	Industrial	3.36 (2.56)	14.89
8. Mountain	Residential and Commercial	3.63 (4.06)	12.60
	Industrial	2.82 (2.35)	9.55
9. Pacific	Residential and Commercial	3.90 (3.18)	12.01
	Industrial	3.06 (2.19)	11.03

Table 8.4

CHANGE IN THE OPTIMAL GENERATING CAPACITY BY REGION, 1980-1990
(in Billions of kW)

Region	Coal	Oil	Natural Gas	Nuclear	Hydroelectric
1. New England	5.0	- 5.1	0.0	4.3	0.0
2. Middle Atlantic	8.3	-12.8	0.0	10.1	0.3
3. East North Central	10.0	-13.2	0.0	16.0	0.0
4. West North Central	8.7	- 1.0	0.0	3.2	0.0
5. South Atlantic	24.8	- 8.1	0.0	9.1	2.8
6. East South Central	12.9	- .5	0.0	12.8	.3
7. West South Central	35.5	- 1.0	-5.8	10.8	.8
8. Mountain	16.3	- 1.2	- .5	2.8	1.3
9. Pacific	9.8	- 8.6	0.0	7.1	4.5

Fuel Use Act. This is most noticeable in the Middle Atlantic region and the East North Central region both of which had considerable oil generating capacity at the start of the 1980s. Natural gas generating capacity in general will not be affected. The exception is the West South Central region that found almost 69 percent of its 1980 generating capacity being natural gas fired. Had the analysis extended beyond 1990, however, there would be a significant decline in natural gas generating capacity due to PIFUA. Hydroelectric capacity will expand primarily in the western portion of the United States where the development potential continues to be the greatest.

In conclusion, it is important to realize that the utility generation process described is dynamic in that demands, costs, and the environmental and energy related legislation continually change. This will necessarily affect the evolution, for example, of the optimal configuration of generating capacity. As an example, if political and institutional considerations continue to weigh heavily with regard to the additon of nuclear capacity as they have in recent years, then one would expect to realize a larger addition to coal-fired generating capacity and considerably smaller additions to nuclear capacity.

Author
Noel D. Uri
Economic Research Service
U.S. Department of Agriculture
Washington, D.C. 20005

References

Baughman, M.L., P.L. Joskow and D.P. Kamat, (1979). Electric Power in the United States: Models and Policy Analysis, Cambridge: MIT Press, Inc.

Baumol, W.J., (1968). "On the Social Rate of Discount," The American Economic Review, 58: 788-802.

Bradford, D.F., (1975). "Constraints on Government Investment Opportunities and the Choice of Discount Rate," American Economic Review, 65: 802-819.

Council on Environmental Quality. (1972). The Economic Impact of Pollution Control, U.S. Government Printing Office, Washington, D.C.

Data Resources Incorporated, (1980). Energy Review, Autumn 1980, Data Resources Incorporated, Lexington.

Department of Energy, (1980). Annual Report to Congress 1979, U.S. Government Printing Office, Washington, D.C.

Department of Energy, (1983). 1982 Annual Energy Outlook, U.S. Government Printing Office, Washington, D.C.

Federal Energy Regulatory Commission, (1978). Air Pollution and the Regulated Electric Power and Natural Gas Industries

Gramlich, E.M. (1981). Benefit-Cost Analysis of Government Programs, Englewood Cliffs: Prentice-Hall.

Joint Committee on Atomic Energy, (1973). Understanding the National Energy Dilemma," U.S. Government Printing Office, Washington, D.C.

Mohring, H., (1970). "The Peak Load Pricing Problem with Increasing Returns and Pricing Constraints," The American Economic Review, 60: 693-705.

National Regulatory Institute, (1981). Capacity Expansion and Reliability Evaluation System.

Takayama, T. and N.D. Uri, (1983). "A Note on Spatial and Temporal Price and Allocation Modeling: Quadratic Programming or Linear Complementarity Programming," Regional Science and Urban Economics, 13: 455-470.

Taylor, L.D., (1976). The Demand for Energy: A Survey of Price and Income Elasticities, University of Arizona.

Turvey, R., (1969). "Marginal Cost," Economic Journal, 79: 282-299.

Turvey, R. and D. Anderson, (1977). Electricity Economics, Baltimore: Johns Hopkins University Press.

Uri, N.D., (1982). The Demand for Energy and Conservation in the United States, Greenwich: JAI Press.

9 Alternative national policies and the location patterns of energy-related facilities

GEORGE PROVENZANO *U.S. Environmental Protection Agency*

Introduction

Significant differences in energy facility location patterns and, hence, the spatial distribution of energy-related environmental impacts are associated with potential national energy development policies. The optimal energy facility location pattern for a policy that, for example, emphasizes utilization of both coal and nuclear resources will differ greatly from the optimal pattern associated with a policy that places a moratorium on constructing nuclear power plants. An understanding of the manner in which energy policy changes of this kind affect location choices for energy production activities, therefore, is essential in coordinating energy development and environmental resources management at the regional and subregional levels.

One area in which information regarding potential energy facility location patterns is especially important concerns that of obtaining sufficient water supplies to expand steam electric power generation and to develop synthetic fuels from coal industries. On a per unit of output basis, both industries require large quantitites of water for cooling purposes. In the case of synfuels production, large amounts of water are also needed as a material input into the various processes. Therefore, the extent to which regions are able to accommodate future development of these industries ultimately depends on planning efforts that coordinate location-specific options for providing needed water supplies with the construction of new energy production facilities. Some background information on this problem can be found in the U.S. Water Resources Council (1974a, 1974b, 1978), Dobson et al. (1977), Harte and El-Gasseir (1978), Probstein and Gold (1978), and the U.S. Department of Energy (1979).

Accordingly, this Chapter discusses the formulation and application of a large scale multiperiod, multiplant, multimarket linear programming model to the problem of coordinating the joint development of a region's energy and water resources. The model simulates the regional expansion of steam electric power generation and high Btu coal gasification industries; it simultaneously appraises investment and production alternatives for these industries and assigns new energy production facilities to spatially dispersed sources of water and coal in a manner that minimizes the total costs of meeting future energy demands.

As a demonstration of its capabilities, the model is used to identify and evaluate for a case study region, the regional changes in energy facility location patterns that might be induced by changes in national energy development policies or by changes in policies for allocating water to that end. With respect to energy, this study examines the locational shifts that may be induced by the two policies that were recently debated at the national level: (1) encouraging the rapid development of synfuels-from-coal industry (coal gasification), and (2) declaring a moratorium on starting construction of additional nuclear power plants. Although the model that is presented is crude in some points, its basic function is to provide insight into the interaction between energy and water resources development policies within a region. In this regard, information provided by the model can be used by planners in coordinating energy and water resources development decisions.

Planning for Regional Energy and Water Resources Development

The problem of coordinating regional energy and water resources development requires allocating or assigning new energy facilities to locations with sufficient water supplies for use in energy production. Because location decisions are inherently part of new plant investment decisions, the regional coordination problem involves a comparative cost analysis of a large number of potential investment alternatives for energy production and water use. The kinds of alternatives that must be compared include: (1) choices among alternative types and sizes of energy production facilities and their corresponding water use requirements (nuclear power plants, coal fired power plants, and coal gasification plants), (2) choices among alternative options for water reuse and recovery (cooling ponds or cooling towers), and (3) choices among alternative location possibilities with respect to available water supplies (rivers, reservoirs or lakes).

A comparative cost analysis of this kind is further complicated by the fact that regional energy investment, and hence, location decision variables strongly interact at a point in time and over time. This temporal and spatial interaction occurs for a number of reasons which are best illustrated using three examples from the electric utility industry, although similar kinds of interaction can be found in other energy production industries as well.

(1) At a point in time, different types of power plants have complementary functions within a modern interconnected power supply system. In terms of cost structure, large nuclear and fossil fuel base local plants have high capital but lower generation costs; intermediate size fossil fuel plants have lower capital costs but higher generation costs; and gas turbine peaking plants have the lowest capital but highest generation costs. To meet continuously fluctuating power demands at least cost, power plants are connected or dispatched to the load in a sequence that minimizes total generation and transmission costs. Large economic nuclear and fossil baseload plants are connected first; intermediate fossil plants are connected as the load increases; and finally gas turbine peaking plants with the highest generation costs are connected for the peak loads.

(2) Investment decision variables for a power system interact with operating variables through time. Because of the complementary functions of the different types of plants, the optimal mix of plant types and sizes in the system at a point in time involves balancing potential economies of scale from larger plants against the opportunity costs of temporary excess capacity. The optimal mix of plants, therefore, depends on the sum of the discounted present values of both annualized capital and generation costs for the set of existing and future

plants in the system.

(3) Decisions to add new plants are made in the context of an "inherited" set of plants that have expected operating lifetimes and opportunity costs of replacement. The fact that a power supply system expands within the spatial context of an existing network of plants, transmisison lines and local centers may affect future location decisions in at lest two ways. First, of the candidate sites for new plants, those sites that are located near existing load centers or along existing transmission line right-of-ways may be economically more attractive to develop. Second, two or more neighboring utilities may jointly develop one site in order to take advantage of economies of scale embodied in large units.

Because of these complex economic and technical interactions between investment and operating variables, engineers, economists and operations researchers have developed mathematical programming models to determine optimum investment plans for power supply systems. Linear programming models were first applied to the problem of minimizing power generation investment costs in France in the 1950s, i.e., see Anderson (1972) and Massé and Gibrat (1957). In recent years the problem of determining least cost investment plans has also been formulated as a mixed integer linear program by Gately (1970) and Scherer (1977), as a dynamic program by Braun and Cady (1973), as a nonlinear program by Bessiere (1970), as a mixed integer, chance constrained program by Noonan and Giglio (1977), and by Scherer and Joe (1977) to accomodate discrete plant-size variables and stochastic aspects of plant-sizing decisions.

Basic Description of the Model

The model and applications that are discussed below have been adapted from linear programming models for planning optimal investments in electric power generating facilities. This particular model differs from previous optimal investments for power generation models in two respects. First, because of the need to focus on location specific alternatives for supplying water for energy production, the present model emphasizes and combines the determination of optimal locations of new energy facilities with the determination of the optimal mix of types and sizes of new energy production capacity. Second, the present model includes the simultaneous determination of optimal investment strategies for steam electric power generation and coal gasification industries subject to available water resources.

Specifically, a multiperiod, multiplant, multimarket linear programming assignment model is formulated. The objective of the model is to minimize the regional sum of the discounted present values of capital, production, and transmission costs incurred in supplying future demands for electricity and gas, i.e. see Uri (1975) for a discussion of the associated efficiency gains. Decision variables in the model include: choice of nuclear, coal fired, and gas turbine power generating capacity; size, location, and sequence of additions of new steam electric and gas production and transmission.

Optimization occurs simultaneously over several time periods. The model selects a minimum-cost set of locations for new energy facilities from a larger set of prescreened candidate areas. Construction of new steam electric and coal gasification plants takes place within the context of an existing set of spatially dispersed energy production facilities. All plants are connected by a network of high voltage transmission lines and gas pipelines to substations and spatially dispersed points of demand for electricity and gas. Steam electric power plants that were constructed prior to the base year of analysis are gradually retired over the course of the planning horizon. Optimum additions of new generating capacity, therefore, include additions required to meet growing power demands as well as additions required to replace retired power plants.

The model's assignment of new energy production facilities to candidate areas is influenced by water supply considerations in the following two ways: (1) The size and sequence of new additions to capacity are constrained by water availability for energy production at various points within a region. Each candidate area that the model evaluates as a location for a new energy production facility must possess sufficient surface water supplies from river or potential reservoir sources to meet the maximum gross withdrawal requirements of at least one of the large scale steam electric or coal gasification plants considered in the study. (2) The selection of a location for a new energy production facility is dependent on capital costs which include associated water procurement and utilization costs. In particular, reservoir construction costs, which are site-specific in the model, have an important effect on the economic viability of a candidate site for a new plant.

The evaluations provided by the linear programming model represent optimized responses to a regional objective function of least cost energy production. This formulation provides an indication of the direction in which the economic costs of expansion, operation and transmission will encourage energy production to shift. The results of the model must be cautiously interpreted because not all responses by energy producers will be toward minimizing the costs of supply. For example, the extent to which energy producers may weigh the importance of government subsidies, environmental aesthetics or local community impacts in siting new facilities is not reflected in the least cost solution obtained from this model.

Finally, a linear programming model of this kind is designed to give only approximate solutions to some of the countless engineering-economic problems encountered in energy system planning. The essential function of the model is to identify general trends regarding how many and what types of plants to build and approximately when and where to build them. Once these basic features of the future energy production system and corresponding water use patterns have been blocked out, and once the sensitivity of energy development strategies to policies affecting a major system component such as water availability for energy production has been established, then more detailed studies of the impacts of energy development on water resources can be made using simulation methods.

The following notation is used in formulating the multiperiod, multiplant, multimarket linear programming model described above. Let:

- t denote discrete time periods within the planning horizon; $t = 1,...,T$.
- δ denote energy production facilities, for example, a nuclear base load, fossil base load, fossil intermediate load, or peak load generating station or coal gasification plant; $\delta = 1,...,D$.
- τ denote energy transmission systems, for example, high voltage transmission lines or gas pipeline.
- ν denote the energy commodities electricity and gas; $\nu = 1,...N$.

i denote the location of the origin of energy transmission which may be a power plant, coal gasification plant, or a substation; $i = 1,\ldots,I$.

j denote the location of the destination of energy transmission which may be a substation, storage area or demand point; $j = 1,\ldots,J$.

k denote for electricity the different instantaneous levels of power demand, base load, intermediate load, and peak load levels, within each time period; $k = 1,\ldots,K$. (The k subscript is only applicable for electricty.)

$x^{\delta\tau\nu}_{tvijk}$ denote the level of production and transmission of energy commodity ν at location i using production facility δ and shipping from i to j using transmission system.

$x^{\tau\nu}_{tvijk}$ denote the level of transmission of energy commodity ν from i to j using transmission system τ.

$c^{\delta\tau\nu}_{tvijk}$ denote the unit costs of producing energy commodity ν using facility δ at location i and shipping it to j via transmission system τ.

$c^{\tau\nu}_{tvijk}$ denote the unit transmission costs for shipping energy commodity ν from i to j using transmission system τ.[3]

$w^{\delta\nu}_{vi}$ denote the variable quantity of plant capacity δ for producing ν that can be added at location i.

$c^{\delta\nu}_{vi}$ denote the unit capital cost of plant capacity constructed at location i.

y^{ν}_{tjk} denote the instantaneous power demand in megawatts during subperiod k at load center j.

y^{ν}_{tj} denote the consumption of energy commodity ν at location j.

μ denote a systemwide margin of reserve capacity for producing electricity which is needed for peak demands above expectations.

σ_{ij} denote the loss factor for transmission losses between i and j. The loss factor is the product of the percentage loss per mile and the distance between i and j.

θ_k denote the number of hours in subperiod k within each period.

$\theta_{tvi}^{\delta\nu}$ denote the fraction of a power plant at i that is available for net continuous generation during each period.

$\xi_{tvi}^{\delta\nu}$ denote the annual capacity factor for a power plant i during each period.

$a_{vi}^{\delta\nu}$ denote the quantity of water required to produce a unit of energy commodity ν using production facility δ.

b_i denote the quantity of water available for energy production at location i.

The objective of the model is to minimize the discounted present value of total plant investment, energy production and transmission costs:

$$\sum_{\nu\delta v i}\sum\sum\sum c_{vi}^{\delta\nu} w_{vi}^{\delta\nu} + \sum_{\nu t v i j k}\sum\sum\sum\sum\sum c_{tvijk}^{\delta\tau\nu} x_{tvijk}^{\delta\tau\nu} \theta_k$$

$$+ \sum_{\nu t v i j k}\sum\sum\sum\sum\sum c_{tvijk}^{\tau\nu} x_{tvijk}^{\tau\nu} \theta_k \tag{1}$$

costs are minimized subject to the following system constraints.

The first constraint states that the installed generating capacity of the integrated regional power supply system must be sufficient to meet the regional peak load demand for each time period. This is the peak power guarantee condition. In order to minimize the probability of not having enough capacity, the available installed capacity must be sufficient to meet the expected peak demand with a margin of reserve capacity μ that allows for peak demands above mean expectations. The left side of this constraint is the sum of existing plus new generating capacity that has accumulated from all previous periods, v - t,...,t.

$$\sum_{\delta v i}\sum\sum w_{vi}^{\delta} \quad (1 + \mu) \sum_{\delta v i j}\sum\sum\sum x_{tvijk}^{\delta\tau\nu}; \; \forall t \text{ and } k = 1 \tag{2}$$

This form of the constraint implicitly assumes that the peak load demands occur simultaneously at all load centers within the region. If the region in question is very large, for example such as a multistate region, it is likely that peak loads within the region will occur at different times. A regional "diversity factor" may be added to adjust for the nonsimultaneous occurrence of the peak load demands within a region.

Similarly, for gas production in each time period the second constraint states that the installed capacity of an integrated regional gas supply system must be sufficient to meet total regional production needs. Although there is a peak load period for gas consumption, in some regions gas can be stored, allowing the buildup of supplies to meet the peak. Gas storage permits large efficient SNG plants to operate on a continuous basis without having to adjust output on an hour-to-hour basis in meeting demands. As a result, there is little or no need to build enough capacity to meet expected peak demands with a margin of reserve.

$$\sum\sum\sum_{\delta v i} w^{\delta\nu}_{vi} \qquad \sum\sum\sum\sum_{\delta v i j} x^{\delta\tau\nu}_{tvij} ; \ \forall\ t \tag{2a}$$

There are now a set of related limitations defined by constraints 3 to 7. The transmission of electric power from generating stations and substations, minus any transmission losses, must be sufficient to meet instantaneous power demands at each regional load center.

$$\sum\sum\sum_{\delta v i} x^{\delta\tau\nu}_{tvijk}\ (1 - \sigma_{ij}) + \sum\sum_{vi} x^{\tau\nu}_{tvijk}\ (1 - \sigma_{ij}) \qquad y^{\nu}_{tjk} \tag{3}$$

$\forall$t, j, and k.

Shipments of synthetic natural gas from all plants plus shipments of natural gas must be sufficient to meet levels of gas consumption at each regional demand point.

$$\sum\sum\sum_{\delta v i} x^{\delta\tau\nu}_{tvij} + \sum_{i} x^{\tau\nu}_{tij} \qquad y^{\nu}_{tj} ; \ \forall t \text{ and } j. \tag{3a}$$

Because electricity cannot be stored, transmission into each substation must be equal to transmission out.

$$\sum\sum\sum_{\delta v i} x^{\delta\tau\nu}_{tvijk} (1 - \sigma_{ij}) + \sum\sum_{vi} x^{\tau\nu}_{tvijk} (1 - \sigma_{ij}) =$$

$$\sum\sum_{vj'} x^{\tau\nu}_{tvjj'k}, \forall t,k, \text{ and } j \neq j \qquad (4)$$

No plant can produce energy at a level that is greater than its available capacity.

$$\sum_{j} x^{\delta\tau\nu}_{tvijk} \quad \phi^{\delta\nu}_{tvi} \; w^{\delta\nu}_{vi}, \forall t, v, k, i \text{ and } \delta \qquad (5)$$

The available capacity of each existing plant in the system at the initial time period t = 1 is fixed and is equal to the capital stock inherited from all previous periods. That is

$$\sum_{v} w^{\delta\nu}_{vi} = \hat{w}^{\delta\nu}_{li}, \forall \delta \text{ and v is over -t,...,1} \qquad (5a)$$

and where i denotes a plant constructed prior to the base year of analysis.

The capacity of each new plant that is added to the system during future periods, t over 2, 3,...,T is constrained by an upper bound which limits the maximum size of each plant type that can be built at a particular site.

$$0 \quad \sum_{v} w^{\delta\nu}_{vi} \quad \hat{w}^{\delta\nu}_{i}, \forall \delta \text{ and v is over 2, 3,...T} \qquad (5b)$$

and where i denotes a plant investment alternative.

A final set of constraints limits the electric energy supply guarantee conditions which relate instantaneous power generation to the annual electric energy demands at each regional load center.

$$\sum\sum\sum\sum_{\delta vik} \xi^{\delta\nu}_{tvi} \; w^{\delta\nu}_{vi} \; \theta_k \quad \sum\sum\sum\sum\sum_{\delta vijk} x^{\delta\tau\nu}_{tviji} \; \theta_k, \forall t. \qquad (6)$$

$$\sum\sum\sum\sum\sum_{\delta vijk} x^{\delta\tau\nu}_{tvijk} (1 - \sigma_{ij})\theta_k + \sum\sum\sum\sum_{vijk} x^{\tau\nu}_{tvijk} \qquad (7)$$

$$(1 - \sigma_{ij})\theta_k \quad y_{tj}, \forall t$$

The plant capacity factor is the expected annual level of generation for each power plant. Plant capacity factors are dependent on the size, age, fuel type, and operating characteristics of each plant.

As is the case with many linear programming analyses, the optimal levels of operation and expansion that the above model selects are heavily dependent on the parameters inserted in the demand constraints. The regional levels and characteristics of power demand (megawatts) and electric energy consumption (megawatt hours) that are used in the model are developed within the context of annual load duration curves for each utility. An annual load duration curve is constructed by rearranging the hourly power demands that occur during a year in descending order of magnitude. The maximum or annual peak load demand is placed farthest left, and each succeeding hourly load is placed next to is in descending order. The integral of the load duration curve is the annual consumption of electric energy in the utility service area.

Figure 9.1 illustrates a typical annual load duration curve. For a linear programming model, the annual curve must be approximated by k = 1,...,k discrete blocks representing subperiods within a year. Since the width of each block represents the number of hours in each subperiod, total annual energy consumption can be approximated by adding up the areas of all of the blocks. The left-hand side of each block extended up to the load duration curve is the instantaneous power demand in each subperiod.

$$\sum\sum_{\delta} a_{vi}^{\delta\nu} w_{vi}^{\delta\nu} \quad b_i, \ \forall i. \tag{8}$$

Total water use for energy production at the site i is limited to the net available supply. Net available supply may be defined in terms of sustained yields for reservoirs or expected flow rates for rivers.

Application of the Model

The model that is formulated in the previous section can be implemented for any region. In order to illustrate the types of information that can be obtained, an application based on the Illinois coal industry is presented here. For this application, the model is used to determine optimal spatial and temporal patterns for energy development activities for a

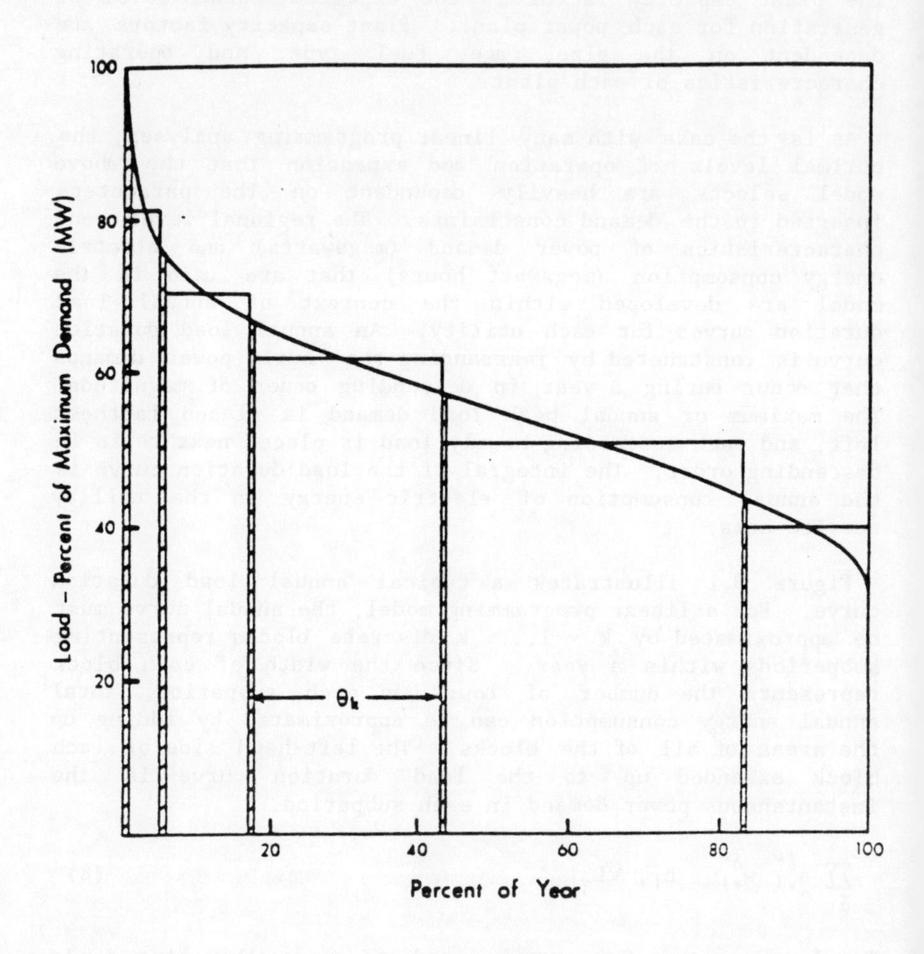

Figure 9.1

ANNUAL LOAD DURATION CURVE

30 year planning horizon that is subdivided into three 10-year planning segments.

For the base year time period, nominally 1972 to 1974, the model contains production and transmission activities for 51 existing base, intermediate and peak load plants having a combined generating capacity of over 25,000 megawatts (Mwe). In the model these plants are interconnected by transmission linkages to 35 substations and 14 regional load centers, as shown in Figure 9.2. These linkages correspond to the major transmission corridors, intermediate transmission points and electricity consumption centers in Illinois. The model does not include any interstate transmission linkages.

For the three future investment periods, nominally the early 1980s, early 1990s and early 2000s, the model contains potential location specific investment and production activities for new energy facilities. In addition to basic plant construction costs, the cost coefficients for the investment activities include a number of expenses related to environmental control. Cost coefficients for potential plants on reservoir sites include the costs of reservoir construction; cost coefficients for potential coal fired power plants include the costs of sulfur dioxide scrubbers and flyash precipitators; and cost coefficients for potential nuclear plants in seismically active zones, include a proportionate cost premium for additional structural reinforcement.

Cost coefficients for future energy production activities include production and transmission costs. Transmission costs are a function of the distances from locations for new energy facilities to the bearest substations in the existing transmission grid.

The locations or candidate areas for new energy facilities are townships. Townships are 36 square mile areas that provide a regular geographic grid in the state. In preparation for evaluation of the model, townships were prescreened using statewide resource maps to determine their potential suitability for supporting the operation of large scale energy production facilities, i.e., see Smith and Stall (1975). The screening criteria included the availability of water, the availability of coal, proximity to population centers and presence of seismic activity. For this study, the prescreening procedure resulted in the following area selections: (1) 68 candidate areas for 2000 MWe nuclear plants, 52 river sites and 16 reservoir sites, (2) 48

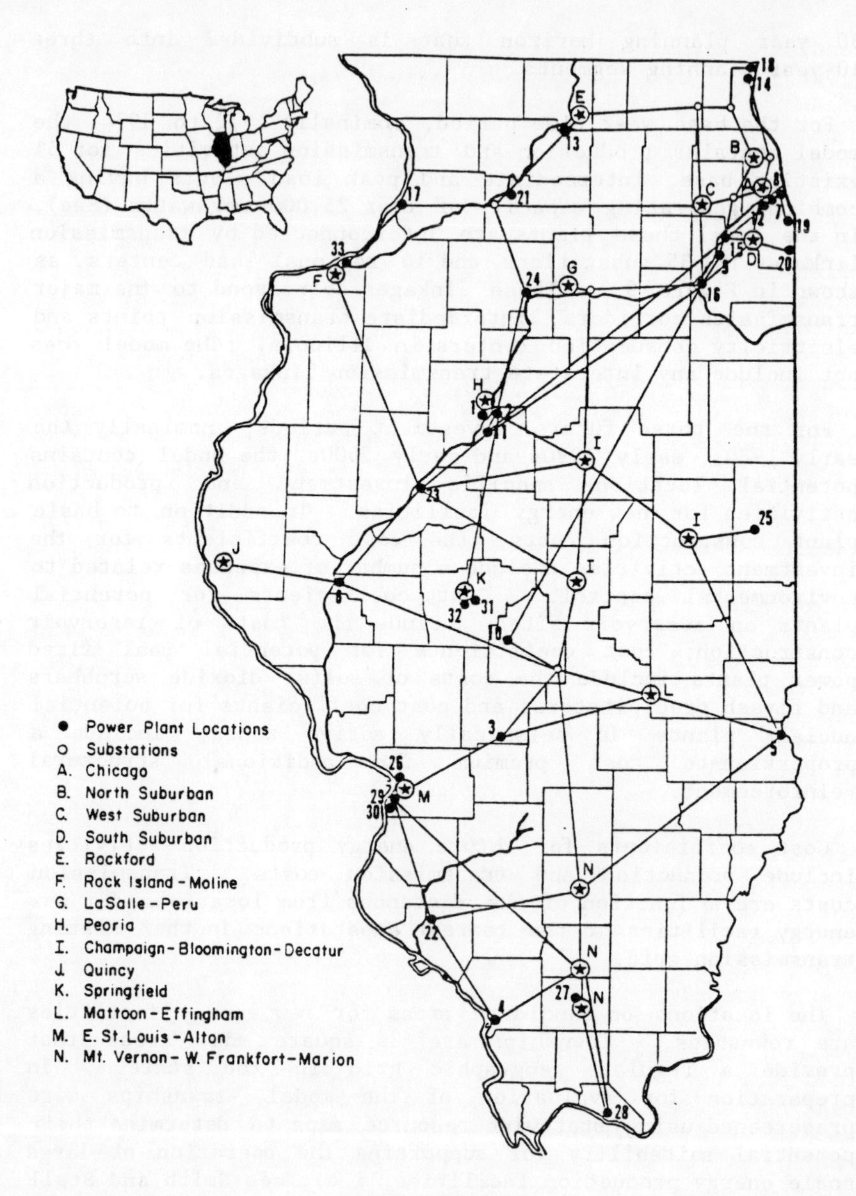

Figure 9.2

MAJOR POWER PLANTS AND TRANSMISSION LINES IN ILLINOIS, 1972-74

candidate areas for 2000 MWe minemouth, coalfired plants, 15 river sites and 33 reservoir sites, and (3) 24 candidate areas for 250 million standard cubic feet per day (scfd) minemouth, coal gasification plants, 11 river sites and 13 reservoir sites.

Because activities for transporting coal or water were not included in the model, a large number of candidate areas which can supply the above plant types with just one of these resources, were not included in the analysis. In spite of this assumption, the model that was implemented is quite large, having approximately 7,150 activities and 2,500 constraints. In the interest of brevity, many additional details concerning the prescreening process and the estimation of the model's parameter values can be found in Provenzano (1977).

Results of the Application

Information on the optimal spatial and temporal location patterns, optimal mixes of power generating capacity and average costs of power generation is presented for six hypothetical energy development scenarios. The additions of new power generating capacity represent amounts that will be needed to supply future growth in the demand for electricity as well was to replace retirements of old plants occurring during the planning horizon. These additions also include sufficient new capacity to meet peak loads that are above projected expectations. A statewide reserve requirement of approximately 20 percent was used in this study as being sufficient for this purpose.

For all of the scenarios, the consumption of electric energy for all uses at each of the regional load centers in Illinois is projected to grow at an average annual rate of 5 percent at each of the 14 regional laod centers. Regional load factors, on the other hand, are projected to remain at 1972 levels for the entire planning horizon. Because there is considerable regional variation in these load factors within Illinois, regional peak load power demands are projected to grow with corresponding regional variation throughout the state. For all scenarios, gas demand for all uses in the state is projected to grow at an annual rate of 1 percent, and interstate pipeline deliveries and supplies of gas from other sources are assumed to decline at a rate of 4 percent. In this analysis coal gasification plants are constructed solely for the purpose of offsetting the projected deficit between demand and supply in Illinois.

Scenario Ia considers only the expansion of steam electric power generation and provides a basis of comparison with alternative development scenarios. Scenario Ib combines steam electric power generation with rapid development, beginning in the early 1990s, of a high Btu coal gasification industry.

Scenario IIa examines the expansion of steam electric power generation under constraints prohibiting further construction of nuclear power plants. In this scenario, four new nuclear plants that are scheduled for completion in the 1980s are included in optimal additions of new generation capacity. No additional nuclear facilities are permitted thereafter. Scenario IIb again combines rapid development of a high Btu coal gasification industry with the growth in power generation but with the restriction on nuclear power plant construction.

To examine impacts of energy development that may occur as a consequence of the implementation of a policy that limits water availability for energy production, Scenarios Ic and IIc, which are companions to Ib and IIb, impose cumulative limitations on the quantity of water that can be withdrawn from rivers for energy related uses. These constraints limit cumulative withdrawals for energy production to 10 percent of the average 7-day, 10-year low flows for the major rivers in and bordering Illinois.

Figures 9.3 and 9.4 illustrate the optimum spatial and temporal development patterns for growth Scenarios Ia and Ib. The maps show approximate locations for the optimum set of energy production facilities selected by the model. These locations represent the minimum cost set of new energy production facilities and locations that will be needed to meet projected energy demands.

River and reservoir locations in the immediate proximity of large energy markets are relatively more attractive for new facilities because of lower power transmission costs. In the synfuels development scenario, the model selects a number of locations for coal gasification plants along the Wabash River. Although these locations are considerable distances from the major gas markets in northern Illinois, the extra costs of gas transmission from this region are more than offset by higher plant construction costs at reservoir

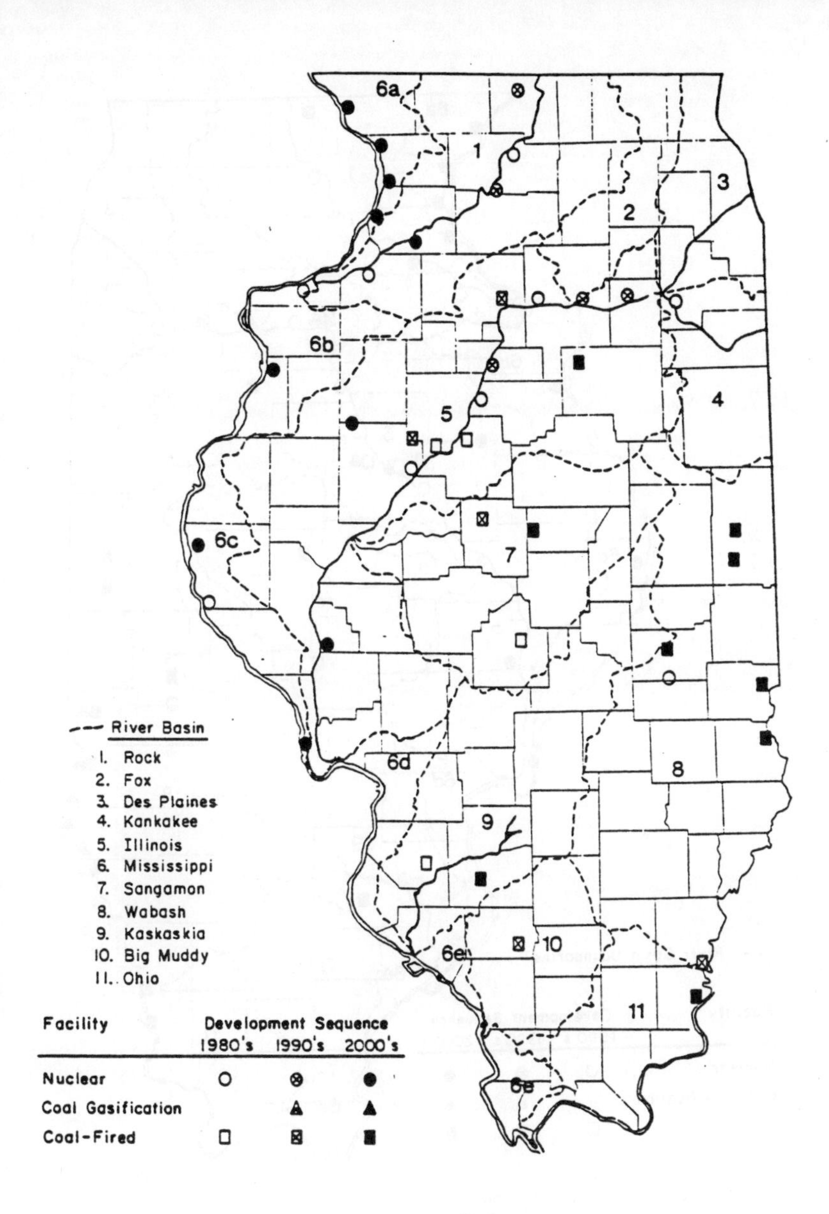

Figure 9.3

DEVELOPMENT SCENARIO 1a: OPTIMAL SPATIAL AND TEMPORAL DEVELOPMENT PATTERNS FOR NEW ENERGY PRODUCTION FACILITIES

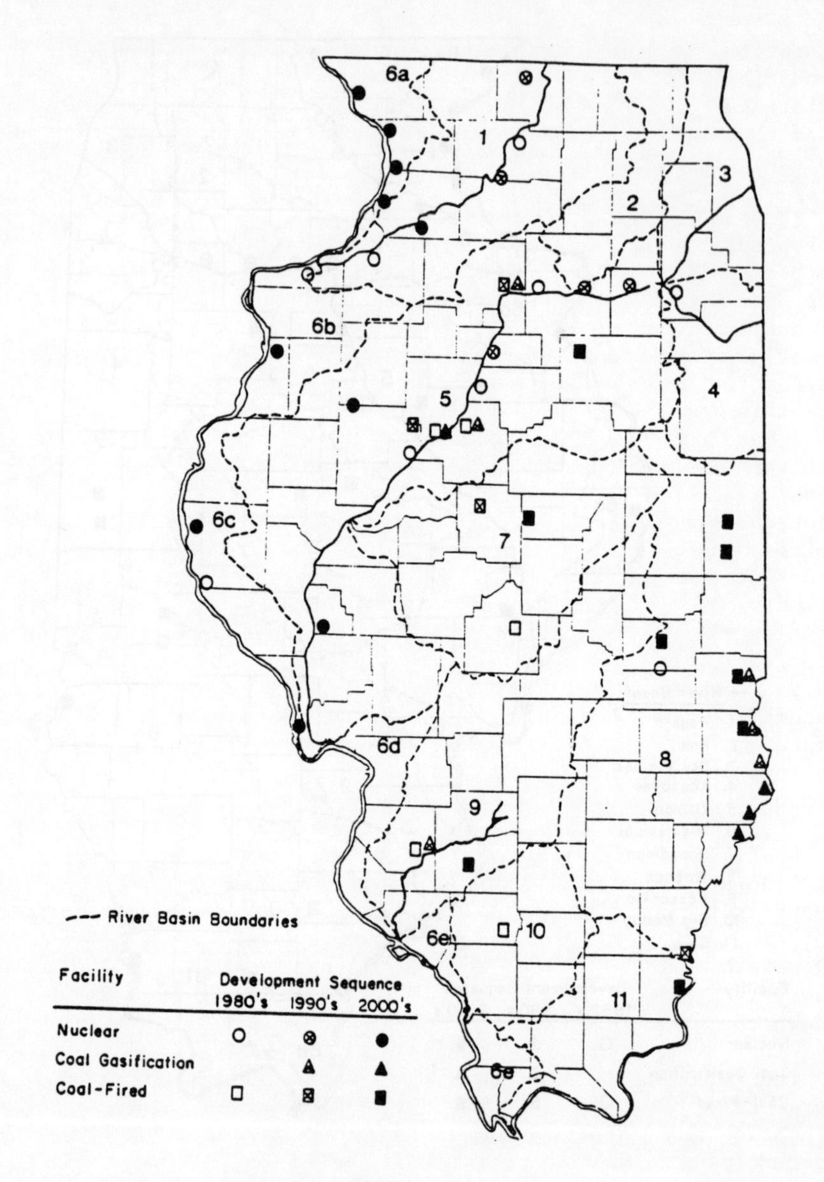

Figure 9.4

DEVELOPMENT SCENARIO 1b: OPTIMAL SPATIAL AND TEMPORAL DEVELOPMENT PATTERNS FOR NEW ENERGY PRODUCTION FACILITIES

locations in the central and southern part of the state. In addition, locations along the Wabash are also within short distances of a major north-south gas pipleline (Midwestern Gas Transmission) that services the northern part of the state.

Temporally, the model projects that development will proceed away from major energy demand centers. As might be expected, lower development cost locations that are closest to demand centers are committed in the first 10 years; locations that are somewhat more distant and, hence, more costly from a transmission standpoint are committed in the second 10 years, and so on. The progression away from demand centers in siting is in part dependent on an assumption that new baseload capacity cannot be added at sites where existing units have been retired. Power plants that are currently in operation are located primarily within the state's metropolitan areas. Although future development of these sites woudl be very attractive from an economic standpoint, current federal regulations make them very difficult, if not impossible, to use for new large scale plants. The U.S. Nuclear Regulatory Commission, for example, prohibits siting nuclear power plants within major population centers, and the U.S. Environmental Protection Agency's regulations for achieving the primary ambient air quality standards currently make it extremely difficult to site new coal fired power plants in nonattainment areas such as the Chicago, Peoria and East St. Lous metropolitan areas.

Spatially, therefore, development proceeds down the Illinois River away from Chicago, and in the upriver and downriver directions on the Illinois River away from Peoria. Development also proceeds down the Rock River away from Rockford and in both directions along the Mississippi River away from Rock Island-Moline. Finally, development proceeds down the Wabash River.

The relative costs of construction and proximity to markets are also key determinants in the model's selection of location and type of new generating capacity for meeting future power demands. Figures 9.3 and 9.4 indicate a decided preference by the model for assigning new capacity to river locations which have associated construction costs that are relatively lower than those at reservoir locations. The maps also indicate a preference by the model for nuclear power plants in spite of the fact that unit construction costs for nuclear plants are currently higher than unit construction costs for coal fired plants equipped with gas desulfurization equipment. These preferences reflect the relative importance of large projected demands for electric power in the Chicago metropolitan and northern Illinois regions and the comparative economic advantage of meeting those large demands with nuclear plants that are located closer to the point of consumption rather than with minemouth, coal fired plants located in central and southern Illinois, a considerable distance from these load centers.

The importance of the Chicago metropolitan and northern Illinois load centers is also apparent in Tables 9.1 and 9.2. These tables present estimates of the optimal additions of energy production capacity by plant and location in Illinois with the basin numbers in the tables corresponding to the numbered regions in Figures 9.3 and 9.4. The heavy concentrations of additions to capacity along the Rock, Illinois and Mississippi Rivers in northern Illinois indicated a projected intensive use for these rivers as locations for power plants which will be needed to supply the future demands for electricity in the northern Illinois region. These spatial patterns of power plant locations that the model has produced for the early 1980s are very similar to the pattern that is actually emerging in the announcements of new plant sites to be developed in the next decade.

The rapid development of a coal gasification industry does not have any impact on the optimal mix or pattern of power plant locations when there are no restrictions on water supplies for energy production (Table 9.2 compared to Table 9.1). In other words, for these scenarios, the model indicates that the concurrent expansion of synfuels production and power generation does not result in regional competition for available water that is sufficiently intense to alter the type or location of new power generation capacity.

Figures 9.5 and 9.6 illustrate optimum spatial and temporal development patterns for growth Scenarios IIa and IIb, scenarios that hypothesize a major prohibition on the construction of nuclear power plants. Compared to the base case scenarios, a moratorium on nuclear power after 1990 results in substantial shifts in the projected pattern of energy development. With the foreclosure of the nuclear option, the model projects more intensive development in the coal-rich areas of central and southern Illinois and less intensive development in the vicinity of the major energy consumption centers in the norther part of the state. In addition, because of the small number of minemouth candidate

Table 9.1

DEVELOPMENT SCENARIO 1a:
OPTIMAL ADDITIONS OF NEW ENERGY PRODUCTION CAPACITY BY RIVER BASIN IN ILLINOIS (capacity units)

River Basin	Nuclear (MWe)						Coal Fired (MWe)					
	River			Reservoir			River			Reservoir		
	1980	1990	2000	1980	1990	2000	1980	1990	2000	1980	1990	2000
1. Rock River	533	5739	3728									
2. Fox River												
3. Des Plaines River												
4. Kankanee River	2000											
5. Illinois River	1053	9429	2703			2000	4000	845	1156		2000	2000
6a. Mississippi River (north)			8000									
6b. Mississippi River (north central)	105	325	1562									
6c. Mississippi River (central)	669	614	1715									
6d. Mississippi River (south central)												
6e. Mississippi River (south)												
7. Sangamon River										240	1856	2718
8. Wabash River				1006	633	361		1230	4193			4671
9. Kaskaskia River							406	1594				2000
10. Big Muddy River											2000	
11. Ohio River									2000			
TOTAL	4360	16107	17708	1006	633	2361	4406	3669	7349	240	5856	11389

Table 9.2

DEVELOPMENT SCENARIO 1b:
OPTIMAL ADDITIONS OF NEW ENERGY PRODUCTION CAPACITY BY RIVER BASIN IN ILLINOIS
(capacity units)

River Basin	Nuclear (MWe)						Coal Fired (MWe)						Coal Gasification (106 acfd)					
	River			Reservoir			River			Reservoir			River			Reservoir		
	1980	1990	2000	1980	1990	2000	1980	1990	2000	1980	1990	2000	1980	1990	2000	1980	1990	2000
1. Rock River	533	5739	3728															
2. Fox River																		
3. Des Plaines River																		
4. Kankanee River	2000																	
5. Illinois River	1053	9429	2703			2000	4000	845	1156		2000	2000		428	146			
6a. Mississippi River (north)			8000															
6b. Mississippi River (north central)	105	325	1562															
6c. Mississippi River (central)	669	614	1715															
6d. Mississippi River (south central)																		
6e. Mississippi River (south)																		
7. Sangamon River										240	1856	2718						
8. Wabash River				1006	633	361		1230	4193			4671		700	775			
9. Kaskaskia River							406	1594				2000		60	48			
10. Big Muddy River											2000							
11. Ohio River									2000									
TOTAL	4360	16107	17708	1006	633	2361	4406	3669	7349	240	5856	11389		1188	969			

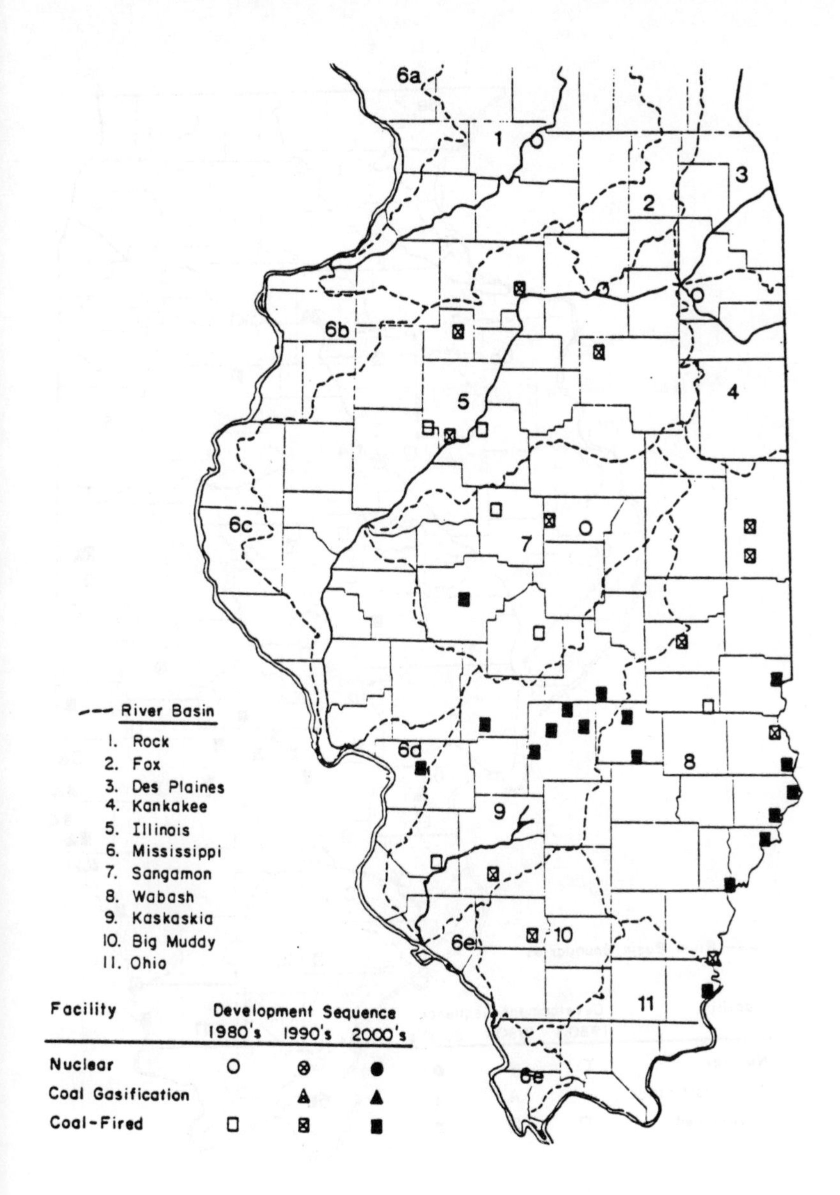

Figure 9.5

DEVELOPMENT SCENARIO 11a: OPTIMAL SPATIAL AND TEMPORAL DEVELOPMENT PATTERNS FOR NEW ENERGY PRODUCTION FACILITIES

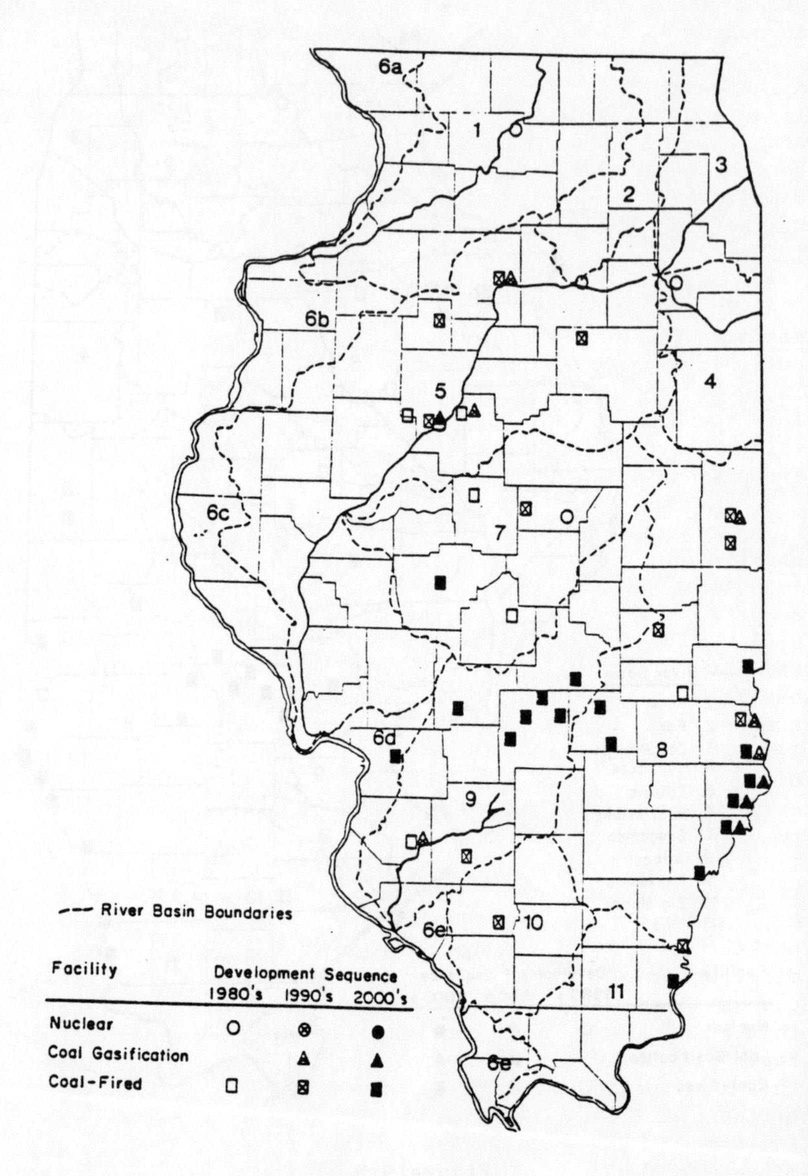

Figure 9.6

DEVELOPMENT SCENARIO 11b: OPTIMAL SPATIAL AND TEMPORAL DEVELOPMENT PATTERNS FOR NEW ENERGY PRODUCTION FACILITIES

areas along rivers, the pattern of development in these scenarios is concentrated at reservoir sites.

The projected extent of the capacity mix and locational impacts of a nuclear moratorium are presented in Tables 9.3 and 9.4. Temporally, the effects of the moratorium do not become apparent until the 1990s because of the large commitments to nuclear power that major electric utilities in northern Illinois have made for meeting power demands in the 1980s.

As in the base case, a policy of rapid development of coal gasification does not bring about any marked changes in the optimal pattern of facility locations (Table 9.4 compared to Table 9.3). In these scenarios the additional water demands for the coal gasification industry are apparently not extensive enough to alter the expansion patterns of the power industry.

In contrast, the imposition of cumulative withdrawal constraints produces some major changes in both the optimal locations and capacity mixes in scenarios without (Table 9.5 compared to Table 9.2) and with (Table 9.6 compared to Table 9.4) a nuclear moratorium. Withdrawal constraints effectively limit the capacity of the smaller river basins-Rock, Kankakee, Illinois, Kaskaskia and Wabash to support new energy development in the early 1990s. This limitation causes the model to alter the optimal composition of new capacity in two ways. The model initially (in the early 1990s) substitutes reservoir locations for coal fired power plants for the power plant locations that are displaced from smaller rivers. After the most economically attractive reservoir locations are developed, the model then (in the early 2000s) substitutes locations on large rivers, primarily nuclear power plant locations on the Mississippi, for displaced plant locations on small rivers. The model, of course, makes these substitutions on the basis of cost. In this analysis the construction of coal fired power plants at reservoir locations in central Illinois is less costly than the construction of nuclear capacity on the Mississippi in northern Illinois, but the development of nuclear plants on the upper Mississippi is less costly than the construction of minemouth plants in deep southern Illinois. These shifts are apparent in Table 9.5 and, to a greater extent, in Table 9.6 where a nuclear moratorium would intensify regional competition for water in central and southern Illinois.

Table 9.3

DEVELOPMENT SCENARIO 11a: OPTIMAL ADDITIONS TO NEW ENERGY PRODUCTION CAPACITY BY RIVER BASIN IN ILLINOIS (capacity units)

River Basin	Nuclear (MWe)						Coal Fired (MWe)					
	River			Reservoir			River			Reservoir		
	1980	1990	2000	1980	1990	2000	1980	1990	2000	1980	1990	2000
1. Rock River	2240											
2. Fox River												
3. Des Plaines River												
4. Kankanee River	2240											
5. Illinois River	2156						292	4633	1075	489	5257	254
6a. Mississippi River (north)												
6b. Mississippi River (north central)												
6c. Mississippi River (central)												
6d. Mississippi River (south central)												
6e. Mississippi River (south)												
7. Sangamon River										240	4296	3463
8. Wabash River				1900				2760	12174	70	5570	6185
9. Kaskaskia River							320	1679				13774
10. Big Muddy River											2000	
11. Ohio River									2000			
TOTAL	6636			1900			612	9072	15249	799	17123	25676

Table 9.4

DEVELOPMENT SCENARIO 11b:
OPTIMAL ADDITIONS TO NEW ENERGY PRODUCTION CAPACITY BY RIVER BASIN IN ILLINOIS
(capacity units)

River Basin	Nuclear (MWe)						Coal Fired (MWe)						Coal Gasification (106 acfd)					
	River			Reservoir			River			Reservoir			River			Reservoir		
	1980	1990	2000	1980	1990	2000	1980	1990	2000	1980	1990	2000	1980	1990	2000	1980	1990	2000
1. Rock River	2240																	
2. Fox River																		
3. Des Plaines River																		
4. Kankanee River	2240																	
5. Illinois River	2156						292	4633	1075	489	5257	254		428	146			
6a. Mississippi River (north)																		
6b. Mississippi River (north central)																		
6c. Mississippi River (central)																		
6d. Mississippi River (south central)												2000						
6e. Mississippi River (south)																		
7. Sangamon River				1900						240	4296	3463						
8. Wabash River								2760	12174	70	5570	6185		450	775		250	
9. Kaskaskia River							321	1679				13774		60	48			
10. Big Muddy River											2000							
11. Ohio River									2000									
TOTAL	6636			1900			613	9072	15249	799	17123	25676		938	969		250	

Table 9.5

DEVELOPMENT SCENARIO 11c:
OPTIMAL ADDITIONS TO NEW ENERGY PRODUCTION CAPACITY BY RIVER BASIN IN ILLINOIS
(capacity units)

River Basin	Nuclear (MWe)						Coal Fired (MWe)						Coal Gasification (106 acfd)					
	River			Reservoir			River			Reservoir			River			Reservoir		
	1980	1990	2000	1980	1990	2000	1980	1990	2000	1980	1990	2000	1980	1990	2000	1980	1990	2000
1. Rock River	1143	2903																
2. Fox River																		
3. Des Plaines River																		
4. Kankanee River	1144																	
5. Illinois River	1053	9213	2407			4128	4000	562			4000	1432		178	146			222
6a. Mississippi River (north)	71	81	7847			683												
6b. Mississippi River (north central)	266	283	4365															
6c. Mississippi River (central)	669	614	4598															
6d. Mississippi River (south central)												64						
6e. Mississippi River (south)																		
7. Sangamon River						2000				240	3171	2589						170
8. Wabash River				1006	633	361						5659		950	106			250
9. Kaskaskia River							421	1579				2000		60	75			
10. Big Muddy River											2000							
11. Ohio River								1231	769									
TOTAL	4360	13094	19217	1006	633	7172	4421	3372	769	240	9171	11774		1188	327			642

Table 9.6

DEVELOPMENT SCENARIO 11c:
OPTIMAL ADDITIONS TO NEW ENERGY PRODUCTION CAPACITY BY RIVER BASIN IN ILLINOIS
(capacity units)

River Basin	Nuclear (MWe)						Coal Fired (MWe)						Coal Gasification (106 acfd)					
	River			Reservoir			River			Reservoir			River			Reservoir		
	1980	1990	2000	1980	1990	2000	1980	1990	2000	1980	1990	2000	1980	1990	2000	1980	1990	2000
1. Rock River	2240																	
2. Fox River																		
3. Des Plaines River																		
4. Kankanee River	2240																	
5. Illinois River	2156						292	4633	1075	489	5257	2140		428	146			181
6a. Mississippi River (north)																		
6b. Mississippi River (north central)																		
6c. Mississippi River (central)																		
6d. Mississippi River (south central)												2000						
6e. Mississippi River (south)																		
7. Sangamon River				1900						240	5270	2490						170
8. Wabash River								1428		70	5570	14360		700	148			250
9. Kaskaskia River							321	1679			226	15774		60	75			
10. Big Muddy River											2000	1375						
11. Ohio River								356	1644									
TOTAL	6636			1900			613	8096	2719	579	18323	38139		1188	369			611

The spatial and temporal location patterns for the nuclear moratorium scenarios obviously reflect the stringent assumption that all coal fired plants must be minemouth facilities. By using the model to examine altneratives in whcih coal is transported to river sites, for example, in nothern Illinois, a somewhat less concentrated optimal spatial pattern may have been obtained. Such alternatives clearly would have higher variable costs than the minemouth coal plants because on a per unit output basis, power transmission costs are much less than coal transport costs over the range of distances being modelled here. The model would, therefore, favor coal transport alternatives only if the construction cost differential between reservoir and river sites is large enough to offset the costs of transporting coal to the river sites.

In regard to costs, the optimal power plant mix and optimal power generation levels determined by the model provide a means for estimating the expected levelized average cost of supplying electricity. Levelized average cost can be regarded as a "lowest common denominator" yardstick for comparing the economic differences among scenarios. The levelized average cost for the region can be written as:

$$AC = \frac{(FC \times CRF) + VC}{Q} \tag{9}$$

The variables included in this definitions are as follows: AC equals levelized annual average costs in cents per kilowatthour (kWh), FC equals cumulative investment costs for new generating capacity, CRF equals the capital recovery factor for computing annual capital costs as a percentage of first cost; VC equals annual variable costs such as fuel costs and variable operation and maintenance costs; and Q equals annual system output in kWh.

Using the optimal investment and power generation levels, the components of AC can be computed as follows:

$$FC = \sum_{\nu \delta v i}\sum\sum\sum c_{vi}^{\delta\nu} \bar{w}_{vi}^{\delta\nu} \tag{10}$$

$$VC = \sum_{\nu \delta v i j k}\sum\sum\sum\sum\sum c_{tvijk}^{\delta\tau\nu} \bar{x}_{tvijk}^{\delta\tau\nu} \theta_k \tag{11}$$

$$Q = \sum_{\delta v i j k}\sum\sum\sum \bar{x}_{tviji}^{\delta\tau\nu} \theta_k \tag{12}$$

Assuming a capital recovery factor of 9 percent, the levelized average costs for the terminal year in the planning horizon for each of the eight scenarios are presented in Table 9.7.

Overall, the average costs of supplying electricity are relatively insensitive to the kinds of policy changes examined here. The results indicate that the largest change in these costs would stem from the imposition of limitations on future construction of nuclear plants. The approximately 5 percent projected increase in average costs is in line with the 3 to 6 percent nuclear moratorium induced increases in average costs reported by Joskow and Rozanski (1977).

The relative unresponsiveness in costs in part reflects the capability of the region in question to accommodate large scale energy development at least as far as having sufficient coal and water resources are concerned. Additional research, along the lines presented here, will be needed to assess whether the region's capability can be as flexible in the face of additional environmental constraints such as those for protecting air and water quality and agricultural land.

Conclusions

This chapter has demonstrated that a multiperiod, multiplant, multimarket linear programming model can provide information that is useful to planners in coordinating regional development of energy and water resources. The model generates information on optimal spatial and temporal patterns of energy facility construction and operation subject to regional constraints on water for energy. Because of the spatially disaggregated nature of this information, it facilitates coordinating location specific options for providing needed water supplies with construction opportunities for new energy production facilities. The model provides information in a manner that is consistent with a minimum cost strategy for regional energy development and in a manner in which cumulative regional energy related water demands do not exceed the water resources available for energy production.

Application of the model to Illinois indicates that optimal energy facility location patterns are quite sensitive to changes in energy and water resources development policies. An analysis of several hypothetical development scenarios revealed that major differences in locational and, hence, environmental impacts may be associated with policy

Table 9.7

ESTIMATED AVERAGE LEVELIZED COST OF SUPPLYING ELECTRICITY IN 2002
(Mills per kWh, 1972 dollars)

	Average Cost	Average Cost Relative to Base Case
Scenario Ia	13.1	-
Scenario Ib	13.3	1.02
Scenario Ic	13.2	1.01
Scenario IIa	13.8	1.05
Scenario IIb	13.7	1.05
Scenario IIc	13.7	1.05

initiatives calling for rapid synfuels development, a nuclear moratorium, and energy related water withdrawal limitations. Although the analysis indicated that these policy changes would not result in substantial increases in the cost of electricity to the consumer, many of the negative environmental spillovers associated with energy development could not be included in the estimated average costs. Additional research is needed to quantify in greater detail the air quality, water quality and land use impacts that correspond to the locational shifts caused by the policy changes.

Author
George Provenzano
U.S. Environmental Protection Agency
Washington, D.C. 20502

References

Anderson, D., (1972). "Models for Determining Least-Cost Investments in Electricity Supply," Bell Journal of Economics and Management Science, 3: 267-299.

Bessiere, F., (1970). "The Investment '82' Model of Electricité de France," Management Science, 17: 192-211.

Braun, C. and K.G. Cady, (1973). An Electric Power System Expansion Model, Ithaca, NY: Cornell University, Cornell Energy Project Paper No. 73-1.

Dobson, J.E., A.D. Shepherd, R.G. Palmer and S. Chiu, (1977). A Nationwide Assessment of Water Quantity Impacts of the National Energy Plan, Volume 1: Summary and Conclusions, Oak Ridge, TN: Oak Ridge National Laboratory.

Gately, D., (1970). Investment Planning for the Electric Power Industry: An Integer Programming Approach, London, Canada: University of Western Ontario, Department of Economics Research Report 7035.

Harte, J. and M. El-Gasseir, (1978). "Water and Energy," Science, 199: 623-634.

Joskow, P.L. and G. Rozanski, (1977). "Effects of a Nuclear Moratorium on Regional Electricity Prices and Fuel Consumption by the Electric Utility Industry," Land Economics, 53: 23-24.

Massé, P. amd R. Gibrat, (1957). "Application of Linear Programming to Investments in the Electric Power Industry," Management Science, 3: 148-166.

Noonan, F. and R.J. Giglio, (1977). "Planning Electric Power Generation: A Nonlinear Mixed Integer Model Employing Benders Decomposition," Management Science, 23: 946-956.

Probstein, R. and H. Gold, (1978). Water in Synthetic Fuel Production: The Technology and Alternatives, Cambridge, MA: MIT Press.

Provenzano, G., (1977). A Linear Programming Model for Assessing the Regional Impacts of Energy Development on Water Resources, Urbana, IL: University of Illinois, Water Resource Center Research Report No. 126.

Scherer, C.H., (1977). Estimating Electric Power System Marginal Costs, Amsterdam: North-Holland Publishing Co.

Scherer, C.H. and L. Joe, (1977). "Electric Power System Planning with Explicit Stochastic Reserves Constraint," Management Science, 23: 978-985.

Smith, W.H. and J.B. Stall, (1975). Coal and Water Resources For Coal Conversion in Illinois, Urbana, IL: Illinois State Water Survey and Illinois State Geological Survey, Cooperative Resources Report No. 4.

U.S. Department of Energy, (1979). National Energy Plan II: Appendix Environmental Trends and Impacts, Washington, D.C.: Office of the Assistant Secretary for Environment.

U.S. Water Resources Council, (1974a). Water Requirements, Availabilities, Constraints and Recommended Federal Actions: Federal Energy Administration Project Independence Blueprint, Final Task Force Report, Washington, D.C.: U.S. Government Printing Office.

U.S. Water Resources Council, (1974b). Water for Energy Self-Sufficiency, Washington, D.C.: U.S. Government Printing Office.

U.S. Water Resources Council, (1978). The Nation's Water Resources: The Second National Water Assessment. Part III. Functional Water Uses, Washington, D.C.: U.S. Government Printing Office.

Uri, N., (1975). "A Spatial Equilibrium Model for Electric Energy," Journal of Regional Science, 15: 323-333.

PART III
AGRICULTURAL MODELS

10 Application of the spatial and temporal price and allocation model to the world food economy

TAKASHI TAKAYAMA *University of Western Australia*
HIDEO HASHIMOTO *The World Bank*
DANG H. NGUYEN *California State Energy Commission*
RICK C. WHITACRE *Illinois State University*

Introduction

Many major commodity markets began to reflect the inflationary and instability problems of the early 1970s. The major grain exporting nations, the United States and Canada, laboring under the fiscal burden of large stocks of grains, began to reduce the stocks steadily at the beginning of the 1970s. However, in 1972 when these stocks reached a low point level, simultaneous crop failures in the USSR, India, China, Australia, Argentina and Canada drove the international grain and soybean prices to alarmingly high levels. Before the shock in the agricultural markets had barely subsided, the second commodity shock hit the world economy because of OPECs influence on the oil market.

In the midst of these circumstances we commenced work on an important related project: "The Projection and Evaluation of Trends and Policies in Agricultural Commodity Supply, Demand, International Trade, and Food Reserves." Funding for the project was provided by the Ford Foundation and by the World Bank. Of the issues dealt with in the project, we discuss the following here: (1) Under what conditions could such a phenomena as prevailed in the agricultural market in 1973 and 1974 agricultural market take place? Is this phenomenon a normal market response or something else that cannot be explained by the market mechanism? (2) What consequences for prices and trade can be expected from changes in policies and supply conditions of the main grain exporting and importing countries? (3) Is U.S. agriculture inherently unstable? What stabilization policies, if any, should be adopted? (4) What would be the effects of Japan's trade liberalization in meats on her own, the U.S., Australian and Canadian consumer expenditures and producer incomes?

To analyze these issues, we developed various world food economy models, which are variants and/or extensions of the spatial and temporal price and allocation (STPA) models developed by Takayama and Judge (1971), and defined in Chapter 2. Because of the asymmetry of the demand and supply coefficient matrices, usual quadratic programming approaches proved to be inappropriate. As explained in Chapter 2, the linear complementarity programming (LCP) approach presented by Takayama (1977) proved to be highly suitable for the kinds of market equilibrium problems described here.

The basic model and its various representations in the world food economy models discussed in this chapter are multi-commodity, multi-region models, i.e., see the Appendix. All of them encompass nine commodities: wheat (W), maize (corn) (M), other grains (G), soybeans (S), soybean meal (Y), soybean oil (Z), beef (B), pork (P), and chicken (C). Although the number of specified regions differs among the models depending upon the issues dealt with, all the models share an important feature. They embody interconnections above commodities through substitution and complementarity and interconnections over regions through trade. In addition, the model was extended to include the temporal dimension for the analysis of the instability issue with respect to U.S. agriculture.

All the models were solved by using MPX-QUAD. The MPX-QUAD software was developed by D. Rarick in 1975 as a natural extension of the then existing LP software MPXIII. MPX-QUAD has the specific purpose of solving the so-called linear complementarity programming problem. Due to unfamiliarity by the users of the term LMCP, the developer used "QUAD" in its title, instead of LCP. It must be understood that the usual quadratic programming (QP) problem can be solved by MPX-QUAD.

Model Analysis Issues

The first issue to be investigated requires the following framework: (1) establish a market-oriented model of the world food economy, and (2) test if the model can reproduce the historical events such as those in 1974. If the model is capable of reproducing the historical events, one may be able to conclude that the basic market structure of the free world agriculture did not change but the entry of the USSR into world agriculture trade, the crop failure in China and South Asia, and the reduced level of stocks of grains in the United States and Canada all worked together to create tight world agricultural markets in the 1974 period.

It is almost impossible to collect data in a uniform time reference for all the commodities and for all the regions concerned. We adopted crop years for grains and marketing years for soybean meal and soybean oil as specified in each region, and the calendar year for meats. For example, the year 1974 for wheat in the United States refers to the year starting with July 1974 through June 1975.

The second issue will be examined in a comparative static framework. Scenarios are developed with respect to reserve build-up and price-elasticities of excess supply and demand quantities in the major grain exporting and importing countries. Comparisons of the solutions of each scenario solution with those of the standard model will show the impact of changes in the various contries' policies and supply conditions on the solution variables.

The third issue wil be tested by developing a series on one-year recursive models that specify only the United States (U) and the rest of the world (ROW) and solve the models recursively. The model solutions show excessive price and output fluctuations, implying that U.S. agriculture has a tendency to fluctuate unless price stabilization policies are implemented. In order to explore how stabilization can be effected, we develop a dynamic model that covers the four years between 1976 and 1980 under various scenarios with respect to yield of maize and ROW's excess demand for maize and wheat. The solutions of the five-year model are utilized to select minimum and maximum prices for price stabilization policies. With such price bands imposed we argue that the U.S. food economy may be stabilized.

The fourth issue, the question of Japan's liberalization of agricultural trade, will be analyzed by developing a five-region model that consists of Japan's major trade partners, i.e., the United States, Canada, Australia, ROW and Japan itself. The model is designed to simulate the situations in 1976. The model results (with and without the trade constraints that existed in that year) will be compared to calculate the impact of Japan's trade liberalization on consumer expenditures and producer incomes of those countries.

In the concluding section we look back and review the efficacy of the present models developed within the STPA framework, regarding the treatment of these various aspects of commodity market projections and policy analyses. We discuss ways of improving these and related quantitative analytical tools and conclude this paper by looking toward frontiers to be explored.

Model Backcasting: The 1974 World Food Economy

The past ten years have witnessed the construction of many diverse world and domestic commodity models, as reviewed in Chapter 2. However, large-scale models in this category such as PIES (Project Independence Evaluation System) which use an iterative LP algorithm in contrast to our single pass-through LCP algorithm have rarely been validated against historical data, i.e., see U.S. Department of Energy (1977). The iterative LP algorithms have also been shown to be less efficient than the LCP algorithms. There is no reason a priori to assume that the market-oriented STPA model can reproduce the market situation of any past year. To test the validity of the world food economy model, we developed a nine-commodity, six-region, one-year model, which was designed to simulate the world food economy in 1974.

The model includes six countries: the United States (U), Canada (C), EEC(9) (E), Japan (J), Australia (A) and the ROW. The parameter values of linear demand and supply functions for 1974 are shown in Tables 10.1 and 10.2. The model solutions are shown in Tables 10.3 to 10.7 and three samples of the international trade flow solution are shown in Tables 10.8 for wheat, 10.9 for maize and 10.10 for beef along with the actual figures (in parentheses). All the prices in this section are expressed in terms of constant 1970 U.S. dollars.

The predictability performance of this model for 1974 is "good" for the United States, "good" for Canada, "good" for Japan (despite some discrepancies in prices -- most likely due to policy interventions by the Japanese Government),

Table 10.1

COEFFICIENTS OF DEMAND AND SUPPLY FUNCTIONS FOR 1974, UNITED STATES

	P_W	P_M	P_G	P_Y	P_Z	P_B	P_P	P_C	P^B	P^C	Intercept
D_W	-89.746	79.372				2.1956			10.484		14483
D_M		-419.00		83.192					57.566		98683
D_G		78.656	-302.34						21.652		36521
D_Y				-21.738					9.4250		10372
D_Z					-.65632						3407.8
D_B						-6.7451					16036
D_P						1.5874	-5.4535	1.7263			7252.3
D_C						.68222	.52129	-1.8407			4358.0
S_B									3.2741		9169.5
S_C		-5.2884								.23968	4555.7

Note: Subscripts refer to commodities for demand quantities (D) and prices (P), and superscripts refer to commodities for supply quantities (S) and prices (P).

Table 10.2

COEFFICIENTS OF DEMAND FUNCTIONS FOR 1974, CANADA, EEC-9, JAPAN, AND AUSTRALIA

	P_W^C	P_M^C	P_G^C	P_B^C	P_P^C	P_W^E	P_B^E	P_P^E	P_W^J	P_B^{RJ}	P_P^J	P_W^A	Intercept
D_W^C	-33.525												10549
D_M^C	2.9081	-33.942											6217.8
D_C^C		75.948	-60.306										9101.0
D_B^C				.11580	.09805								1036.7
D_P^C				.17625	-.28272								615.44
D_W^E food						-27.858							29215
D_B^E							-.80542	.087522					9302.1
D_P^E							.047066	-1.5487					11774
D_W^J food									-11.891	.20398			4898
D_B^J									1.1819	-.08759	.014475		542.9
D_P^J									1.11082	.041399	-.26440		1099.7
D_W^A												-7.4094	3129.18

Note: Subscripts refer to commodities, and superscripts refer to regions.

Table 10.3

ACTUAL STATISTICS AND MODEL SOLUTIONS FOR 1974, UNITED STATES

Commodity	Quantity in '000 MT						Price in US $/MT			
		Demand		Supply			Demand		Supply	
	Carry-in	Actual	Solution	Actual	Solution	Carry-over	Actual	Solution	Actual	Solution
Wheat	8,658*	20,564	20,271	48,751	48,751*	8,901*	104.6	97.2	102.3	96.2
Maize	25,056*	104,939	105,254	134,072	134,072*	9,119*	84.7	86.8	80.1	84.4
Other Grains	7,855*	28,306	28,842	34,306	34,306*	5,222*	76.2	89.9	76.0	89.1
Soybeans	4,651*	21,232	22,016	35,672	35,672*	5,036*	160.4	172.4	158.3	170.3
Soybean Meal	460*	11,341	13,474	15,286	17,430	325*	99.5	111.1	99.5	111.1
Soybean Oil	360*	2,956	3,105	3,451	3,824	254*	460.6	460.6 a/	460.6	460.6
Beef	209*	11,410	11,511	10,515	11,086	289*	626.9	670.9	541.2	585.5
Pork	130*	6,379	6,408	6,253	6,253*	139*	522.5	531.6	519.9	529.0
Chicken	66*	3,937	4,038	4,052	4,158	79*	649.2	573.2	326.8	255.4

a/ A lower bound contraint was used; the corresponding lagrangean multiplier or the quantity discharged to keep price at this artificial level is 231.927 MT.

* Fixed or exogenously determined.

Table 10.4

ACTUAL STATISTICS AND MODEL SOLUTIONS FOR 1974, CANADA

	Quantity in '000 MT						Price in US $/MT			
		Demand		Supply			Demand		Supply	
Commodity	Carry-in	Actual	Solution	Actual	Solution	Carry-over	Actual	Solution	Actual	Solution
Wheat	8,037*	4,805	5,809	13,260	13,260*	8,072	147.6	141.4	134.2	128.1
Maize	217*	3,769	3,872	2,743	2,743*	51*	81.8	81.2	79.5	83.8
Other Grains	5,661	9,986	10,466	13,222	13,222*	5,170*	86.3	79.6	100.3	93.7
Soybeans	NA	775	914	301	301*	NA	161.7	182.3	16.10	NC
Soybean Meal	NA	776	776*	613	723	NA	128.0	123.1	128.0	123.1
Soybean Oil	NA	167	167*	142	167	NA	747.7	462.7	NA	462.7
Beef	24*	966	953	919	919*	20*	1,369.6	1,413.9	705.4	749.7
Pork	15	610	633	633	633*	11*	798.1	819.3	1,205.0	816.7
Chicken	NA	598	NC	609	NC	NA	707.6	NC	490.0	NC

*Fixed or exogenously determined.
NA : not available.
NC : not specified or not applicable.

Table 10.5

ACTUAL STATISTICS AND MODEL SOLUTIONS FOR 1974, EEC-9

	Quantity in '000 MT						Price in US $/MT			
		Demand		Supply			Demand		Supply	
Commodity	Carry-in	Actual	Solution	Actual	Solution	Carry-over	Actual	Solution	Actual	Solution
Wheat (O)	6,968*	29,178	29,667	42,511	42,511*	8,777*	139.7	213.1	119.0	153.6
Wheat (E)	6,968*	12,392	11,799	42,511	42,511*	8,777*	139.7	213.1	119.0	153.6
Maize (O)	3,104*	5,444	5,444*	15,491	15,491*	3,455*	140.0	111.3	96.8	96.5
Maize (E)	3,104	20,706	21,405	15,491	15,491*	3,455*	140.0	111.3	96.8	96.5
O. Grains (O)	3,423	9,622	9,620*	50,054	50,054*	4,939*	95.6	96.0	94.3	89.1
O. Grains (E)	3,423	34,422	39,272	50,054	50,054*	4,939	95.6	96.0	94.3	89.1
Soybeans	NA	9,099	7,756	0	0	NA	169.4	184.5	NA	NC
Soybean Meal	NA	9,917	10,120	7,204	6,141	NA	148.6	123.2	148.6	123.2
Soybean Oil	NA	1,422	1,422*	1,668	1,422	NA	439.0	474.3	109.0	474.3
Beef	NA	6,276	6,602	6,227	6,227	NA	4,090.0	3,596.1	1,175.0	2,773.3
Pork	NA	8,108	8,470	8,470	8,470	NA	2,490.0	2,242.7	1,136.0	1,701.9
Chicken	NA	3,056	3,056*	3,152	3,056	NA	904.0	1,096.5	730.0	778.7

* Fixed or exogenously determined.
(O) A portion of the grain used for food and other purposes.
(E) A portion of the grain used for feeding purposes.
NA: Not available.
NC: Not specified or not applicable.

Table 10.6

ACTUAL STATISTICS AND MODEL SOLUTIONS FOR 1974, JAPAN

Commodity	Carry-in	Quantity in '000 MT				Carry-over	Price in US $/MT			
		Demand		Supply			Demand		Supply	
		Actual	Solution	Actual	Solution		Actual	Solution	Actual	Solution
Wheat (O)	1,110*	4,898	4,487	58	58*	1,130*	99.0	92.9	196.7	190.6
Wheat (E)	1,110*	612	697	58	58*	1,130*	99.0	92.9	196.7	190.6
Maize (O)	842*	1,414	1,414*	44	44*	817*	103.7	112.8	NA	110.4
Maize (E)	842*	7,763	7,147	44	44*	817*	103.7	112.8	NA	110.4
O. Grains (O)	418*	1,084	1,084*	435	435*	416*	98.9	123.4	NA	122.6
O. Grains (E)	418*	6,820	6,457	435	435*	416*	98.9	123.4	NA	122.6
Soybeans	NA	3,614	2,782	710	710	NA	187.2	198.4	354.8	NC
Soybean Meal	NA	2,245	2,237	2,136	2,202	NA	152.8	137.1	NA	137.1
Soybean Oil	NA	529	510	512	510	NA	830.0	490.1	NA	490.1
Beef	NA	384	372	326	300	NA	3,180.9	3,397.1	NA	868.6
Pork	NA	1,039	1,028	966	987	NA	1,228.9	1,189.7	NA	1,187.1
Chicken	NA	749	749	730	726	NA	681.4	610.1	NA	292.3

* Fixed or exogenously determined.
(O) A portion of the grain used for food and other purposes.
(E) A portion of the grain used for feeding purposes.
NA: Not available.
NC: Not specified or not applicable.

Table 10.7

ACTUAL STATISTICS AND MODEL SOLUTIONS FOR 1974, AUSTRALIA

Commodity	Quantity in '000 MT						Price in US $/MT a/			
		Demand a/		Supply			Demand		Supply	
	Carry-in	Actual	Solution	Actual	Solution	Carry-over	Actual	Solution	Actual	Solution
Wheat	1,982*	3,262	2,475	11,551	11,551*	1,788*	93.4	88.3	123.2	118.1
Maize	8*	11	11*	NC	NC	14*	NA	111.2	NA	NC
Other Grains	526*	-1,900	-1,900*	NC	NC	376*	NA	NC	61.4	100.7
Soybeans	NC	41	41*	NC	NC	NC	150.6	196.8	150.6	NC
Soybean Meal	NC	25	25*	NC	NC	NC	117.8	135.5	117.8	NC
Soybean Oil	NC	9	9	NC	NC	NC	588.8	558.6	NA	NC
Beef	NA	-493	-493*	NC	NC	NA	471.5	NC	471.5	515.8
Pork	NA	NC	NC	NC	NC	NA	1,038.0	NC	1,038.0	NC
Chicken	NA	NC	NC	NC	NC	NA	NA	NC	NA	NC

a/ All other commodities, except for wheat, are in terms of net excess demand quantities (a negative quantity denotes net excess supply). The corresponding price solutions are either demand price in the case of net excess demand, or supply price in the case of net excess supply.

* Fixed or exogenously determined.

NA: Not available.

NC: Not specified or not applicable.

Table 10.8

ACTUAL STATISTICS (IN PARENTHESES) AND MODEL SOLUTIONS FOR TRADE FLOWS IN 1974, WHEAT
(000 MT)

Exporter/Importer	U	C	E	J	A	ROW
U	(20,564) 20,270	(0) 0	(1,3965) 0	(3,073) 3,388	(0) 0	(24,912) 24,912*
C	(10) 0	(4,805) 5,809	(2,554) 0	(1,187) 2,226	(0) 0	(7,346) 5,225
E	- NC	- NC	(41,570) 37,470	- NC	- NC	- 5,041
J	- NC	- NC	- NC	(58) 58*	- NC	- NC
A	- 0	- 0	(20) NC	(1,009) 0	(2,925) 2,475	(7,224) 9,076
ROW	NA NC	NA NC	NA NC	NA NC	NA NC	NA NC

* Fixed or exogenously determined.
NA: Not available.
NC: Not specified or not applicable.

Table 10.9

ACTUAL STATISTICS (IN PARENTHESES) AND MODEL SOLUTIONS FOR TRADE FLOWS IN 1974, MAIZE (000 MT)

Exporter/Importer	U	C	E	J	A	ROW
U	(104,939) 105,254	(940) 1,129	(10,617) 11,358	(5,232) 8,517	- 11	(12,396) 7,804
C	- NC	(2,743) 2,743*	- NC	- NC	- NC	- NC
E	- NC	- NC	(15,491) 15,491*	- NC	- NC	NA NC
J	- NC	- NC	- NC	(44) 44*	- NC	- NC
A	- NC	- NC	- NC	- NC	(122) NC	- NC
ROW	NA NC	NA NC	NA NC	NA NC	NA NC	NA NC

* Fixed or exogenously determined.
NA: Not available.
NC: Not specified or not applicable.

Table 10.10

ACTUAL STATISTICS (IN PARENTHESES) AND MODEL SOLUTIONS FOR TRADE FLOWS IN 1974, BEEF (000 MT)

Exporter/Importer	U	C	E	J	A	ROW
U	(10,515) 11,106	(7) 0	(1) 0	(6) 0	(0) NC	(9) NC
C	(17) 0	(919) 919*	NA 0	NA 0	- NC	NA NC
E	(20) NC	- NC	(6,227) 6,227*	- NC	- NC	NA -
J	- NC	- NC	- NC	(326) 300	- NC	- NC
A	(288) 405	(28) 34	(20) 0	(15) 54	(868 NC	(59) 0
ROW	(219) 0	- 0	NA 375	NA 0	NA 0	NA 0

* Fixed or exogenously determined.
NA: Not available.
NC: Not specified or not applicable.

"fair" for the EEC(9) and "poor" for Australia. The better performances for the United States and Canada was probably due to greater detail in the model specifications, i.e., a greater number of demand and supply equations. The opposite is the case for EEC(9) and Australia.

Where sizeable discrepances are found between model solution and actual values in the trade flow matrices, they may reflect non-economic rather than economic ties between pairs of countries involved in trade. For instance, Australia shipped about 1 million metric tons of wheat to Japan in the 1974 season, while the optimal solution states that Canada should be supplying this much more to Japan instead of supplying the EEC(9). The discrepancies may also be due to such factors as: (1) statistical estimation errors in the demand and supply functions, (2) errors in transport cost information, (3) omission of political and/or commercial institutional factors such as long-term contracts between countries, and (4) some combinations of the above factors.

Although several problems were unsolved in this study, the model was able to reproduce the 1974 agricultural economy, particularly that of the United States, fairly well. Because our market-oriented model is fully equipped with interconnections among commodities and over regions, the closeness of the model solution to actual statsitics of the major commodity markets suggests that the experiences in the 1974 world food economy were the consequences of various factors that could be explained within the framework of market mechanism.

Short-Term Analyses of Consequences of Reserve Build-Up Policies

A basic interest of policy decision makers is in projections of demand and trade profiles (price and quantities) when policy and/or supply change(s) is (are) expected in important producing or consuming regions. Nguyen quantified the impact of changes in reserve policies of the major wheat/ maize producing countries (Nguyen 1977). In addition to the six countries (actually, five countries and ROW) specified in the previous subsection, the model was expanded to include the USSR, China, India and Argentina.

The series of experiments were made in a comparative static framework. In other words, results of the scenario models were compared to the solutions of the standard model, termed as Scenario 0 in Table 10.11. Some of the findings expressed in terms of constant 1975 U.S. dollars.

(1) An increase of the U.S. wheat reserves by 2 million tons from 23,760 thousand tons (assumed in the standard model) increased the corresponding wheat price by $19. This price increase was shared by all the other nations. However, its impact on prices of other commodities was nil or negligible. (Scenario 1).

(2) An increase of the U.S. maize reserves by 2 million tons from 16,376 thousand tons caused the corresponding maize price to increase by $6.8 and the wheat price to increase by $3.1 (Scenario 2). These results imply that the elasticity of price with respect to stock changes for wheat was very high (1.88), compared with that of maize (0.48). However, it should be noted that the effect of the maize stock incrase on the wheat price (through the maize price increase) is quite significant and positive.

(3) Simultaneous increases of wheat and maize reserves in the United States raised the prices of these products in just about the same amount as the sum of the price rises resulting from the reserve increase in each product separate (Scenario 3).

(4) An increase in Canadian wheat reserves of 2 million tons affected the total world food price by an amount similar to that of an increase in U.S. wheat reserves. (Scenario 4).

The impact of simultaneous increases in the U.S. wheat and maize reserves under more elastic net excess grain demand or supply was explored in scenarios 5 through 7. (Net excess grain demand/supply are fixed in scenarios 0-4.) In other words, it was assumed that demand and supply could be expressed in functional forms with hypothetical price elasticities. (Further results concerning these elasticities are reported in Chapter 2). Three levels of price elasticities were estimated and reported in Table 10.12: low (Scenario 5), medium (Scenario 6) and high (Scenario 7). In addition, functional-form equations for excess demand and supply were derived from these price elasticities. These equations and simultaneous increases of the U.S. wheat and maize reserves were inserted into the standard model, and solutions of each scenario were compared to the standard

Table 10.11

SOLUTIONS OF PRICES OF SELECTED COMMODITIES
IN SELECTED COUNTRIES IN THE RESERVE POLICY MODEL
(US$/MT)

Commodity	Scenario	United States	Canada	EC-9	India
Wheat					
	0	120.3	128.1	201.3	145.2
	1	139.3	147.2	220.3	164.2
	2	123.4	131.2	204.4	148.2
	3	142.4	150.2	223.4	167.2
	4	139.1	147.6	220.1	164.6
	5	134.0	141.8	215.0	158.8
	6	130.1	138.0	211.1	155.0
	7	128.1	135.8	209.0	152.8
Maize					
	0	99.8	101.9	102.1	NC
	1	100.0	102.1	102.4	NC
	2	106.6	108.7	108.9	NC
	3	106.8	108.9	109.2	NC
	4	100.0	102.2	102.4	NC
	5	106.0	108.1	108.4	NC
	6	105.2	107.3	107.5	NC
	7	104.9	107.1	107.3	NC
Other Grains					
	0	138.2	162.7	194.8	NC
	1	138.2	163.3	195.3	NC
	2	139.9	168.8	200.9	NC
	3	140.0	169.3	201.4	NC
	4	138.2	163.3	195.4	NC
	5	139.7	168.5	200.5	NC
	6	139.4	167.8	199.9	NC
	7	139.8	167.6	199.7	NC

NC: Not specified or not applicable.

Table 10.12

ASSUMED PRICE ELASTICITIES OF EXCESS DEMAND AND SUPPLY IN THE RESERVE POLICY MODEL

Region	Commodity	Excess Demand or Excess Supply	Price Elasticities a/ Low	Medium	High
USSR	Wheat	Excess Demand	-.1	-.2	-.3
USSR	Maize	Excess Demand	-.2	-.4	-.6
India	Wheat	Excess Demand	-.25	-.5	-.75
China	Wheat	Excess Demand	-.05	-.1	-.15
ROW	Wheat	Excess Demand	-.16	-.32	-.48
ROW	Maize	Excess Demand	-.16	-.32	-.48
ROW	O. Grains	Excess Demand	-.16	-.32	-.48
Argentina	Wheat	Excess Supply	.15	.3	.45
Argentina	Miaze	Excess Supply	.15	.3	.45
Australia	O. Grains	Excess Supply	.15	.3	.45

a/ The medium elasticities are taken from the U.S. Department of Agriculture (1971). The low elasticities are assumed to be one half of the medium elasticities, and the high elasticities are assumed to be equal to: medium elasticities + [medium elasticities - low elasticities].

model solutions. The results show that the world food market had more stable price variations under the higher elasticity assumptions for the excess demand or supply functions for the six regions mentioned above.

Reserve build-up in the foregoing scenario analysis can be used as a proxy to evaluate various contingencies affecting the world food economy. For instance "an increase of the U.S. wheat or maize reserve" can be replaced by a case of the withdrawal of U.S. wheat or maize out of the crop year supply quantities due to a government policy decision or to a natural cause. The model developed in this subsection can also be used to examine broad issues relating to policy and/ or supply changes.

The foregoing study revealed two important points from the modeling point of view. The first is the need for research in the evaluation and estimation of price-elasticities of excess demand/supply in countries for which such estimates are not available. These parameters severely affect the relative variability of prices in the world food economy. The second involves the treatment of the end-of-year carry-over quantity of each commodity. In backcasting exercises, this information is known and there is no problem in generating model solutions. However, in short-run policy analyses such as that shown in the previous section, there is always a certain degree of risk involved in fixing these quantities. One way to cope with this problem is to introduce a price-endogenous stock function, which was developed as a behavioural STPA model, by Hashimoto (1977). The risk associated with stock variations can be substantial. For example, the U.S. carry-over quantity of wheat in 1976 was assumed to be 23.76 million metric tons, while the actual carry-over was 32.27 million metric tons. This led us to examine the issues relating stocks to reserves in a dynamic context.

Medium- to Long-Term Analysis of Stabilization Policies

One major issue of the world food economy which has challenged decision makers and researchers in the field of agricultural policy for a considerable time is that of "instability of the world food economy," better known as "feast or famine?" The specter of worldwide famine was raised as soon as food prices escalated in 1972, and pessimists argued as though world food production had indeed reached its maximum capacity. In this section the instability problem of the U.S. food economy in medium-term framework is analyzed and a comparative study of a class of stabilisation policies is presented, according to Hashimoto (1977).

As one can easily see, developing a nine-commodity, ten-region model with the network system connecting all the regions for each and all commodities is not an easy task. In this section we restrict our focus to the U.S. feed economy only, recognizing that this forces us to assume the fixity of ROW's excess demands (i.e., demands for U.S. exports), which may result in an overestimation (or at least biased estimation) of the price and quantity reactions for the U.S. food economy. All prices reported are given in terms of constant 1975 U.S. dollars.

Before checking for the stability of the U.S. food economy from a system point of view, we first proceed to examine the stability of individual markets and of sub-markets. For this purpose we use a simplified model consisting of the maize, wheat and soybeam sub-sectors. These latter two were adopted as the generators of instability in formulating the following demand and supply systems:

The demand system is given by

$$D_{kt} = \alpha_k - \beta_{kk} PD_{kt} + \sum_{\ell} \beta'_{k\ell} PD_{\ell t}$$

and the supply system is

$$S_{kt} = \gamma_k + \delta_{kk} PS_{k(t-1)} - \sum_{\ell} \delta'_{k\ell} PS_{\ell(t-1)}$$

where

$\alpha_k, \beta_{kk}, \beta'_{k\ell}$ = demand function parameter

$\gamma_k, \delta_{kk}, \delta'_{k\ell}$ = supply function parameter

D_{kt}, S_{kt} = demand or supply quantity

PD_{kt}, PS_{kt} = demand or supply price

k = commodity: W (wheat), M (maize) and S (soybeans)

The coefficient values for wheat, maize and soybeans are presented in Table 10.6.

By inspection of coefficients of the demand and supply functions we find:

$$|\beta_{WW}| > |\delta_{WW}|, \quad |\beta_{MM}| < |\delta_{MM}| \quad \text{and} \quad |\beta_{SS}| < |\delta_{SS}|$$

These relationships indicate that the maize and soybean subsectors are dynamically (cobweb) unstable and explosive, while the wheat subsector is stable. Judged from the ratios

$$\frac{\delta_{MM}}{\beta_{MM}} \text{ and } \frac{\delta_{SS}}{\beta_{SS}}$$

instability seems to be higher in the soybean subsector.

The next logical step is to see how the whole system, containing both stable and unstable subsectors, behaves in a hypothetical environment. For this purpose, we developed a nine-commodity, two-region model that included the United States and the ROW only. It was simulated for eight scenarios defined in terms of hypothetical but historically feasible yields of maize and the ROW's excess demands for wheat and maize. The yearly changes in yield and the ROW's excess demands in each scenario were produced by selecting typical patterns from the past. For example, the sequence of maize yield in Scenario 1 was assumed to be similar to that experienced between 1963 and 1967. By the same token, the ROW's excess demands for wheat and maize in Scenario 1 were assumed to repeat the fluctuations between 1971 and 1975. The year-to-year sequences used in Scenario 1 are shown along with actual statistics in Table 10.14. As it was still a one-year model, it was solved recursively for each year from 1976 to 1980. The carry-in and carry-over quantities were taken from the solutions from the five-year model, which will be discussed later.

As expected, the U.S. food economy was cyclically unstable with respect to soybean production and exhibited infeasible price fluctuations for all commodities; for all scenarios the results became infeasible within three to four years. The process leading to infeasibility, for example, in Scenario 1 as reported in Table 10.15 was as follows. A high yield of maize in 1977 resulted in increased production for that year. The increased production caused a lower price, and caused a shift from the area planted for maize to the area planted for soybeans. This shift subsequently increased soybean production significantly and forced the soybean price downwards to zero. The zero price led to a decreased

Table 10.13

COEFFICIENTS IN THE WHEAT, MAIZE AND SOYBEAN SUBSECTORS

Function and Commodity	Coefficient		
Demand Function			
Wheat	$\beta_{WW} = 56.68$	$\beta_{WW} = 50.10$	$\beta_{WS} = 0$
Maize	$\beta_{MW} = 0$	$\beta_{MM} = 264.5$	$\beta_{MS} = 24.38$
Soybeans	$\beta_{SW} = 0$	$\beta_{SM} = 0$	$\beta_{SS} = 8.045$
Supply Function			
Wheat	$\delta_{WW} = 56.62$	$\delta_{WM} = 0$	$\delta_{WS} = 0$
Maize	$\delta_{MW} = 0$	$\delta_{MW} = 472.4$	$\delta_{MS} = 162.8$
Soybeans	$\delta_{SW} = 0$	$\delta_{SM} = 161.7$	$\delta_{SS} = 92.84$

Table 10.14

ASSUMED YEARLY CHANGES, SCENARIO 1

	Yield of Maize		ROW's Excess Demand for Wheat		ROW's Excess Demand for Maize	
	Assumed	Actual	Assumed	Actual	Assumed	Actual
	-----(MT/HA)------		----------------(million MT)----------------			
1976	4.84	5.52	31.2	20.2	36.8	42.77
1977	5.28	5.70	28.2	24.7	35.2	49.48
1978	5.27	6.33	32.2	23.3	47.4	54.18
1979	5.59	6.89	31.1	32.1	45.7	61.80
1980	4.74	5.71	28.3	39.5	41.3	64.77

Table 10.15

SOLUTIONS OF THE ONE-YEAR MODEL, SCENARIO 1

Commodity	Year	Supply	Demand	Area Planted	Supply Price	Demand Price
		(1,000 MT)		(1,000 HA)	(1975 Constant US$/MT)	
Wheat	1976	55,121	20,609	31,728[a]	94.9	114.5
	1977	55,202	24,836	29,190	11.4	31.1
	1978	50,384	16,703	26,103	294.8	314.4
	1979		(infeasible)			
Soybeans	1976	36,747	22,118	19,951[a]	224.7	258.6
	1977	40,979	25,021	21,428	282.6	316.5
	1978	54,615	28,948	28,185	0	33.8
	1979		(infeasible)			
Beef	1976	11,993	12,826	NC	836.1	916.9
	1977	11,723	12,556	NC	976.9	1,057.6
	1978	11,518	12,351	NC	1,102.6	1,183.3
	1979		(infeasible)			

[a] Exogenously determined.
NC: Not specified or not applicable.

production of soybeans in 1979 and the assumed (fixed) excess demand of the ROW could not be met. Although the process to reach infeasibility differed among the scenarios, it was caused in all the cases by a large shift in the areas planted between maize and soybeans.

The conclusions, however, must be qualified. The instability in the model solutions might have resulted, at least partially, from the following technical assumptions underlying the model:

(1) fixed excess demands in ROW;

(2) linearity in demand and supply equations;

(3) fixed input-output coefficients in the soybean sector, that is, soybean meal and soybean oil were generated in a fixed proportion to the soybeans input; and

(4) fixed carry-over quantities derived outside the model.

For future research, the following improvements are considered important:

(1) One should use non-linear functions for the demand and supply systems and utilize the LCP iterative approach suggested by Mathieson (1979) to obtain a solution;

(2) One should develop several different (operationally acceptable) process representations for the soybeans-soybean meal-soybean-oil subsector (a linear combination of which can be chosen as optimal depending on the market/price conditions); and

(3) One should specifiy a model where carry-over stocks are solved endogenously.

The next question is whether the unstable system can be stabilized. The stabilization scheme tested in this chapter is as follows: (1) set a maxmium and minimum price for all (or some selected) commodities for each year; and (2) let government agencies and/or private enterprises inject or withdraw a sufficient quantity of the relevant commodity to or from markets so that the market price maintains the stipulated maximum or minimum price, once it hits the extremum.

The basic question relating to the above mentioned

stabilization policy is how to find an "appropriate" price band for each commodity. To construct such price bands we developed a five-year model covering the years 1976-1980, and included the nine commodities and the two regions. The model was solved for each of the eight scenarios described above. The terminal carry-over quantity of each commodity was estimated outside these scenario models. For example, the terminal carry-over stock of wheat was assumed to be larger by 10 million tons than the initial carry-in stock, in consideration of the likely increase in stock during the sample model period. By the same token, the terminal carry-over stock of maize was assumed to be larger by 15 million tons than the initial carry-in stock.

Examples of solutions involving Scenario 1 are reported in Table 10.16. Two sets of price bands for the three commodities, wheat, maize and soybeans, were derived from the solutions of the five-year model. For Price Band A, the minimum price for each year was set at the lowest price solution among the eight scenario solutions, while the maximum price was set at the highest price solution for each commodity. For Price Band B, the price was stipulated at the mean of the above mentioned minimum and maximum prices. (As such, Price Band B has a zero width.) For reference purposes, the price band discussed in Johnson (1976) was chosen as Price Band C. The minimum and maximum prices of Price Band C were fixed over time. Among these three, Table 10.17 shows that Price Band C was the widest, followed by Price Bands A and B.

The price band experiments were then conducted by imposing a selected price band on the initial one-year model, and the model was solved for each of the eight scenarios. The quantity of each commodity to be withheld or injected was solved based on the Lagrangean multipliers of the imposed price bands. The solutions of these quantities under Price Band A are shown Table 10.18. The sums of the solved quantities of wheat, maize and soybeans handled by the authorities in order to execute each band policy are then shown in Table 10.19. If one can assume that the handling costs are nearly the same for all three commodities, the stabilization policy with Price Band A is far superior to either Band B or C. Following a policy of Price Band B may result in problems of perpetual vigilance and execution of reserve and release throughout the period, which may constitute an extra burden and thus be a disadvantage from a policy execution and administration point of view, even though prices are perfectly stabilized.

Table 10.16

PARTIAL SOLUTIONS AND ACTUAL STATISTICS (IN PARENTHESIS) OF THE FOOD ECONOMY IN THE FIVE-YEAR MODEL, SCENARIO 1

Quantity		Quantity (1,000 MT)					Price (1975 Constant US$/MT)	
Commodity	Year	Carry-in	Supply	Demand	Trade	Carry-out	Supply	Demand
Wheat	1976	14,780 /b (18,129)	55,121 (58,081)	21,132 (20,549)	31,249 /b (25,859)	17,520 (30,296)	85.0 (95.9)	104.7 (101.1)
	1977	17,520 (30,296)	54,693 (55,270)	22,312 (23,382)	28,228 /b (30,595)	21,674 (32,065)	93.8 (77.1)	113.4 (90.0)
	1978	21,674 (32,065)	55,282 (47,973)	23,286 (22,810)	32,117 /b (32,501)	21,077 (25,151)	102.4 (91.4)	122.2 (103.7)
	1979	21,077 (25,151)	55,282 (57,676)	23,626 (21,313)	31,139 /b (37,428)	21,594 (24,552)	111.4 (103.1)	131.0 (116.0)
	1980	21,594 (24,552)	57,299 (64,046)	25,824 (21,238)	28,288 /b (41,095)	24,780 /b (26,916)	120.2 (94.7)	139.8 (106.7)
Maize	1976	10,465 /b (10,160)	162,077 (159,740)	111,855 (104,673)	36,800 /b (42,774)	23,877 (22,504)	89.5 (80.9)	100.7 (86.5)
	1977	23,886 (22,504)	160,773 (165,230)	111,924 (110,109)	35,209 /b (49,479)	37,527 (28,219)	98.3 (71.6)	109.5 (80.2)
	1978	37,527 (28,219)	159,200 (184,610)	114,114 (125,555)	47,435 /b (54,178) /b	35,178 (33,122)	107.0 (74.0)	118.3 (83.5)
	1979	35,178 (33,122)	171,646 (201,650)	115,936 (131,928)	45,687 (61,798)	45,201 (41,097)	115.8 (73.6)	127.0 (82.1)
	1980	45,201 (41,097)	148,691 (168,860)	127,141 (123,190)	41,285 /b (64,770)	25,466 /b (21,996)	124.6 (82.0)	135.8 (89.5)
Beef	1976	164 /b (164,	12,021 (11,804)	12,768 (12,481)	-833 /b (-863)	250 (211)	849.6 (710.2)	930.3 (824.3)
	1977	250 (211)	11,615 (11,490)	12,448 (12,180)	-833 /b (-797)	250 (148)	1,001.5 (683.2)	1,082.2 (802.0)
	1978	250 (148)	11,411 (11,019)	12,244 (11,818)	-833 /b (-942)	250 (187)	1,126.8 (892.5)	1,207.6 (963.2)
	1979	250 (187)	11,562 (9,748)	12,395 (10,691)	-833 /b (-990)	250 (164)	1,777.2 (1,080.2)	1,253.9 (1107.6)
	1980	250 (164)	10,638 (9,838)	11,521 (10,600)	-833 /b (-835)	200 /b (168)	1,448.3 (896.7)	1,529.0 (962.4)

/a Negative figures indicate U.S. imports.
/b Fixed quantities or quantities bound from below.

Table 10.17

ALTERNATIVE PRICE BANDS
(1975 constant US$/MT)

Year	Price Band a/						Price Band b/			Price Band c/					
	Wheat		Maize		Soybeans					Wheat		Maize		Soybeans	
	Min.	Max.	Min.	Max.	Min.	Max.	Wheat	Maize	Soybeans	Min.	Max.	Min.	Max.	Min.	Max.
1976	85.0	157.6	89.5	118.5	223.5	271.5	121.3	104.0	247.0	82.7	206.8	68.9	172.4	147.0	367.0
1977	93.8	166.4	98.3	127.2	232.2	280.3	130.1	112.8	256.3	82.7	206.8	68.9	172.4	147.0	367.0
1978	102.6	175.2	107.0	136.0	241.1	289.0	138.9	121.5	265.1	82.7	206.8	68.9	172.4	147.0	367.0
1979	111.4	184.0	115.8	144.8	249.9	297.8	147.7	130.3	273.9	82.7	206.8	68.9	172.4	147.0	367.0
1980	120.2	192.8	124.6	153.6	258.7	306.6	156.6	139.1	282.7	82.7	206.8	68.9	172.4	147.0	367.0
Width of Price Bank	72.6		29.0		48.0		0	0	0	124.1		103.5		219.4	

a/ The minimum price in each year was set at the lowest price solutions of the 8 scenarios. The maximum price in each year was set at the highest price solution for each commodity.

b/ The price was set at the mean of Price Band A.

c/ The choice of Price Band C is discussed in Johnson [1976].

Table 10.18

QUANTITIES WITHDRAWN FROM OR INJECTED a/ INTO MARKETS, PRICE BAND A ('000 MT)

Year	Scenario 1			Scenario 2			Scenario 3			Scenario 4		
	Wheat	Maize	Soybeans	Wheat	Maize	Soybeans	Wheat	Maize	Soybeans	Wheat	Maize	Soybeans
1976	0	0	0	0	0	0	0	0	0	0	0	0
1977	2,718	10,351	-19	2,718	10,351	-19	2,718	10,351	-19	2,718	10,351	-19
1978	0	-2,942	4,209	-10,412	-2,942	4,209	0	-10,028	4,209	-10,412	-10,028	4,209
1979	2,381	19,296	-1,048	-3,950	19,296	-1,048	2,381	475	-1,048	-3,950	475	-1,048
1980	4,317	0	4,254	0	0	4,254	3,781	-16,022	4,254	0	-16,022	4,254
Total b/	9,416	32,589	9,530	17,080	32,589	9,530	8,880	36,876	9,530	17,080	36,876	9,350

Year	Scenario 5			Scenario 6			Scenario 7			Scenario 8		
	Wheat	Maize	Soybeans	Wheat	Maize	Soybeans	Wheat	Maize	Soybeans	Wheat	Maize	Soybeans
1976	0	0	0	0	0	0	0	0	0	0	0	0
1977	1,270	-8,889	-19	1,270	-8,889	-19	1,270	-8,889	-19	1,270	-8,889	-19
1978	0	0	-138	-8,990	0	-138	0	0	-138	-10,333	0	-138
1979	0	-3,370	4,063	-5,403	-3,370	4,063	853	-10,967	0	-5,403	-10,967	0
1980	5,196	37,361	-472	0	37,361	-472	5,210	14,821	133	0	14,821	133
Total b/	6,466	49,620	4,692	15,663	49,620	4,692	7,333	34,677	290	178,006	34,677	290

a/ Quantity injected is represented by a negative figure.
b/ Sum of quantitites of withdrawals and injections (signs are not taken into account).

Table 10.19

SUM OF QUANTITIES OF WITHDRAWALS AND INJECTIONS
OF ALL THE EIGHT SCENARIO MODELS
(1,000 MT)

	Wheat	Maize	Soybeans	Total
Price Band A	98,925	307,524	48,084	454,533
Price Band B	183,116	378,370	7,816	569,302
Price Band C	82,873	502,134	213,846	798,853

The system instability shown in the model solutions does not necessarily imply a real world instability. However, recent developments in U.S. agriculture suggest that elements of instability do exist. In retrospect, U.S. agriculture has advanced remarkably well in the past 40 years; crop production almost doubled while the acreage planted remained almost the same. Export volume has increased at least fivefold since the 1950s. The expanded export activity has increased the degree of dependence (riskiness) on foreign demand. Furthermore, both United States and EC policies often have led to more unstable pricing than otherwise. The recent U.S. Federal Government policy of PIK (Payment-in-Kind) is based on a concern about the excess supply of U.S. agricultural products in the face of shrinking (relative to the past trend) foreign demand for them in recent years. As the model experiments showed, because adjustments of production to shifts in the demands of the market-oriented free(r) economies is not likely to stabilize prices and outputs, some sort of price stabilization policy may still be necessary.

The problem facing U.S. agriculture is how to deal with this productive giant during period(s) of normal agriculture production in the rest of the world, while maintaining its health and vitality. Freer agricultural trade, especially the reduction of trade barriers such as import quotas and duties has been called for under the Reagan Administration. Liberalization of trade may increase U.S. farm exports to Japan and Europe. If so, U.S. agricultural problems may be partially alleviated. Realistically, what can the movements toward this trade liberalization accomplish in the future? Let us now turn to this trade policy question, and investigate the potential consequences of Japan's liberalization of trade in meats for the United States, Canada, Australia and the rest of the world.

Potential Consequences of the Liberalization of Japan's Trade in Meats

In economics as in many other social science disciplines, all factors are interdependent. To some extent, this is the nature of international trade in farm products. It was argued in the previous section that the instability of U.S. agricultural markets may be reduced if the protectionist policies of Japan and Europe against U.S. farm exports are removed.

U.S. agricultural exports to Japan in 1980 amounted to $6.1 billion, or about 15 percent of total U.S. farm exports. How much benefit could there be from the anticipated liberalization of Japan's meat trade, which was one of the outcomes of the 1979 multilateral trade negotiations? The benefits to U.S. agriculture up to 1987 have been estimated by Houck (1982) to be only $211 million: $88 million arising from tariff reductions and $123 million from quota increases (mainly beef). In a two-country (U.S.-Japan) model of farm trade, it is almost obvious that U.S. producers benefit from liberalization. However, the answer is not that clear once the trading partners increase in number. Hence, Whitacre (1979) attempted to evaluate the effects of various degrees of trade liberalization of farm products on consumer spending, producer income, and trade of the United States, Japan, Canada, Australia and ROW (EEC(9) plus others), assuming that liberalization could be implemented instantly or in the near future.

The model used to analyze Japanese trade liberalization is basically the same as that presented in Section 2 of this chapter. The model was solved for two scenarios. Model A (or the basic model), which was designed to simulate the situation in 1976, was based on the following constraints:

(1) Domestic producer price of maize in the U.S. must be at least $90/mt ($2.30/bushel), the support price of maize, based on the non-recourse loan program.

(2) Total Japanese beef, pork and poultry imports are restricted to the actual 1976 quantities, and these can be supplied by any exporters.

(3) The U.S. must export at least the 1976 quantities of wheat and other grains to Japan. Without those constraints the U.S. exported all the wheat and other grains to ROW (Europe) and Australia satisfied Japanese imports.

(4) Tariffs are set at the 1976 levels.

In Model B, which was designed to simulate the post-liberalization situation, all the constraints on Japan's meat imports were removed. Some selective model results relating to Japan and the U.S. are shown in Tables 10.20 through 10.25. All of the reported prices are in constant 1977 U.S. dollars.

Table 10.20

IMPACT OF TRADE LIBERALIZATION ON JAPANESE CONSUMPTION

Commodity	Actual Statistics (1975)			Model A			Model B		
	Quantity /a	Price /b	Value /c	Quantity /a	Price /b	Value /c	Quantity /a	Price /b	Value /c
Beef	407	5,575 /d	2,269	442	5,072	2,241	745	1,105	823
Pork	1,058	3,377 /e	3,572	861	3,036	2,614	909	2,190	1,991
Chicken	4,429	934	4,137	756	1,006	761	756	913	690
Subtotal	2,246		7,130	2,059		5,616	24,455		3,504
Wheat	5,578	155 /g	865	5,631	161	907	4,564	155	707
Maize	NA	NA	NA	6,228	121	754	2,268	121	274
Other Grains	NA	116 /h	NA	5,626	127	715	2,049	104	213
Soybean Meal	NA	NA	NA	1,896	118	224	254	35	89
Soybean Oil	___		___	439	1,001	439	59	1,001	59
Subtotal	NA		NA	19,820		3,039	9,194		1,342
Total	NA		NA			8,655			4,846

/a 1000 metric tons.
/b US dollars/m.t.
/c Million US dollars.
/d Retail price of beef in Tokyo, 1975 adjusted for the retail/wholesale spread (retail & wholesale - 1.62).
/e Retail price of pork in Tokyo, 1975 adjusted for the retail/wholesale spread (retail & wholesale - 1.53).
/f Retail price of chicken in Tokyo, 1975 adjusted for the retail/wholesale spread (retail & wholesale - 2.0).
/g Japanese Government resale price of domestic rice, brown basis, average of Grades 1-4, 1975/76.
/h Japanese Government resale price of domestic barley, Grade 2, 1975/76.

NA: Not Available

Table 10.21

IMPACT OF TRADE LIBERALIZATION ON JAPANESE LIVESTOCK PRODUCERS

Commodity	Model A			Model B		
	Quantity[a]	Price[b]	Value[c]	Quantity[a]	Price[b]	Value[c]
Beef	350	2,915.57	1,020.45	0	--	0
Pork	718	1,265.96	908.96	0	--	0
Chicken	756	832.82	629.61	756	753.19	569.41
Total			2,559.02			569.41

[a] 1,000 metric tons.
[b] U.S. Dollars/m.t.
[c] Millions of U.S. dollars.

Table 10.22

IMPACT OF JAPANESE TRADE LIBERALIZATION ON U.S. CONSUMERS

	Actual Statistics (1977)			Model A			Model B		
Commodity	Quantity /a	Price /b	Value /c	Quantity /a	Price /b	Value /c	Quantity /a	Price /b	Value /c
Beef	11,483	1,633/d	18,752	14,066	1,117	15,712	13,892	1,173	16,295
Pork	5,933	1,463	8,680	5,975	1,866	11,149	5,974	1,897	11,333
Chicken	4,429	934	4,137	4,587	707	3,243	4,589	723	3,318
Subtotal	21,845		31,569	24,628		30,104	24,455		30,946
Wheat	23,378	123	2,875	18,207	120	2,185	19,065	113	2,154
Maize	108,210	89	9,631	98,590	89	8,774	96,013	86	8,257
Other Grains	27,900	78	2,176	30,097	89	2,679	32,574	82	2,671
Soybean Meal	14,920	177	2,641	11,170	180	2,011	12,813	98	1,256
Subtotal	174,408		17,323	158,064		15,649	160,465		14,338
Total			48,892			45,753			45,284

/a 1000 metric tons.
/b US dollars/m.t.
/c Million US dollars.
/d Average price in terms of carcass equivalent of choice steers at Omaha, last two quarters of 1977 and first two.
/e Average price in terms of carcass equivalent of barrows and gilts at 7 markets, last two quarters of 1977 and first
/f Average price of broilers, ready to cook at nine cities, for the last two quarters of 1977 and the first two quarters of 1978.
/g Equivalent to $2.72/bu., price for market year 1977/1978 at Kansas City for No. 1 Red Winter Wheat
/h Equivalent to $2.26/bu., price for market year 1977/1978 at Chicago for No.2 yellow corn.
/f Equivalent to $3.54/bu., price for market year 1977/1978 at Kansas City for No.2 milo.
/j Equivalent to $160/short ton, price quotation of June 14, 1978 at Decatur, Illinois

Table 10.23

IMPACT OF JAPANESE TRADE LIBERALIZATION
ON U.S. AGRICULTURAL PRODUCTION

Commodity	Model A			Model B		
	Quantity[a]	Price[b]	Value[c]	Quantity[a]	Price[b]	Value[c]
Beef	13,327	872	11,621	13,457	928	12,488
Pork	5,920	1,500	8,880	5,920	1,531	9,064
Chicken	4,586	475	2,178	4,789	491	2,351
Subtotal	24,833		22,679	24,166		23,903
Wheat	60,139	114	6,856	60,139	108	6,495
Maize	152,400	83	12,649	152,400	83	12,649
Other Grains	34,391	88	3,026	35,391	81	2,867
Soybeans	43,980	219	9,632	43,980	153	6,729
Subtotal	290,910		32,163	290,910		28,740
Total			54,842			52,643

[a] 1,000 metric tons.
[b] U.S. dollars/m.t.
[c] Millions of U.S. dollars.

Table 10.24

SIMULATED CHANGES IN TRADE FLOWS RESULTING FROM JAPANESE TRADE LIBERALIZATION, BEEF (1,000 MT)

Exporter		U.S.	Canada	Australia	R.O.W.
Importer:					
United States	Actual	--	(51)	(310)	(328)
	Model A	--	184	555	--
	Model B	--	190	244	--
Canada	Actual	(14)	--	(35)	(60)
	Model A	--	--	30	--
	Model B	--	--	30	--
Japan	Actual	(7)	--	(72)	(4)
	Model A	--	--	92	--
	Model B	--	--	745	--
R.O.W.	Actual	(12)	(8)	(137)	--
	Model A	--	--	--	--
	Model B	--	--	--	--

Table 10.25

SIMULATED CHANGES IN TRADE FLOWS RESULTING FROM JAPANESE TRADE LIBERALIZATION, PORK (1,000 MT)

Exporter		U.S.	Canada	Australia	R.O.W.
Importer:					
United States	Actual	--	(13)	--	(130)
	Model A	--	55	--	--
	Model B	--	54	--	--
Canada	Actual	(72)	--	--	(2)
	Model A	--	--	--	--
	Model B	--	--	--	--
Japan	Actual	(24)	(35)	--	(51)
	Model A	--	--	--	149
	Model B	--	--	--	--
R.O.W.	Actual	(11)	--	--	--
	Model A	--	--	--	--
	Model B	--	--	--	--

The results show that Japanese consumers' expenditures for livestock products declined to almost one-half of the 1976 expenditure as a result of trade liberalization. The reduction in expenditure is due mostly to the drastic call in prices, although Table 10.20 shows that beef consumption quantity almost doubles. On the other hand, Japanese producers' incomes plunge to nearly one-fifth of the 1976 level, as shown in Table 10.21. The net benefit to the Japanese economy was $1,797 billion, after allowing for the income loss of the livestock producers to be fully compensated.

The U.S. situation is a little more complicated than for Japan. In the multi-region competitive framework, the United States has to compete with Australia, Canada and the ROW for the Japanese agricultural markets. As is shown in Tables 10.24 and 10.25 (trade flows--beef and pork) for instance, the Japanese beef market would be almost completely monopolized by Australia, and the pork market would be taken away from the United States and Canada by the ROW (not specified). The disappearance of the livestock industry (except poultry) in Japan under trade liberalization leads to the U.S. grain producers suffering a sizeable loss, due to decreases in feed grain and soybean exports to Japan. The lossess given in Table 10.23 are estimated at $2.28 billion. The savings of U.S. consumers derived from reduced prices of grains and soybean products are $0.469 billion. The net benefit to the U.S. economy from Japanese liberalization of its meats trade amounts to a negative $1.811 billion.

All in all, the Japanese economy would benefit most from its trade liberalization. However, the effect on the U.S. economy seems to be ambiguous, contrary to the general expectations of U.S. policy makers and researchers. Please note that the quantity of Japanese livestock (especially beef) consumption may increase much more than the model solutions (Model B) indicate if the Japanese demand functions are convex to the origin (like a rectangular hyperbola) at the much lower price (around $1,000/ton). In this case the meat exports from the U.S. may even increase, stimulating the U.S. grains and soybean industries (though to a lesser extent than before due, ironically, to more efficient livestock feeding practices in the U.S. than in Japan).

Among the distinctive features of the results from the multi-country, multi-commodity model applied to the 1976 trade situation, one should recognize that these quantitative conclusions cannot be derived from commodity-by-commodity studies; only an integrated system approach can unravel the interrelationships among these commodities over several countries importantly involved in trade. In terms of policy conclusions, there necessarily exist a series of considerations in relation to the implementation of a policy such as the full liberalization of Japan's meat and grain trade. It may take several years before such a policy is fully implemented. During this period the agricultural production (supply) conditions and technology and consumption of farm products in each and all the regions in the world may change to such an extent that the conclusions reached in this study are invalidated. Therefore, serious students of agricultural policy (including trade policy) must pay due attention to the feasibility and implementation aspects of the model conclusions and to likely future changes in these conclusions. In other words, in-depth, cabinet-level policy studies should only begin at the point where we left the studies presented in this chapter.

Hayami presents his view on this subject as follows: "Having achieved rapid economic growth and having clearly established the comparative advantage for its industry, Japan is inexorably faced with pressures for liberalization of agricultural imports. However, if this liberalization of agricultural imports is to mean a destruction of domestic agriculture, it will be resisted not only by the farmers but by all people who value the contributions which agriculture makes to society above and beyond its purely economic aspects. Herein lies the conflict between international harmony and agricultural protection," i.e., from Castle and Hemmi (1982, p. 376). Our conclusions in this section have to be evaluated within this context by the trading partners involved.

Conclusions

In this section, we summarize some of the unique features of the STPA modeling of the world food economy as employed above, and their implications for policy analyses.

The first important feature of these world food economy models is that multi-commodity linkages among major farm products (except for some specialty crops and fruit) have been established, even though the linkages are a first rough-cut representation derived in linear functional form. This modeling approach can be termed an "integrated agricultural commodity systems approach" or a "systems approach" for short. So far a large number of single commodity policy studies have been published, subject to the caveat that further study which would include other commodities than the one in the study may be required to reach more balanced policy conclusions. No operational multi-commodity modeling system for policy analysis had been developed subsequent to the present system of STPA models. However, obvious precursors existed (using different philosophical and algorithmic approaches) such as the USDA-GOL model and the Japanese Ministry of Agriculture and Forestry model. As shown earlier, all nine commodities are interconnected (with varying degrees of closeness). These connections play an important role in some policy analyses, as found in the impact analysis of grain reserve changes on certain international commodity markets.

Secondly, the systems approach was extended to cover the time dimension whereby system stability could be examined for the U.S. food economy. Commodity-by-commodity examinations revealed that the wheat market was (cobweb) stable, the maize market unstable, and soybean market unstable. The degree of instability of the soybean market was found to be greater than in the maize market. There was, however, some hope that the whole nine-commodity system might produce relatively stable behaviour over time. This hope was not justified, as shown in the recursive simulation exercises presented above. If the system is stable, that is, either monotonically converging or cyclically converging then, as Samuelson and Burmeister (1978) argue, no stabilization policy (intervention) is needed. In the case of the U.S. food economy as modeled here, system stability was found to be non-existent and hence we argued that some form of stabilization scheme might be necessary.

The third feature is related to the treatment of stochastic behaviour. Starting with Waugh (1944), simplified, static and stochastic price stabilization arguments have been proposed. However, they have ignored storage costs, administrative and operational costs, multiple-commodity interactions, trends in crop and livestock yield increases and consumer tastes (wheat and meat in Japan) or producer tastes (feed grains in the USSR), i.e., see Labys (1980). The arguments thus remain highly theoretical and quite ineffective for policy prescription. Stochastic price behaviour may be introduced if the number of scenarios is increased ad infinitum, but this is a luxury that no large-scale modeler can enjoy at this stage. Our resuts were thus presented based on a limited number of scenario exercises.

We believe that this research project has marked a modest first step toward developing a world food economy model in an integrated system framework. As such, there are many aspects that may require correction, further elaboration and improvement.

The first important change which should be incorporated in the present modeling system is the proper recognition of the difference in the Northern and Southern Hemisphere cropping seasons. For short-run analysis, this will prove to be crucially important. A modeling framework that can differentiate the cropping seasons is already available in the STPA dynamic models. Estimation of the requisite demand functions is a remaining problem and one which we believe to be solvable.

The second issue relates to the linearity assumption adopted and the related estimation of parameters. The linear demand and supply functions employed in the STPA models are first approximations to reality. The linearity of the system is not essential, if more efficient (and less costly) algorithms for solving non-linear programming problems can be developed. At this stage, however, we would still recommend the STPA approach or iterative STPA approach over others on the basis of their computational efficiency. In these three studies we have used the single equation, ordinary least squares estimation method to estimate the demand and supply equation parameters. A more satisfactory estimator, from the integrated systems point of view, is a simultaneous equations systems estimator, and future studies should correct this situation.

The last issus is more fundamental and philosophical than technical. Modeling activities such as those presented in this chapter must serve specific purposes important for policy makers. Policy changes, such as the on-going trade liberalization of agricultural commodities in Japan, require detailed impact studies of the policy changes and careful vigilance of the effects of the policy changes on the various parties over some period of time.

We have presented in this chapter, some prototypical approaches in analyzing market situations and evaluating economic policies related to farm products in the United States, Europe, Australia, Japan, Canada and the rest of the world. We hope that this type of modeling framework will be vigorously pursued by the trade and/or agriculture policy makers in major trading countries and international organizations for similar or wider purposes than those to which our models were put in this chapter.

Appendix

Variable and Model Definition

The common modeling framework of the STPA world food economy models are presented in this appendix as concisely as technically possible.

Notation

1. Indices

i, j	=	regions
k, ℓ	=	commodities
m,	=	types of livestock
t, τ	=	time periods

2. Variables

D_{kit}	=	demand quantity of the k-th commodity in the i-th region in the t-th time period,
D'_{kit}	=	per capita demand quantity of the k-th commodity in the i-th region in the t-th period,
S_{kit}	=	supply quantity of the k-th commodity in the i-th region in the t-th period,
T_{kijt}	=	quantity of the k-th commodity shipped from the i-th region to the j-th region in the t-th period,
$Z_{kit(t+1)}$	=	quantity of the k-th commodity carried-over in the i-th regin from the t-th period to the (t+1)-th period,
A_{kit}	=	planted area for the k-th commodity in the i-th region in the t-th period,
L_{mit}	=	number of the m-th livestock in the i-th region in the t-th period,

C_{kit} = the quantity of soybeans (the k-th commodity) that is crushed into soybean meal and soybean oil in the i-th region in the t-th period,

F_{kit} = the quantity of feed grains (the k-th commodity) used for feeding in the i-th region in the t-th period,

MD_{kit} = market demand price of the k-th commodity in the i-th region in the t-th period,

PD_{kit} = regional demand price of the k-th commodity in the i-th region in the t-th period,

MS_{kit} = market supply price of the k-th commodity in the i-th region in the t-th period,

PS_{kit} = regional supply price of the k-th commodity in the i-th region in the t-th period,

$PC_{k\ell it}$ = proceeds gained from sales of soybean meal or soybean oil (the ℓ-th commodity) that is processed by crushing soybeans (the k-th commodity) in the i-th region in the t-th period,

PF_{kit} = proceeds gained from sales of feed grains (the k-th commodity) for feeding.

3. Slack Variables

Each of the above variables has a counterpart slack variable denoted by the initial letter W.

4. Exogenous Coefficients and Parameters

c_{kit} = unit costs other than cost of feed grains in producing meats (the k-th commodity) in the i-th region in the t-th period,

h_{kit} = unit transportation costs of the k-th commodity from the i-th region to the j-th region in the t-th period,

g_{kit} = marketing margin for sales of the k-th commodity in the i-th region in the t-th period,

$s_{kit(t+1)}$ = unit storage costs of the k-th commodity in the i-th region carried-over from the t-th period to the (t+1)-th period,

PI_{it} = per capita income in the i-th region in the t-th period,

TR_t = time trend,

α_{kit} = the constant intercept of the demand function for the k-th commodity in the i-th region in the t-th period,

$\beta_{k\ell it}$, $\beta'_{k\ell it}$ = the slope coefficient of the ℓ-th commodity's price in the demand function for the k-th commodity in the i-th region in the t-th period,

γ_{kit} = the constant intercept of the supply function of the k-th commodity in the i-th region in the t-th period,

$\delta_{k\ell it}$, = the slope coefficient of the ℓ-th commodity's price in the supply function of the k-th commodity in the i-th region in the t-th period,

ξ_{kit} = the slope coefficient of the own lagged variable in the function of area planted for the k-th commodity in the i-th region in the t-th period,

η_{kmit} = the slope coefficient of the number of the m-th livestock in the supply function of the k-th commodity in the i-th region in the t-th period,

λ_{mit} = the constant intercept of the function for the m-th livestock number in the i-th region in the t-th period,

μ_{mit} = the slope coefficient of the livestock number in the m-th livestock number function in the i-th region in the t-th period,

$\nu_{m\ell it(t-\tau)}$ $\nu'_{m\ell it(t-\tau)}$ = the slope coefficient of the (t-τ) year's price of the ℓ-th commodity in the m-th livestock number function in the i-th region in the t-th period,

ξ_{kit} = the slope coefficient of per capita income in the per capita demand function for the k-th commodity in the i-th region in the t-th period,

θ_{kit} = the slope coefficient of the time trend in the per capita demand function for the k-th commodity in the i-th region in the t-th period,

$\phi_{k\ell it}$ = input-output coefficient for soybean crushing, i.e., the amount of soybeans (the k-th commodity) required to produce a unit amount of soybean meal or soybean oil (the ℓ-th commodity) in the i-th region in the t-th period,

$\psi_{k\ell it}$ = input-output coefficient for livestock feeding, i.e., the amount of feed grains (the k-th commodity) used for feeding to produce a unit amount of meats (the ℓ-th commodity) in the i-th region in the t-th period.

Specification of Functional-Form Equations and Input-Output Relationships

1. Demand

Demand for food commodities (wheat for food use, meats and soybean oil) and demand for feed commodities (wheat for feed use, maize, other feed grains and soybean meal) were estimated by different specifications.

a. Food Commodities

Demand for food commodities was first estimated on a per capita basis and then transformed into total demand by multiplying population. Per capita demand for each food commodity was estimated on the own (demand) price, demand prices of substitutes, per capital income and time trend (which was expected to represent the change in taste) in functional form. The typical form is:

$$D'_{kit} = \alpha_{kit} + \sum \beta_{k\ell it} PD_{k\ell it} + \xi_{kit} PI_{it} + \theta_{kit} TR_t$$

b. Feed Commodities

Demand for feed commodities is expressed either in a functional form or as an input-output relationship. The demand function for each feed commodity was estimated on the own (demand) price, demand prices of substitutes, supply prices of meats and time-lagged numbers of each type of livestock. The typical form is:

$$D_{kit} = \alpha_{kit} + \sum_{\ell} \beta_{k\ell it} PD_{k\ell it} + \sum_{\ell} \beta'_{k\ell it} PS_{k\ell it}$$

$$+ \sum_{\tau} \sum_{m} L_{mi(t-\tau)}$$

The general form of the input-output relationship is:

$$F_{kit} = \sum \psi_{k\ell it} S_{\ell it}$$

2. Supply

Supply functions of grains and meats were estimated by different specifications.

a. Grains

Supply of grains is decomposed into planted area and yield. The planted area for each grain was estimated on one-year time-lagged planted area, one-year time-lagged own supply price and supply prices of substitutes in production in a functional form. The typical form is:

$$A_{kit} = \gamma_{kit} + \xi_{kit} A_{ki(t-1)} + \sum_{\ell} \delta_{k\ell it} PS_{k\ell i(t-1)}$$

Yield was treated exogenously or estimated on a time trend.

b. Meats

Supply of each kind of meat was estimated on the own (supply) price, demand prices of feed grains and the number of the lievestock associated with the meat concerned. The typical form is:

$$S_{kit} = \gamma_{kit} + \delta_{kkit} PS_{kit} + \sum_{\ell} \delta_{k\ell it} PD_{kit}$$

$$+ \sum_{m} \eta_{kmit} L_{mit}$$

3. Livestock Number

The number of each type of livestock was estimated on the number of that livestock in the preceding years, time-lagged supply price of the meat associated with the livestock concerned and time-lagged demand prices of feed grains in a functional form. The typical form is:

$$L_{mit} + \lambda_{mit} + \mu_{mit} L_{mi(t-1)} + \sum_{\tau} \sum_{m} \nu_{kmit(t-\tau)} PS_{kmi(t-\tau)}$$

$$+ \sum_{\tau} \sum_{m} \nu'_{kmit(t-\tau)} PD_{kmi(t-\tau)}$$

4. Soybean Crushing Activity

Crushing of soybeans and production of soybean meal and soybean oil were represented by input-output relationships in the following way:

$$C_{kit} = \phi_{k\ell it} S_{\ell it}$$

5. Livestock Feeding Activity

Grain feeding and production of meats were represented by input-output relationships in the following way:

$$F_{kit} = \psi_{k\ell it} S_{\ell it}$$

Market Equilibrium Conditions

The market equilibrium conditions of the world feed economy model can be classified into three types of conditions that regulate:

(1) quantity and price variables,

(2) those among the price variables and the relationships with their counterpart quantity variables; and

(3) those among the quantity variables and the relationships with their counterpart variables.

The market equilibrium conditions of our model are explained in this order; however, those for the soybean crushing activity will be put together and the same is the case for the livestock feeding activity. In the relations listed below, all of the endogenous and then slack variables are non-negative.

1. Demand and Supply Functions

After all the functional-form demand and supply functions explained before are converted into their reduced forms; the market equilibrium conditions regulating the demand and supply functions are formulated as follows:

$$WPD_{kit} \equiv D_{kit} + \sum_{\ell} \beta_{k\ell it} PD_{\ell it} - \alpha_{kit} \text{ and } WPD_{kit} \cdot PD_{kit} = 0$$

$$WPS_{kit} \equiv S_{kit} + \sum_{\tau} \sum_{\ell} \delta_{k\ell it(t-\tau)} PS_{\ell i(t-\tau)} + \gamma_{kit} \text{ and}$$

$$WPS_{kit} \cdot PS_{kit} = 0$$

2. Relationships among Price Variables and Relationships of Those Variables with Their Counterpart Quantity Variables

$$WD_{kit} \equiv MD_{kit} - PD_{kit} \geq 0 \text{ and } WD_{kit} \cdot D_{kit} = 0$$

$$WS_{kit} \equiv PS_{kit} - MS_{kit} \geq 0 \text{ and } WS_{kit} \cdot S_{kit} = 0$$

$$WT_{kijt} \equiv MS_{kit} - MD_{kjt} + g_{kit} + h_{kijt} \geq 0 \text{ and}$$

$$WT_{kijt} \cdot T_{kijt} = 0$$

$$WZ_{kit(t+1)} \equiv MS_{ki(t+1)} + MS_{kit} + s_{kit(t+1)} \geq 0 \text{ and}$$

$$WZ_{kit(t+1)} \cdot Z_{kit(t+1)} = 0$$

3. Relationships Among Quantity Variables and Relationships of Those Variables with Their Counterpart Price Variables

$$WMD_{kit} \equiv -D_{kit} + \sum_j T_{kjit} \geq 0 \text{ and } WMD_{kit} \cdot MD_{kit} = 0$$

$$WMS_{kit} \equiv S_{kit} - \sum T_{kijt} + Z_{ki(t-1)t} - Z_{kit(t-1)} \geq 0$$

$$WMS_{kit} \cdot MS_{kit} = 0$$

4. Soybean Crushing Activity

$$WS_{\ell it} = - MS_{\ell it} + \phi_{k\ell it}\, PC_{k\ell it} \geq 0 \text{ and } WS_{\ell it} \cdot S_{\ell it} = 0$$

$$WC_{kit} = - \sum_{\ell} \phi_{k\ell it} + MD_{kit} \geq 0 \text{ and } WC_{kit} \cdot C_{kit} = 0$$

$$WPC_{k\ell it} = - \phi_{k\ell it}\, S_{\ell it} + C_{kit} \geq \text{ and } WPC_{k\ell it} \cdot PC_{k\ell it} = 0$$

$$WMD_{kit} = - C_{kit} + D_{kit} \geq \text{ and } WMD_{kit} \cdot MD_{kit} = 0$$

5. Livestock Feeding Activity

$$WS_{\ell it} = - MS_{\ell it} + \sum_k \psi_{k\ell it}\, PF_{kit} \geq 0 \text{ and } WS_{\ell it} \cdot S_{\ell it} = 0$$

$$WF_{kit} = - PF_{kit} + MD_{kit} \geq 0 \text{ and } WF_{kit} \cdot F_{kit} = 0$$

$$WPF_{kit} = - \sum_{\ell} \psi_{k\ell it}\, S_{\ell it} + F_{kit} \geq 0 \text{ and } WPF_{kit} \cdot PF_{kit} = 0$$

$$WMD_{kit} = - C_{kit} + D_{kit} \geq \text{ and } WMD_{kit} \cdot MD_{kit} = 0$$

Authors
Takashi Takayama
Department of Economics
University of Western Australia
Perth, Australia 6009

Hideo Hashimoto
Commodity Studies and Projections Division
The World Bank
Washington, D.C. 20433

Dang H. Nguyen
The California State Energy Commission
Sacramento, CA 95814

Rick C. Whitacre
Department of Economics
Illinois State University
Normal, IL 61761

Acknowledgment
This article has been based on the following Ph.D. dissertations generated in response to the aforementioned project issues defined in the introduction to this Chapter: Nguyen (1977) for the first and second issues, Hashimoto (1977) for the third issue, and Whitacre (1979) for the fourth issue. We acknowledge the contribution of those who participated in this project. Any errors and omissions committed in this Chapter remain the responsibility of the authors.

References

Burmeister, E., (1978). "Is Price Stabilization Theoretically Desirable?" in F.G. Adams and S. Klein (eds.) Stabilizing World Commodity Markets, Lexington: Lexington Books.

Castle, E.N. and K. Hemmi (eds.), (1982). U.S.-Japanese Agricultural Trade Relations, Washington, D.C.: Resources for the Future.

Hashimoto, H., (1977). "World Food Projection Models, Projections and Policy Evaluation," unpublished Ph.D. dissertation, University of Illinois.

Houck, J.P., (1982). "Agreements and Policy in U.S.-Japanese Agriculture Trade," in E.N. Castle and K. Hemmi (eds.) U.S. - Japanese Agricultural Trade Relations, Washington, D.C.

Johnson, G., (1973). World Agriculture in Disarray, London: McMillan.

Johnson, S., (1976). "Analysis of a Grain Reserve Plan," in U.S. Department of Agriculture, Analyses of Grain Reserves, Economic Research Service Report No. 634, Washington, D.C.: U.S. Government Printing Office.

Labys, W.C., (1980). "Commodity Price Stabilization Models: A Review and Appraisal," Journal of Policy Modeling, 2: 121-36.

Nguyen, H.D., (1977). "Word Food Projection Models and Short-Run World Trade and Reserve Policy Evaluations," unpublished Ph.D. dissertation, University of Illinois.

Takayama, T. and G.G. Judge, (1971). Spatial and Temporal Price and Allocation Models, Amsterdam: North-Holland Publishing Co.

Takayama, T., (1977). "An Application of Spatial and Temporal Price Equilibrium Models to World Energy Modeling," Papers of Regional Science Association, XLI: 43-58.

U.S. Department of Agriculture, (1971). "World Demand Prospects for Grain in 1980 with Emphasis on Trade by the Less Developed Countries," Foreign Agricultural Economic Report No. 75, Washington, D.C.: U.S. Government Printing Office.

U.S. Department of Energy, (1977). Energy Information Administration; PIES (Project Independence Evaluation System) Integrating Model Documentation, Washington, D.C.

Waugh, F.V., (1944). "Does the Consumer Benefit from Price Stabilization?" Quarterly Journal of Economics, 58: 602-614.

Whitacre, R.C., (1979). "An Evaluation of Japanese Agricultural Trade Policies with a Multiregion Multicommodity Model," unpublished Ph.D. dissertation, University of Illinois.

11 Linking farm and sector models in spatial equilibrium analysis: an application to ozone standards as they affect Corn Belt agriculture

BRUCE McCARL *Oregon State University*
DEBORAH BROWN *Purdue University*
RICHARD ADAMS *University of Wyoming*
JAMES PHEASANT *University of Florida*

Introduction

Economists have devoted considerable effort to the assessment of the consequences of policy or technically induced changes on participants within the agricultural sector. Many types of changes have been examined. For example, Freeman (1979) reviews approaches examining the consequences of environmental change; Feder, Just and Zilberman (1983) examine the consequences of changes on agriculture. The assessments of such changes have been done at a number of different levels of generality within the agricultural sector. (We will refer to the above set of stimuli as change or induced change from here on.)

In particular there have been assessments of the benefits of change done at both the farm and sectoral levels. Analysis at these two different levels potentially leads to quite different results. For example, it is not difficult to imagine a case where the analysis on a single Corn Belt farm would lead to the conclusion that a ban on pesticides without effective substitutes would lead to Corn Belt farmers receiving less income. But conversely, when considering a similar ban where the pesticide is widely used throughout the Corn Belt on commodities subject to inelastic demand, it is likely that an increase in the welfare of the farm sector would occur while consumers' would lose. Thus, there are potential differences in the results of technical evaluations depending upon the level at which the evaluations are done. This argues for considering broader implications in evaluation of induced change rather than simply the farm level effects as economists have traditionally done. For example, McCarl and Spreen (1980); and Norton and Schiefer (1980) review such larger efforts.

However, there is another aspect to the situation. The evaluation of changes at the sectoral level often require one to sacrifice micro economic detail in order to keep the size of the problem tractable. This can have serious consequences. For example, when doing appraisals of induced change with aggregate models, such as those used by Baumes (1978) or Burton (1982), one often finds extreme specialization in production (solutions where whole regions are devoted to a single crop). This situation usually leads to the imposition of inflexible "flexibility" constraints, as indicated by Sahi and Craddock (1974). However, McCarl (1982a) recently argued that a way to avoid this specialization in production and thereby generate more sensible results within a sectoral analysis was to link a number of micro models with the sector model through a Dantzig and Wolfe (1960) decomposition type of scheme using heuristic procedures. Thus, a major purpose of this paper is to implement the McCarl methodological proposal in the context of induced change analysis.

The induced change analysis that will be used as a case study for implementing this procedure involves benefit assessments to environmental change as manifest in changes in ambient ozone concentration levels in the Corn Belt. Agriculture has been identified as one of the priority research areas when examining vegetative effects of ozone and other pollutants. The resultant benefit estimates are an important input into the process by which secondary national ambient air quality standards are established, i.e., see Adams (1983). Economic assessments of the consequences of changes in ozone or other pollutant concentrations are also useful for the formation of environmental research policies, i.e., see Adams and McCarl (1983). Further, benefit assessments are now required as a measure of regulatory efficiency. Thus, a second purpose of this Chapter is to report on a regional analysis of the consequences of changes in ozone concentration levels on agriculture in the Corn Belt.

The methodology we are using is one which basically falls under the broad class of spatial and temporal price and allocation (STPA) modeling. We are using a disaggregated sector model of the United States economy, similar to the models discussed in Judge and Takayama (1973), Takayama and Judge (1971), Duloy and Norton (1973), McCarl and Spreen (1980), and Norton and Schiefer (1980).

Basic Methodology

The methodology used herein is patterned after the discussion in the paper by McCarl (1982a, p. 770). Both a farm model and a sector model were used. The farm model (REPFARM, McCarl 1982b) was implemented for six representative farms in the Corn Belt. These representative farms were developed by Brown and Pheasant. Each farm model was run under a large set of alternative crop prices to develop a set of whole farm plans which consisted of mixtures of corn, soybeans, wheat, oats and double crop soybean acreages. In turn, these whole farm plans were used to generate activities for the sector model (originally developed by Baumes (1978) and documented in Chattin, McCarl and Baumes (1983) utilizing the USDA FEDS budgets. Subsequently, the sector model was solved under the alternative ambient ozone scenarios. Thus, the informal procedure proposed by McCarl (1982a) was utilized in which the presentative farm models were used to pregenerate a number of activities be utilized as done when using Dantzig-Wolfe decomposition procedure.

We now turn our attention to a discussion of the farm model, the sector model and the air pollution appraisal methodology.

<u>The Farm Model</u>

The farm model used was the REPFARM programming model, i.e., see McCarl (1982b) and McCarl and Pheasant (1983). This model was used to develop represenative farms for four different areas in Iowa (Northeast, South, Central, and West) and two ares in Indiana (North and South) by Brown and Pheasant. The REPFARM model facilitated a definition of various possibilities involving continuous corn, rotation corn (rotated with soybeans), rotation soybeans, oats, single crop soybeans, wheat and double crop soybeans in the six areas utilziing location specific timing of planting and harvesting, along with different sequences of other crop cultural operations and different yields for each crop by type (continuous, etc.) planting, and harvesting date. These models were detailed micro-economic linear programming models with approximately 250 columns and 220 rows. The data were based on agricultural statistics, extension reports, existing models and expert opinion, i.e., see Brown and Pheasant (1983) for details. The models were run with five different corn prices ranging from $1.75 to $2.75 with each of 12 different soybean to corn ratios ranging from $2 to $3 and with five different wheat prices ranging $2.03 to $4.28. This yielded 300 different price ratios for each of the six representative farms. The data were summarized to yield a series of unique crop mixes (i.e., land use patterns) and accompanying yields for each of the repsentative farms.

The Sectoral Model

The sectoral model utilized was adapted from the model developed by Baumes (1978) which is documented in Chattin, McCarl and Baumes (1983) utilizing the data developed by Burton (1982) updated to 1980. The sector model is an activity analysis spatial equilibrium model structured as was the Duloy and Norton (1973) model for Mexico. The model, however, was solved under constant elasticity demand curves using the MINOS software package (Murtaugh and Saunders). It is structured (in a two-region example) as in Figure 11.1. The model encompasses production, processing, domestic demand, export demand, and imports. A simplified tableau appears in Figure 11.2.

The basic data utilized in the model are the U.S. Department of Agriculture Firm Enterprise Data System (FEDS) budgets. The United States is disaggregated into ten regions consisting of the 50 states but the mid-West (Iowa, Indiana, Ohio, Illinois, Missouri) was disaggregated into 12 subregions. The primary and secondary crop coverage are as given in Tables 11.1 and 11.2. For the purpose of this study, the FEDS budgets as reformatted by Burton (1982) were updated to 1980, using 1980 yields, acreages, and prices. The miscellaneous production costs were altered following the procedures outlined in Fajardo, McCarl, and Thompson (1981), or Baumes (1982). (These procedures involve calculating miscellaneous costs, so that the miscellaneous costs exactly equalled the difference between the value of production and the cost of the endogenously priced inputs within the model.

Definition of crop production alternatives was handled in two ways depending on the region. Crop production for regions outside the Corn Belt was held at 1980 actual levels using the FEDS budgets to directly define activities. Within

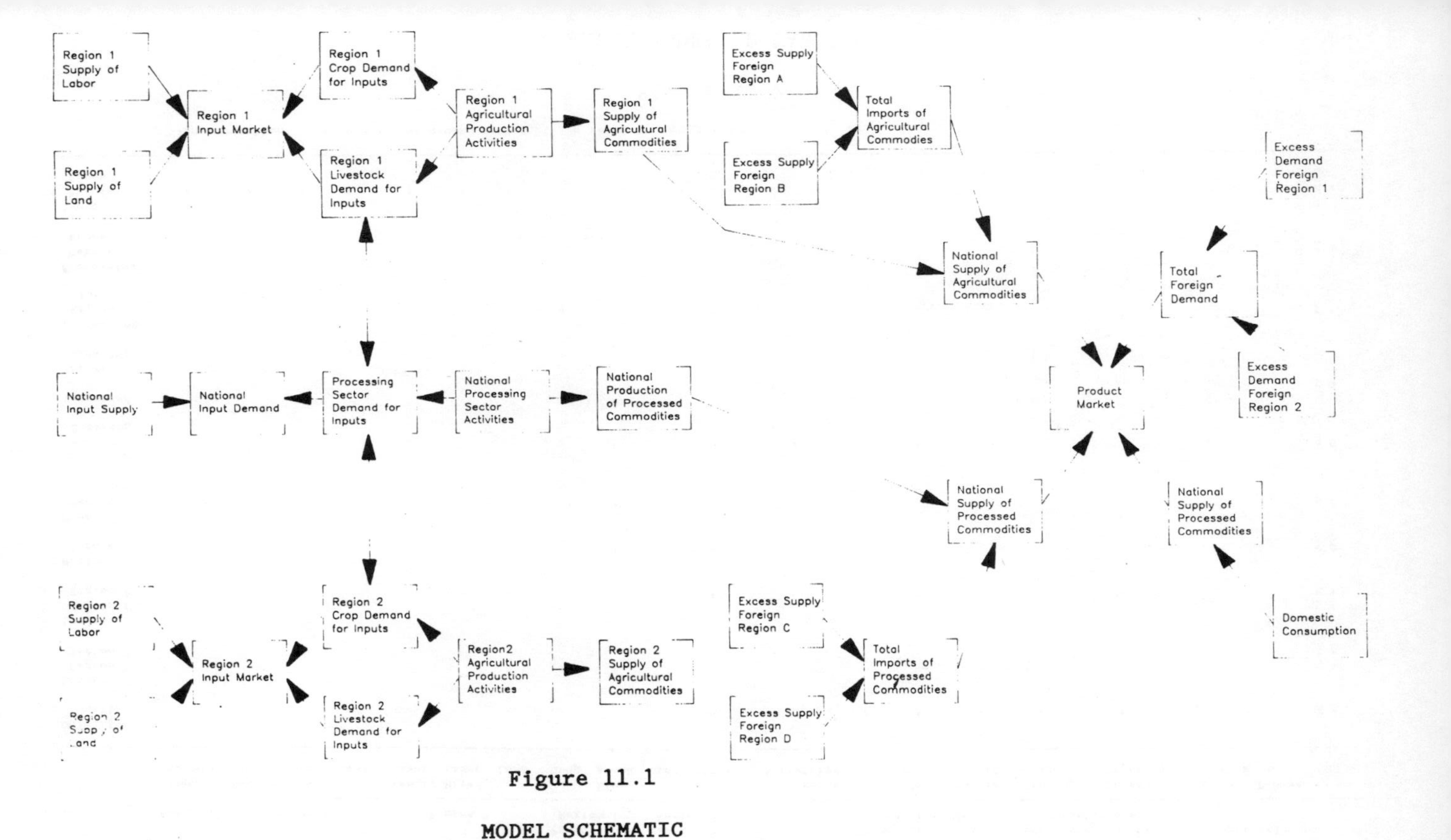

Figure 11.1

MODEL SCHEMATIC

Variables	National	Region 1			Region 2			Production Region 1		Production Region 2			Demand - Primary Products Domestic Use			Demand - Processed Products Domestic Use		Importation			
	Input Supply	Family Labor	Hired Labor	Land	Family Labor	Hired Labor	Land	Crop	Live-stock	Crop	Live-stock	Processing Activities	Crop	Live-stock	Foreign (Exports)	Consump-tion	Foreign (Exports)	Crop	Live-stock	Proces-sed	RHS
Objective Function	-	-	-	-	-	-	-	-	-	-	-	-	+	+	+	+	+				≤ +
Labor:																					
Region 1				-				+	+												≤ '
Region 2							-			+	+										≤ '
Land:																					
Region 1				-				+	+												≤ '
Region 2							-			+	+										≤ +
National Inputs	-							+	+	+	+										≤ 0
Crop Market Clearing								+	-	+	-							-			≤ 0
Livestock Market Clearing									-		-	+		+					-		≤ 0
Processed Goods Market Clearing												-				+	+			-	≤ 0
Production Regula-tions								+	+	+	+										≤ '
Processing Regula-tions												+									≤ +
Input Regula-tions	+	+	+	+	+	+	+														≤ '

Sign convention: (+) - usage or demand source; (-) - yield or supply source.

Figure 11.2

SAMPLE MODEL LP TABLEAU

Table 11.1

PRIMARY COMMODITIES INCLUDED IN THE MODEL

Commodity	Units
Field Crop Commodities	
Cotton	1000 bales
Corn	1000 bushels
Soybeans	1000 bushels
Wheat	1000 bushels
Sorghum	1000 bushels
Oats	1000 bushels
Barley	1000 bushels
Rice	1000 cwt
Sugar cane	1000 tons
Sugar beets	1000 tons
Silage	1000 tons
Hay	1000 tons
Residues	
Corn stover	1000 tons
Sorghum	1000 tons
Small grain	1000 tons
Rice	1000 tons
Sugar cane	1000 tons
Livestock Commodities	
Milk	1000 cwt
Culled dairy cows	1000 head
Culled dairy calves	1000 head
Culled beef cows	1000 head
Live heifers	1000 cwt
Live calves	1000 cwt
Non fed beef available for slaughter	1000 cwt
Fed beef available for slaughter	1000 cwt
Calves available for slaughter	1000 cwt
Feeder pigs	1000 cwt
Hogs available for slaughter	1000 cwt

Table 11.2

SECONDARY OR PROCESSED COMMODITIES INCLUDED IN THE MODEL

Commodity	Units
Soybean meal	1000 lbs.
Soybean oil	1000 cwt.
Raw sugar	1000 tons
Feed grain	1000 lbs.
Protein supplement dairy feed	1000 lbs.
High protein livestock feed	1000 lbs.
High protein swine feed	1000 lbs.
Low protein swine feed	1000 lbs.
Poultry feed	1000 lbs.
Veal	1000 cwt.
Non-fed beef	1000 cwt.
Fed beef	1000 cwt.
Pork	1000 cwt.
Alcohol	1000 gallons
Brewers mash	1000 lbs.

the Corn Belt, activities were formed by aggregating the corn, soybean, oats, and wheat activities according to the whole farm crop mix plans geneated by the representative farm models. Specifically, when the micro economic model was run under a particular price ratio, it yielded a particular combination of crops. These included, for example, 45 percent corn, 35 percent soybeans, and 20 percent wheat with associated yields. The crop budgets were then aggregated into a budget for a single whole farm multiple crop plan. This was done by multiplying each item within each individual crop budget by the percent of each crop, then summing into a composite budget. For example the fertilization expense in the composite budget under the example crop mix above would be 45 percent of the corn fertilization expense plus 35 percent of the soybean fertilization expense plus 20 percent of the wheat fertilization expense.

In addition, yields within these composite budgets were developed as follows. A base ratio was selected from the micro-economic model giving a typical cropping pattern which led to the 1980 yield statistics. Then the yield for a particular price ratio was divided by the base yield to obtain the proportional relationship between yield under the crop mix and base yields. Subsequently, the FEDS crop budget yield was multiplied by this number and by the proportion of corn to generate the corn yield for the multiple crop budget. Thus, if the crop mix represented 90 percent corn, whereas in the base situation there was 50 percent corn, then the yield procedure above would potentially account for a reduction in corn yields experienced in the micro model due to less favorable corn planting conditions. This particular activity formation methodology was used for all crop mixes which were substantially different as generated by the representative farm model, i.e., a large number of crop mixes were duplicated under the price runs.

The representative farm models did not possess a one-to-one relationship to the regions defined within the model. Thus, the following procedures were used. The four areas of Iowa used the State average Iowa crop budgets from the FEDS data and the appropriate crop mix was applied to each. The two areas in Indiana used the FEDS State level Indiana budgets and crop mixes generated for the two regions in Indiana; two regions were defined in Illinois and these used the corresponding two regions in Indiana. Three regions were defined in Ohio: (1) the Southern part of Ohio was defined using the Ohio crop budgets and crop mixes generated from the southern Indiana Model; (2) the northwestern part of Ohio was generated using the northern Indiana crop budget mixes and the Ohio budgets; and (3) the northeastern part of Ohio was generated using the Ohio FEDS budgets and the northeastern Iowa budgets. Missouri was generated using a southern Iowa crop mix and the Missouri budgets. These assignments and budget regions were based on expert opinion.

Demand levels for products and the supply prices are drawn from 1980 agricultural statistics. Elasticities are used from Burton (1982).

Development of Air Pollution Appraisal

The procedures above are used to establish a base model. In performing the air pollution-environmental change assessment the model was run three times. A number of other experiments were run as described in Adams and McCarl (1983). The base model is assumed to reflect actual ambient ozone concentrations for 1980. That is, the yields used in the 1980 model should already incorporate the effects of ozone on crop production for the 1980 crop year. These actual ambient ozone concentrations are associated with the current secondary national ozone standard of 0.12 parts per million hourly maximum not to be exceeded more than once per year. The alterative ozone standards scenarios imposed are: (1) an assumed improvement in air quality intended to portray a more restrictive Federal Standard of 0.08 parts per million not to be exceeded more than once per year, and (2) a scenario that portrays an increase in ozone levels (or a degradation in air quality) to correspond to a relaxation in the Federal standard to 0.16 ppm not to be exceeded more than once per year. The alternative ozone secondary standards are translated into changes in crop yield through use of dose-response functions relating ozone dose levels to crop yields.

These functions were generated primarily by the U.S. Environmental Protection Agency's National Crop Loss Assessment Network (NCLAN), an interdisciplinary, multi-state research program designed to measure the effects of air pollution on important agricultural crops. The response function from the NCLAN and related crop research are reported in Heck et al. (1982). By inserting the appropriate ambient ozone dose levels that correspond to the 0.08 and 0.16 ppm standards into the crop dose response functions for corn (Coker cultivar), soybeans (Corsey cultivar) and wheat (Oasis cultivar from Heck et al., the direct physical consequence of ozone on yields are predicted. These predicted yields then serve to drive the base model.

The NCLAN and related response functions from Heck et al. predict that when the ozone standard is reduced to 0.08 parts per million, corn yeilds are unaffected. Soybean yields increase from 7 percent to 12 percent depending upon location; and wheat and oat yields increase 2 percent to 3 percent. On the other hand, when the ozone standard is relaxed to 0.16 parts per million, corn yields fall by 3 percent. Soybean yields fall by between 15 percent and 19 percent depending upon location; and wheat and oat yields fall by 3 percent to 4 percent. Thus, an improvement in air quality (a reduction in ozone) would be expected to increase soybean and wheat production relative to corn, whereas a decrease in air quality (an increase in ozone) would potentially lead to a relative increase in corn and possibly wheat production at the expense of soybeans.

Given the importance of the Corn Belt as a producer of these commodities, it would be unrealistic to assume fixed prices. Thus, a microeconomic analysis could yield different results when compared to a sectoral analysis. In a sectoral analysis one would expect the price effects in terms of corn and soybeans to dampen some of the adjustment that would occur in the micro model. The analysis of the three ozone scenarios was implemented as follows. The base model was run to reflect environmental conditions corresponding to the present 0.12 parts per million standard. Then, all yields in the base models were adjusted by the state specific yield loss estimates developed from the NCLAN response functions to simulate the 0.08 and 0.16 ppm analyses, all other factors held constant. The model was rerun with the results (the pattern of production, prices and the magnitudes of consumers' plus producers' surplus) interpreted as the economic effects of the changes in ozone secondary standards.

Model Calibration

Before beginning a discussion of the results of this analysis, we should discuss the calibration of the sector model, particularly in light of the methodological objectives within this paper. The first step in assembling the sector model was to run the model in the same fashion as it had been run by Burton (1982) or Baumes (1978), without the whole farm plan crop mix activities. This was done in order to obtain information on whether the model could feasibly replicate 1980 actual acreages. Thus, all activities in the model were held at their 1980 levels and tests were done on model feasibility. The model could not reproduce the 1980 production pattern until data errors were corrected and land statistics reconciled. Subsequently comparisons were done to see how well the model reproduced 1980 prices and quantities. During this analysis, it was discovered that the demand and export figures for 1980 were not consistent with the production figures. This was due to dynamic linkages not captured in the model; for example, stocks were not treated and there was a large drawdown in corn stocks in 1980. At this point, the decision was made to not try to reproduce 1980 quantities but rather to try to reproduce the prices. (The decision was arrived at because we felt short-run dynamic linkages should not play a large role in an assessment, where long-run phenomena such as changes in air quality were being investigated.) Thus, the export demand curve was adjusted to the point at which the prevailing 1980 price, the quantity exported was equal to the difference between 1980 production and 1980 domestic consumption for livestock and other direct usages.

Given these results the model data were accepted as valid for experimentation and the crop mixes entered. All restraints on the Corn Belt cropping activities were removed, although 50 percent flexibility constraints were maintained on the activities which were not involved with the corn, soybeans, wheat, and oats. The activities replaced for these crops were the whole farm crop plans and the model was run. The base model then corresponded closely with the 1980 actuals (Table 11.3).

Scenario Analysis

Following the above procedures, the model was solved under the yield assumptions representing the three air quality pollution scenarios: the present federal standard (i.e., the base) and the two alternatives. The results of these hypothetical standards are compared with the base model as shown in Table 11.4. Differences between the base case and the two alternative standards represent the estimated benefits of ozone control or costs of ozone increases to society. There are several things about the results that are worth noting. First, as one would expect from the generally inelastic nature of agricultural demand, the agricultural sector benefits from the presence of air pollution. That is, a reduction in the amount of ozone leads to a slight decrease in the total producers' surplus within the agricultural sector. Conversely, an increase in ozone concentration leads

Table 11.3

COMPARISON OF BASE MODEL RESULTS WITH 1980 ACTUAL VALUES

Variable	Base Model	Actual Values
Production by Crop		
Corn (mil.bu)	6,726.0	6,647.5
Soybeans (mil.bu)	1,789.5	1,817.1
Wheat (mil.bu)	2,384.4	2,369.7
Prices by Crop		
Corn ($/bu)	$3.27	$3.27
Soybeans ($/bu)	$7.68	$7.61
Wheat ($/bu)	$3.90	$3.96

Table 11.4

SCENARIO RESULTS OF AIR POLLUTION ANALYSIS

	Base Model Solution	.08 PPM Scenario		.16 PPM Scenario	
		Model Solution	% of Base	Model Solution	% of Base
Total Social Welfare (mil. $)	121,577	121,598	100.0	120,570	99.0
Total Producers' Surplus (mil. $)	16,182	16,096	99.5	17,677	109.0
Domestic Consumers' Surplus (mil. $)	95,338	95,398	100.1	93,552	98.0
Export Consumers' Surplus (mil. $)	10,055	10,105	100.5	9,349	93.0
Total Consumer' Surplus (mil. $)	105,394	105,502	100.1	102,901	97.5
Corn Production (mil./bu)	6,726	6,728	100.0	6,608	98.2
Corn Price ($/bu)	$3.27	$3.26	99.7	$3.53	108.0
Soybean Production (mil./bu)	1,779	1,785	100.3	1,630	91.6
Soybean Price ($/bu)	$7.68	$7.66	99.7	$8.25	108.0
Wheat Production (mil./bu)	2,384	2,385	100.0	2,443	102.5
Wheat Price ($/bu)	$3.90	$3.89	100.0	$3.71	95.1

to a slight increase in welfare within the agricutural sector. However, these results do not hold for society as a whole. A decrease in concentration leads to an increase in social welfare (sum of ordinary consumers' surplus and producer quasi-rents) of about $21 million, whereas a degradation in air quality (increase in ozone) leads to a societal welfare loss of approximately $1 billion. The segment of society which is most affected is export consumers, as an increase in ozone concentration leads to a 7 percent reduction in their welfare. The increase in air pollutants also leads to a 7 percent decrease in the value of agricultural exchange earnings. Thus, there is an important tradeoff between air quality and exports. There is no such dramatic effect when air quality improves (ozone decreases) as the level of exports and the level of exports and consumers' surplus remains approximately constant.

As expected, a reduction in ozone does lead to a slight increase in soybean production, whereas an increase in ozone leads to a decrease in soybean production. Somewhat unexpectedly an increase in the amount of ambient ozone, while leading to a relatively large decline in the amount of soybeans produced, also leads to a decline in corn production. This is because corn is not only directly affected by ozone increases (a 3 percent loss in production at 0.16 ppm) but is also indirectly affected in that corn is quite commonly rotated with soybeans. The reduction in soybean acreage thus implies an increase in the cost of producing corn because continuous corn acreage will have to be expanded as opposed to rotation corn acreage, resulting in a small decline in the amount of corn being produced. On the other hand, there is a 9 percent decline in the amount of soybeans being produced, and 8 percent increase in soybeans prices. Simultaneously wheat production is expanded slightly as the corn-soybean rotation acreage shifts somewhat into wheat. This is accompanied by a decline in wheat prices.

The analysis confirms some of the benefits of appraising the technical change at the regional rather than farm level. Namely, in the micro analysis done preceding this study a decline in air quality with fixed prices was shown to lead directly to a decline of producer welfare, whereas an increase in air quality leads to an increase in producer welfare, i.e., see Brown and Pheasant (1983). The opposite direction of effects are found here. Simultaneously, Brown and Pheasant show much more dramatic shifts in terms of production patterns. For example, they found that the acreage of soybeans was reduced to zero in some of the regions under the extreme air pollution scenarios. The minimum effect in the Brown and Pheasant models across the farms in the various states was a halving of soybean acreage. On the other hand, in this analysis the largest production reduction is on the order of 11 percent; thus, the sectoral analysis produces more conservative estimates in terms of assessing the consequences of air pollution on regional crop production (which we feel are more realistic).

The combined micro and macro analyses also indicates benefits although these currently can be demonstrated qualitiatively. Experiments were not developed to analyze the difference between the conventional sector model and a sector model done with crop mix activities. Further this would be difficult due to lack of basis for comparison. The crop mix data from the micro model portrayed the rotation effects. Namely, although one would naively expect corn production to increase at the expense of soybean production under the relaxed ozone standard (0.16 ppm), corn and rotation soybeans constitute a joint product. A reduction in the acreage of soybeans thus leads to an increase in corn production costs such that it did not merit increasing corn, rather the model implied substitution toward other crops.

Conclusions

While the primary focus of this chapter is methodological, the empirical case example does provide some insight into performing environmental benefits analyses. Thus, concluding comments fall into two categories: (1) methodological and (2) empirical. In terms of methodological development, this paper implemented the procedures suggested by McCarl (1982b), using a linear programming model to generate crop mix activities which in turn were integrated into a sector model. In this setting, the procedures of McCarl needed some modification to adjust for the yield changes which accompany changes in crop mix (due to less timely operations when planting and harvesting a crop). Although not attempted here it may also be desirable to incorporate changes in factor usage which could accompany such changes in yields or changes in the intensity of cropping. The McCarl procedure worked satisfactorily, although no detailed attempt was made to appraise the adequacy of this procedure vis a vis traditional policy analysis procedures. The authors believe researchers should consider using this approach, as it provides a desirable theoretical link between micro-economic behaviour and sectoral modeling.

In terms of empirical content, the assessment of the ozone control benefits revealed relatively minor gains to society from reductions in ozone, but substantial losses with further degradation of quality air, i.e., an estimate of $1 billion in losses from the relaxed ozone scenario. At a sectoral level, an increase in ozone is an effective form of supply control and when acting against the somewhat inelastic demand curves of the included commodities results in an increase in agriculture's welfare (producer quasi-rents), although society's welfare falls. It also appears from the analysis that there also is clear tradeoff between air pollution and exchange earnings with increases in air pollution leading to decreases in the amount and value of agricultural exports.

In summary, spatial equilibrium analysis and the sector modeling based on the Dantzig-Wolfe decomposition procedure proved to be an adequate method for appraising agricultural adjustments in the context of the environmental policy analysis. While this study has concentrated on the assessment methodology, a companion study by Adams and McCarl (1983) used updated response information to provide more definititve benefits estimates and addressed a broader range of environmental policy issues.

Authors
Bruce McCarl
Department of Agricultural and Resource Economics
Oregon State University
Corvallis, OR 97331

Deborah Brown
Department of Agricultural Economics
Purdue University
West Lafayette, IN 47907

Richard Adams
Department of Agricultural and Resource Economics
University of Wyoming
Laramie, WY 82070

James Pheasant
Department of Food and Resource Economics
University of Florida
Gainesville, FL 32611

Acknowledgment
Although the research described in this chapter has been funded in part by the United States Environmental Protection Agency through a cooperative agreement (R810296) to Oregon State University, it has not been subjected to the Agency's required peer and policy review and therefore does not necessarily reflect the views of the Agency and no official endorsement should be inferred. This research was also partially supported by the Oregon State and Purdue Agricultural Experiment Stations and the International Plant Protection Center. See Technical Paper No. 6937 of the Oregon State Agricultural Experiment Station. The authors wish to thank Martha Smith, Mike Hanrahan, Andy Lau, and the NCLAN Research Management Committee for aid in generating data for this study.

References

Adams, R.M., (1983). "Issues in Assessing the Benefits of Ambient Ozone Control," Environmental International.

Adams, R.M. and B. McCarl, (1983). "Assessing the Benefits of Alternative Oxident Standards on Agriculture: The Role of Response Information," Unpublished paper, Oregon State University.

Baumes, H., (1978). "A Partial Equilibrium Sector Model of U.S. Agriculture Open to Trade: A Domestic Agricultural and Agricultural Trade Policy Analysis," unpublished Ph.D. Thesis, Purdue University.

Brown, D. and J. Pheasant, (1983). "A Linear Programming Assessment of Economic Damages to Midwest Agriculture Due to Ozone," Final Report to Environmental Protection Agency Purchase Contracts.

Burton, R., (1982). "Reduced Herbicide Availability: An Analysis of the Economic Impacts on U.S. Agriculture," unpublished Ph. D. Thesis, Purdue University.

Chattin, B., B. McCarl and H. Baumes, Jr., (1983). "User's Guide and Documentation for a Partial Equilibrium Sector Model of U.S. Agriculture," Agricultural Experiment Station Bulletin No. 414, Purdue University.

Dantzig, G. and P. Wolfe, (1960). "Decomposition Principle for Linear Porgrams," <u>Operations Research</u> 8: 101-111.

Duloy, J. and R. Norton, (1973). "CHAC: A Programming Model of Mexican Agriculture," in L. Goreux and A. Manne (eds.) <u>Multilevel Planning: Case Studies in Mexico</u>, Amsterdam: North-Holland Publishing Co.

Fajardo, D., B. McCarl and R. Thompson, (1981). "A Multi-commodity Analysis of Trade Policy Effects: The Case of Nicaraguan Agriculture," <u>American Journal of Agricultural Economics</u> 63: 23-21.

Feder, G., R. Just and D. Zilberman, (1983). "Adoption of Agricultural Innovations in Developing Countries: A Survey," World Bank Staff Working Paper No. 542.

Freeman, A., (1979). <u>The Benefits of Environmental Improvements</u>, Baltimore: Johns Hopkins University Press.

Hayami, Y. and W. Peterson, (1979). "Technical Change in Agriculture," in L. Day (ed.) <u>A Survey of Agricultural Economics Literature</u>, Minneapols: University of Minnesota Press.

Heck, W., O. Taylor, R. Adams, G. Bingham, J. Miller, E. Preston and L. Weinstein, (1982). "Assessment of Crop Loss from Ozone," <u>Journal of the Air Pollution Control Association</u> 32: 358-361.

Judge, G. and T. Takayama, (1973). Studies in Economic Planning Over Space and Time Amsterdam: North-Holland Publishing Company.

McCarl, B., (1982a). "Cropping Activities in Agricultural Sector Models: A Methodological Proposal," American Journal of Agricultural Economics, 64: 768-772.

McCarl, B., (1982b). "REPFARM: Design, Calculation and Interpretation of the Linear Programming Model," Agricultural Experiment Station Bulletin No, 385, Purdue University.

McCarl, B. and J. Pheasant, (1983). "REPFARM: Documentation of the Computer Model," Agricultural Experiment Station Bulletin No. 409, Purdue University.

McCarl, B. and T. Spreen, (1980). "Price Endogenous Mathematical Programming as a Tool for Sector Analysis," American Journal of Agricultural Economics 62: 87-102.

Murtagh, B. and M. Saunders, (1977). "MINOS User's Guide," Report SOL 77-9, Department Operations Research, Stanford University, Stanford, CA.

Norton, R. and G. Schiefer, (1980). "Agricultural Sector Programming Models: A Review," European Review of Agricultural Economics 7: 229-264.

Sahi, R. and W. Craddock, (1974). "Estimation of Flexibility Coefficients for Recursive Programming Models: Alternative Approaches," American Journal of Agricultural Economics 56: 344-350.

Takayama, T. and G. Judge, (1971). Spatial and Temporal Price and Allocation Models. Amsterdam: North-Holland Publishing Company.

U.S. Department of Agriculture, Economic Research Service, (1982). Costs of Producing Selected Crops in the United States: Final 1979, 1980, and Preliminary for 1981. Prepared for the Committee on Agriculture, Nutrition, and Forestry, United States Senate. U.S. Government Printing Office, Washington, D.C.

12 World wheat trade: implications for U.S. exports

FORREST D. HOLLAND *Purdue University*
JERRY A. SHARPLES *U.S. Department of Agriculture*

Introduction

A very important parameter for U.S. grains policy research is the elasticity of export demand. In one parameter, it summarizes the net impact on the United States of many forces in the rest of the world affecting wheat trade. Consequently, it is at the same time very useful and very difficult to estimate. Many assumptions must be made in the estimation process to reduce the problem to manageable size and to bridge data gaps.

This study examines the short-run price elasticity of demand for U.S. wheat exports, which according to Tweeten (1967) and Bredah (1979) should be labeled as E_{ef}. No econometric estimation is attempted; rather, the research results of others are put into a comprehensive framework in order to obtain: (1) estimates of the elasticity under various assumptions, and (2) a priority listing of where to focus research to improve these estimates.

The focus here is on a short-run estimate of E_{ef}. A short-run estimate may be differentiated from a longer-run estimate by the potential sources of adjustment to price changes that are assumed for each. The short-run elasticity of U.S. export demand measures consumption and carryover wheat stock adjustments in the rest of the world relative to changes in the annual U.S. wheat export price, but it does not measure any production response or change in policy. It is assumed that the period of adjustment, one marketing year, is too short for either production or government policy in other countries to respond to a change in the annual price at which the U.S. exports wheat. In the longer run, however, consumption, production and policy do adjust to longer run changes in the U.S. wheat export price. Foreign stock adjustments are generally not included in a long-run estimate of the elasticity of demand for U.S. exports. Stocks are held primarily for pipeline or speculative purposes. Speculation is a short-run phenomenon and pipeline quantities are not considered to be price responsive.

In this study, six factors affecting the short-run elasticity of demand for U.S. wheat exports (E_{ef}) are examined. They are: (1) the demand for domestic wheat consumption in other countries, (2) demand for stocks, (3) wheat policy, (4) supply of foreign exhcnage, (5) trade agreements and (6) transportation costs. The unique contribution of this study is to introduce all six factors into a farily simple world trade model in order to obtain a more comprehensive estimate of E_{ef}.

One finds many different estimates of E_{ef} in the literature, each based upon different assumptions. Early work by Tweeten (1967) and Johnson (1977) suggested that the long-run E_{ef} could be very elastic (value of -6 or greater) Gallagher, et al. (1981) estimated a short-run value of -.413 for E_{ef} for all U.S. wheat exports and -.72 for commercial exports to nonsocialist countries. In POLYSIM by Ray and Richardson (1978) the short-run value of E_{ef} is -.5 and the long-run value is -1.5, while in WHEATSIM by Sharples (1980) the short-run E_{ef} is set at -.4. In these two simulators (POLYSIM and WHEATSIM) used by the U.S. Department of Agriculture for policy analysis, the values of E_{ef} are analysts' judgment; they are not empirical estimates.

For this study the world is divided into 20 regions consisting of five net wheat exporters and 15 net importers. Regions are defined according to location, importance in wheat trade and pricing policies. A partial, price equilibrium model is formulated which incorporates all six factors mentioned above. By manipulating the model,an estimate of E_{ef} is obtained. The objective throughout is to observe how the various factors relate to the estimate of E_{ef}, the short-run elasticity of demand for U.S. wheat exports.

The Spatial Model

The spatial price equilibrium problem may be stated mathematically as a surplus maximization problem or equivalently as a set of equilibrium conditions. We have chosen to state the problem in terms of equilibrium conditions.

Find: $\bar{P}_i$, $\bar{P}_j$, $\bar{S}_i$, $\bar{D}_j$, and $\bar{X}_{ij}$

Such that: $\bar{S}_i = S_i(\bar{P}_i) = \sum_j \bar{X}_{ij}$

$$\bar{D}_j = D_j(\bar{P}_j) = \sum_i \bar{X}_{ij}$$

$$\sum_i \bar{S}_i = \sum_j \bar{D}_j$$

Subject to: $SL_i \leq S_i \leq SU_i$

$$DL_j \leq D_j \leq DU_j$$

$$XL_{ij} \leq X_{ij} \leq XU_{ij}$$

$$P_i > 0$$

$$P_j = \min_i L(P_i) \text{ for } XL_{ij} < X_{ij} < XU_{ij}$$

where: i = 1, n sources (exporters)

j = 1, m sinks (importers)

P_i = source price

P_j = sink price

S_i = excess supply of ith source

D_j = excess demand of jth sink

X_{ij} = flow from i^{th} source to j^{th} sink

SL_i = lower bound on S_i

SU_i = upper bound on S_i

DL_j = lower bound on D_j

DU_j = upper bound on D_j

XL_{ij} = lower bound on X_{ij}

XU_{ij} = upper bound on X_{ij}

L = price linkage function containing source and sink exchange rates, tariffs, and transport costs.

The excess supply and demand schedules may be simple schedules which map from a commodity price or they may be composite schedules, containing for instance beginning inventory, a production schedule, a domestic use schedule, and an ending inventory schedule. In multiple commodity or multiple form (processing) models, the excess quantity schedules may depend on more than one price and/or upon other quantities. In general, we would prefer a model solution technique which imposes as few constraints as possible upon the form and composition of the excess quantity schedules.

The market constraints and trade flow constraints may be used to modify the competitive model to reflect real world policies. The market constraints may correspond to actual import/export quotas or may be used to model price band policies. The trade flow constraints may reflect bilateral trade agreements and selective embargoes or other politically induced trade barriers.

In its simplest form, the price linkage function states that if a sink and source are trade partners, then their prices must differ by exactly the cost of transportation. In the more general form, exchange rates and export/import tariffs are also included.

Several different techniques have been used to solve the spatial equilibrium problem. The two most common approaches are Quadratic Programming (QP) and Reactive Programming (REP). Both of these techniques have inherent limitations which may be overcome to some extent by using Nonlinear Programming (NP). Fixed-point algorithms such as that used by the authors allow even more model flexibility than NP.

The most severe limitation of the QP approach for solving spatial equilibrium problems is that the excess supply and demand schedules must be linear. This constraint becomes particularly troublesome when there is evidence to suggest the excess functions are nonlinear and the model is to be used for anlysis which drives the solution point substantially away from the base solution. The linearity limitation may be overcome somewhat by forming piecewise linear functions, but this is an approximation at best and rapidly increases the size of the problem. Composite excess functions (fixed domestic supply with a demand function and an ending stocks function in the model) may be modeled in a QP framework by adding the functions together or adding "markets" to the model. Adding the functions together can result in erroneous model results depending upon the price intercepts of the functions, and adding markets increases the problem size.

The REP method allows linear and constant elasticity excess demand schedules and scalar, linear, and constant elasticity excess supply schedules. Other functional forms may be used if the modeler is willing to recode portions of the computer program. One limitation of REP is that the excess schedules must be price dependent. This leads to the requirement that composite excess functions must be entered as separate demand or supply schedules. A second and more serious limitation is that REP does not allow constraints on the trade flows among regions. The most recent version of the REP algorithm available allows for one or two commodity models. King and Gunn (1981) describe the ReP algorithm and provide several examples of its use.

The NP method may be used to model spatial equilibrium problems with complicated, smooth, nonlinear excess demand and supply schedules, import and export quotas, and trade flow constraints. In order to use a NP algorithm the modeler must formulate an objective function, the derivatives of the objective function, and be able to program these into a computer. Even with small problems, formulating the objective function and its derivative can be a time consuming process. First the user must determine whether a primal or dual formation is appropriate; then formulate the corresponding objective function and its derivatives; and finally program the objective function and detivatives. If the problem involves multiple commodities or time periods or processing activities, the objective function and derivatives become even more complicated. Rowse (1981) has used the NP package MINOS to solve spatial equilibrium modeling problems.

The fixed-point algorithm presently used, the Vector Sandwich Method, allows outstanding flexibility in excess schedule functional form. As with NP, the schedules may be scalar, linear, or nonlinear. In addition, the Vector Sandwich

Method allows semi-smooth and correspondence schedules. A semi-smooth excess quantity schedule is such that its derivative with respect to price is discontinous. For example, an inventory schedule with a quantity minimum representative working stocks is semi-smooth. A correspondence schedule is such that the mapping from price to quantity is point to set rather than point to point. For example, a linear programming model of a production process results in an excess supply schedule which is stepped and thus a correspondence. Furthermore, the Vector Sandwich Method allows composite excess schedules which may contain any of the aforementioned functional forms. The only restriction on the excess quantity schedule is that the supply (demand) schedule must contain no downward (upward) sloping segments. The Vector Sandwich Method's capability to handle semi-smooth functions directly leads to simple modeling of market quotas. Trade flow constraints are enforced by examining the constraint quantity and the price linkage functions. For constraints which are binding, the algorithm enforces them, then moves to the next lowest cost supplier.

In its present form, the version of the Vector Sandwich Method algorithm used by the authors requires the user to code three FORTRAN program units. The first is a main program which sets quota levels, trade flow constraints, transport costs, exchange rates and tariffs and then calls the solution algorithm and report writers. The other two subprograms calculate the excess supply and excess demand in quantity dependent form, returning a vector of quantities given a vector of prices. The authors believe that this programming algorithm is much easier and less prone to error than the objective function and derivative programming required by the NP method.

Both the QP and the NP approach to solving a spatial equilibrium problem are based upon an objective function involving a surplus measure. Neither the REP or Vector Sandwich Method require an objective function. These latter algorithms work directly with the equilibrium conditions, but the method by which these algorithms arrive at an approximate equilibrium is quite different. In the next section, we present a simple descriptive discussion of the workings of the Vector Sandwich Method.

The Vector Sandwich Method

The Vector Sandwich Method is one of a class of algorithms

referred to by various authors as fixed-point, equilibria, homotopy, or path-following algorithms. No particular term dominates, but all the algorithms in the class are path-following in the sense that given an initial point they follow a path leading to an equilibrium point.

Kuhn and MacKinnon (1975) orginally developed the Vector Sandwich Method to solve general equilibrium problems. The algorithm was subsequently applied to the generalized transportation problem (spatial price equilibrium) by MacKinnon (1975). The authors have used the algorithm to solve simultaneous nonsmooth, nonlinear equation systems in market simulation models and to solve spatial equilibrium problems.

The Vector Sandwich Method is a basic approximation algorithm. The solution space is divided into nice sets called simplices and a sophisticated search procedure is used to generate a path leading to an equilibrium point. The algorithm moves from simplex to simplex following a set of rules. On each simplex a piecewise linear approximation of the underlying equation system is formed. Since the simplices are associated with piecewise linear approximations of the underlying equilibrium, the algorithm also forms a piecewise linear approximation to the solution path, as it follows a path from the initial solution to an equilibrium.

In order to move from an initial solution to an equilibrium, the algorithm needs only price vectors and the quantity vectors associated with the price vectors. There is no objective function and derivatives, or system of path following differential equations to evaluate. This results in marked flexibility in market equation formulation and makes the algorithm relatively easy to use.

The inner workings of the algorithms are much more mathematically complex than the above description implies. The Vector Sandwich Method is a complementary pivot algorithm which involves pivoting on the simplex vertices and basis changes associated with labeling vectors and vertex weights. From an empirical viewpoint the mathematical structure of the algorithm is not that important. What is important is that this algorithm and others similar to it can be used to solve empirical equilibrium problems. The algorithm does have two interesting computational properties. First, given some very mild assumptions concerning the division of the solution space into simplices and the relationship between the piecewise linear approximations on adjacent simplices, the algorithm cannot cycle; covergence is guaranteed. Second, because of the construction of the Vector Sandwich Method algorithm, the accuracy of the solution is limited only by computer accuracy in evaluating the excess demand and supply schedules and forming vertex weights. Zangwill and Garcia (1981) present a detailed discussion of simplicial approximation and differential equation procedures for computing equilibria.

The Empirical Model

A point of departure is the work of Bredahl, et al. (1979) who show that:

$$E_{ef} = \sum_j E_{pj} E_{edj} \frac{Q_{mj}}{Q_{ef}} - \sum E_{pi} E_{esi} \frac{Q_{xi}}{Q_{ef}} \qquad (1)$$

where E_{pi} and E_{pj} are the elasticities of transmission between the U.S. wheat price (herein used as the "world price") and the internal wheat price in the ith exporting country or the jth importing country. E_{edj} is the elasticity of excess demand of the jth importer. E_{esi} is the elasticity of excess supply of the ith exporter. Q_{mj} and Q_{xi} are the net quantities imported and exported, respectively. And Q_{ef} is the quantity of U.S. wheat exports. After dividing the world into regions, they construct an estimate of E_{ef} based upon regional estimates of the parameters in (1). The assume $E_p = 0$ for all exporters, Europe, Japan, and U.S.S.R. All other countries are combined into one region called Rest of World(ROW). They then show that if $E_{ed} = -1.5$ and $E_p = 1.0$ for the ROW, then $E_{ef} = -1.67$. They say that of the several estimates they obtained, "This estimate . . . may be the closest approximation of the real world." Since production in the ROW is allowed to be price responsive, theirs is a longer-run estimate.

Equation (1) provides a useful means for showing how country-level excess demand elasticities and price transmission elasticities impact the estimate of E_{ef}. For our purposes, however, it is convenient to change the equation to

$$E_{ef} = \sum E_{mj} \frac{Q_{mj}}{Q_{ef}} - \sum E_{xi} \frac{Q_{xi}}{Q_{ef}} \qquad (2)$$

where E_{mj} is the world-price elasticity of demand for the jth

region's purchases of wheat and E_{xi} is the world-price elasticity of excess supply for export region i. These changes are justified below.

Wheat Importing Regions

Fifteen of the twenty regions reported in Table 12.1 are net importers of wheat. The estimate of E_m is a function of domestic demand, wheat policy and the supply of foreign exchange in the jth importing region. We assume that for all fifteen regions world price transmission is zero, i.e., domestic wheat policies completely sever the link between the world price and the domestic price. Bredahl, et al. (1979) and Zward and Meilke's (1979) show that this assumption is not unreasonable, especially in the short run. A detailed current analysis by country, however, probably would indicate that some regions exhibit a positive elasticity of price transmission.

For some importers, however, limited foreign exchange may force a negative relationship between the world wheat price and wheat imports. This argument is developed by Abbott (1979), Islam (1978), Schmitz, et al. (1981), and others. To illustrate, suppose a country's domestic supply and demand conditions were such that large quantities of wheat would be imported if adequate foreign exchange was available. But because of an extreme shortage of reserves, that country rations a specified quantity of reserves for wheat purchases. If the world wheat price were low, relatively large purchases could be made, but possibly still not enough to meet potential needs. If the world price were to double, however, the quantity imported would need to be halved, because of the fixed quantity of reserves allocated to wheat purchases. In this example the world-price elasticity of excess demand would be unitary. The short-run impact of the reserves constraint would dominate domestic supply and demand conditions. It would also thwart domestic policies from providing consumers with adequate quantities of wheat at a fixed price. In other words, imports of wheat by country with a price transmission elasticity E_{pj} of zero might still be quite responsive to world price.

The People's Republic of China seems to fit the above description. Internal wheat prices are not yet related to world prices. The government purchases wheat to fill the gap between consumption needs and supply. Foreign exchange reserves are very limited. And it has been China's policy to use the foreign exchange earned from rice exports to pay for

Table 12.1

REGION NAMES AND COMPOSITION

Region Name	Canada
Canada	Canada
United States	United States
Central America	Belize, Costa Rica, El Salvador, Guatemala, Honduras, Mexico, Nicaragua, Panama, and Caribbean Islands
Brazil	Brazil
Argentina	Argentina
Other South America	Bolivia, Chile, Colombia, Ecuador, Guiana, Guyana, Paraguay, Peru, Surinam, Uruguay, and Venezuela
European Community	Belgium, Denmark, France, Greece, Ireland, Italy Luxemborg, Netherlands, United Kingdom, and West Germany
Other Western Europe	Austria, Finland, Iceland, Malta, Norway, Portugal, Spain, Sweden, and Switzerland
Eastern Europe	Albania, Bulgaria, Czechoslovakia, East Germany, Hungary, Poland, Romania, and Yugoslavia
Soviet Union	Soviet Union
China	China
Japan	Japan
East Asia	Brunei, Hong Kong, Malaysia, North Korea, Papua, New Guinea, Philippines, Singapore, South Korea, Taiwan, and West Samoa
Southeast Asia	Burma, Cambodia, Laos, Vietnam, and Thailand
South Asia	Afghanistan, Bangladesh, Bhutan, India, Nepal. Pakistan, and Sri Lanka
West Asia	Bahrain, Cyprus, Iran, Iraq, Israel, Jordon, Kuwait, Lebanon, North Yemen, Oman, Qatar, Saudi Arabia, South Yemen, Syria, Turkey, and United Arab Emirates
North Africa	Algeria, Egypt, Morocco, Libya, and Tunisia

Table 12.1 cont'd

Central Africa	Angola, Beninm Burundi, Cameroon, Central African Republic, Chad, Congo, Djibouti, Ethiopia, Gabon, Gambia, Ghana, Guinea, Guinea-Bissau, Ivory Coast, Kenya, Liberia, Madagascar, Malawi, Mali, Mauritania, Mauritius, Mozambique, Niger, Nigeria, Reunion, Rwanda, Senegal, Sierra Leone, Somali Republic, Tanzania, Togo, and Uganda
South Africa	Botswana, Lesotho, Namibia, South Africa, and Swaziland
Australia	Australia

wheat purchases, i.e., see Tang and Stone (1980), and personal interview by Sharples with Chinese agricultural officials. Thus, China's wheat imports would be a function of both rice export earnings and world wheat price. Theoretically, one would expect the world-price elasticity of demand for wheat imports in this case to be unitary. A complicating factor, however, is that international rice and wheat prices are positively correlated so that when the world wheat price is high, foreign exchange earnings also tend to be high. The world-price elasticity of excess demand by China then would be observed as somewhat inelastic.

If foreign exhange reserves do in fact have an impact upon wheat imports then one would expect to find (1) a positive relationship between wheat imports and the supply of reserves, and (2) a negative (inelastic) relationship between world wheat price and wheat imports. Empirical work on these relationships is scarce. Abbott (1976), using 1951-1973 data, found some evidence that the scarcity of reserves had an impact upon wheat imports in selected developing countries. Using pooled time series (1976-1979) and cross-section data from 9 middle-income countries, Jabara (1982) found that the quantity of foreign exchange reserves available to a country had a significant but small impact on the quantity of wheat imported. And as hypothesized here, imports of wheat were negatively related to the world price. The world price elasticity of wheat import demand was -.2. China and other countries with lower per capita income (and greater foreign exchange problems) were not included in either study.

Islam (1978) examined the foreign exchange reserves issue for rice imports by Southeast Asian countries. He assumed that the world price was not a factor in determining rice production or domestic demand. Government-controlled imports, however, were modeled as a function of both world price and the supply of foreign exchange. He found using 1953-72 data that reserve holdings limited rice imports in India, Pakistan, Korea and the Philippines, but not in Malaysia or Sri Lanka. He also found surprisingly large world-price elasticities of rice import demand, e.g., -6 for India and -8 for Pakistan.

Here foreign exchange reserves are assumed to limit wheat imports in many developing countries. No econometric estimation is attempted. The research issue being addressed at this point is, "How important is this factor in determining the value of E_{ef}?" For those countries with exchange constraints, a negative relationship between world price and wheat imports is assumed to be caused by the limited reserves. Following Schmitz, et al. (1981, Chapter 6), and results of Jabara (1982), many developing countries are hypothesized to have a value of E_m between 0 and -1.0, with those countries with larger reserves being closer to zero. Hypothesized values of E_m are listed in Table 12.2 for each importing region. Seven regions are assumed to have no foreign exchange constraint on wheat imports. The Central American region and Brazil are assumed to have a minor foreign exchange constraint. The Other South American and East Asian regions are assumed to face intermediate constraints. For Central Africa, South Asia, Southeast Asia, and China, foreign exchange is assumed to be a serious limitation of wheat imports.

Wheat Exporting Regions

There is evidence of some transmission of world wheat prices to internal markets in Canada, Argentina, and Australia. For example, in Canada privately-held wheat stocks and the quantity fed to livestock appear to be sensitive to movements in world wheat prices. The price of wheat for food consumption, however, was shown to be controlled by Spriggs (1981). Argentina's grain market is now more open to world market forces and there is some evidence that in Australia, even though the wheat price faced by consumers is fixed, there is according to Spriggs (1978) a negative relationship between stocks and world price. Thus, the degree of world price transmission is not the same to all wheat users within a given wheat exporting country. For this reason the elasticity of world price transmission (E_{pi} in equation (1)) is replaced by a world price elasticity of excess supply (E_{xi} in equation (2)). The value of E_x for the ith exporter incorporates the weighted affects of price transmission and domestic price elasticities of the various domestic demand functions (food use, feed use, and stocks). The values of E_x for each exporter is shown in Table 12.3.

Elasticity Estimation

The first step in the estimation process is to construct a partial equilibrium wheat trade model incorporating all the assumptions of equation (2) for the base period (average of wheat trade in 1979/80, and 1980/81, and 1981/82 wheat marketing years). To this is added a matrix of wheat shipping costs and a set of constraints representing bilateral trade agreements that existed in the base period.

Table 12.2

NEW WHEAT IMPORTERS AND ASSUMED ELASTICITIES, BASE PERIOD
(1000 Metric Tons)

Importing Region	Net Imports[a]	Elasticity of Excess Demand
Central America	3,600	-.2
Brazil	4,300	-.2
Other South America	3,800	-.4
Other Western Europe	1,500	0
Eastern Europe	5,300	0
Soviet Union	15,100	0
China	11,800	-.8
Japan	5,500	0
East Asia	6,300	-.4
Southeast Asia	800	-.8
South Asia	3,500	-.8
West Asia	7,000	0
North Africa	11,000	0
Central Africa	4,000	-.8
South Africa	100	0

[a]Annual average of the 1979/80, 1980/81, and 1981/82 wheat marketing years. Calculated from International Wheat Council World Wheat Statistics, various issues.

Table 12.3

NET WHEAT EXPORTS, DOMESTIC USE AND ENDING STOCKS, ASSUMED ELASTICITIES AND CALCULATED EXCESS SUPPLY ELASTICITIES, BASE PERIOD
(1000 Metric Tons)

Exporting Region	Net Exports[1]	Domestic Use[1]	Ending Stocks[1]	Excess Supply	Domestic Use[3]	Ending Stocks[3]
Canada	16,000	5,400	9,600	.70	-.3	-1.0
United States	43,000	22,000	27,000	.68	-.1	-1.0
Argentina	4,100	4,400	600	.14	-.1	-.2
European Community	7,800	---	---	0	---	---
Australia	12,100	3,700	3,200	.11	0	-.4

[1]Annual average of the 1979/80, 1980/81, and 1981/82 wheat marketing years. Calculated from International Wheat Council World Wheat Statistics, various issues and Foreign Agricultural Circular, "Grains", USDA, various issues.

[2]
$$E_{xi} = \frac{(DS_i)(E_{dsi}) + (DD_i)(E_{ddi})}{-X_i}$$

where E_{xi} = elasticity of excess supply,
X_i = quantity exported,
E_{dsi} = elasticity of demand for stocks,
DS_i = quantity of stocks,
E_{ddi} = elasticity of demand for domestic use,
DD_i = quantity of domestic use

[3]Based upon estimates in Lattimore and Zwart (1978), Spriggs (1978), Spriggs (1981), and McKinzie (1979).

An equilibrium solution is then obtained that approximates the base period net wheat trade by region and, hopefully, the base period trade flows between regions. The final step is to vary the quantity of wheat shipped from the United States in order to obtain alternative world trade equilibria. As the quantity exported by the United States increases, the U.S. export price is expected to fall. A plot of these export prices and quantitites traces out the U.S. export demand curve. The elasticity of this curve is our estimate of E_{ef} which includes all the assumptions of equation (2) plus transportation costs and bilateral trade agreements.

A nonlinear and expanded version of the Shei and Thompson (1977) wheat trade model is used. In the model each of the fifteen net importing regions has a constant elasticity excess demand fucntion which passes through the point representing the base period price and quantity imported. Base period quantities and assumed elasticities are listed in Table 12.2. For the price responsive exporting countries, the model includes a constant elasticity demand function for ending stocks, a constant elasticity domestic demand function, and a constant quantity supplied. From these are derived an excess supply function for each exporter. Each function is defined to pass through the base period price-quantity point.

The wheat trade model contains many trade constraints, as shown in Table 12.4. All but one of the constraints to exports from the United States, Canada, Australia, Argentina, and the European Community represent bilateral trade agreements that existed during the base period, 1979/80 to 1981/82. The eight importing regions with perfectly inelastic excess demand functions have equality constraints on total quantity imported from all sources. These are set at the quantity traded during the base period, as shown in Table 12.2. The European Community and Other Western Europe are both importers and exporters of wheat. In the model they are forced to import and export the base period quantities. Estimates of transportation rates between the major exporters and importers are given in Table 12.5.

A competitive equilibrium solution is obtained in the wheat trade model using the Vector Sandwich Method. Actual trade for the base period is shown in Table 12.6, and the model solution is reproduced as Table 12.7. In the model solution the United States exported 43 million tons of wheat at $177 per ton. In the solution the quantities traded by each region duplicated actual regional net trade. The specific

Table 12.4

CONSTRAINTS REPRESENTING BILATERAL AGREEMENTS
AND PRICE INSULATED MARKETS
(1000 Metric Tons)

	Source						
Destination	Canada	United States	Argen-tina	EEC-10	R.O.W. Europe	Aust-ralia	Total
Central America	≥ 300	≥ 600					
Brazil	≥ 500						
South America							
EEC-10							= 4500
Other W. Europe		≥ 75					= 2200
Eastern Europe	≥ 500	≥ 750					= 15100
Soviet Union	≥ 3200	≥ 3000	≥ 3000[a]				= 15100
China	≥ 2800	≥ 5100	≥ 200	≥ 500		≥ 2000	
Japan	≥ 1300					≥ 900	= 5500
East Asia		≥ 575				≥ 600	
Southeast Asia							
South Asia							
West Asia	≥ 150		≥ 200			≥ 400	= 6800
North Africa	≥ 350	≥ 2000		≥ 800		≥ 1000	= 11000
Central Africa							
South Africa							= 100
Total				= 12300	= 800		

[a]Political constraint rather than an actual bilateral agreement.

Sources for Bilateral Agreements: Webb and Wilson (1981), Vogt (1982), Jabara (1982), various issues of the FAS Foreign Agricultural Circular for Grains, and various issues of IWC World Wheat Statistics.

Table 12.5

BASE PERIOD TRANSPORT RATES
($ per Metric Tons)

Destination	Source					
	Canada	United States	Argentina	EEC-10	R.O.W. Europe	Australia
Central America	19.3[a]	13.8	25.1	(20.0)	(25.0)	(27.5)
Brazil	(21.0)	(15.0)	(15.0)	(20.0)	(25.0)	(27.5)
Other S. America	23.0	16.5	20.5	21.7	(25.0)	25.8
EEC-10	13.2	12.0	25.3		(12.0)	33.2
Other W. Europe	15.4	15.6	25.0	(12.0)		39.6[a]
Eastern Europe	16.0	20.2	25.6	12.3	(12.5)	28.0
Soviet Union	16.3	19.8	25.1	(15.0)	(15.0)	19.7
China	28.2	26.4	35.2	(30.0)	(35.0)	23.2[a]
Japan	20.3	16.6	26.1	26.8[a]	(30.0)	18.2
East Asia	26.6	28.2	34.0	(30.0)	(35.0)	23.2
Southeast Asia	38.8[a]	48.2	(27.5)	35.1[a]	(40.0)	21.2
South Asia	37.0	44.2	26.8	39.0	(40.0)	28.0
West Asia	23.5	30.4	31.8	18.1	(20.0)	35.3
North Africa	26.5	30.1	27.0	14.6	(15.0)	32.3
Central Africa	31.2	40.0	28.5	31.6[a]	(30.0)	32.9
South Africa	35.4[a]	34.5	32.1[a]	(35.0)	(35.0)	25.8[a]

Note: [a] indicates less than ten observations
() indicates an estimate not based upon actual charges

Source: Derived from Harrer and Binkley (1979).

Table 12.6

ACTUAL BASE PERIOD TRADE FLOWS AND IMPORT-EXPORT TOTALS
(1000 Metric Tons)

	Source						
Destination	Canada	United States	Argen-tina	EEC-10	R.O.W. Europe	Aust-ralia	Total
Central America	1300	2000		300			3600
Brazil	1200	2500	600	50			4350
Other South America	50	3450	250	50			3800
EEC-10	1950	2450	50				4450
Other W. Europe	200	1400		550			2150
Eastern Europe	1400	1450		2150	250	50	5300
Soviet Union	3600	4600	2700	1050	250	2500	14700
China	2800	6350	300	250		2150	11850
Japan	1350	3350				1000	5700
East Asia	100	4450		250		1400	6200
Southeast Asia		100		250	50	150	550
South Asia	250	1850		550		750	3400
West Asia	600	2300	200	1200	50	2500	6850
North Africa	900	4150		4000	150	1700	10900
Central Africa	200	2000		1600	50	200	4050
South Africa		150					150
Other		50		50			100
Total	15900	42600	4100	12300	800	12400	78100

Source: Derived from International Wheat Council World Wheat Statistics.

Table 12.7

BASE SOLUTION TRADE FLOWS AND IMPORT-EXPORT TOTALS
(1000 Metric Tons)

	Source						
Destination	Canada	United States	Argentina	EEC-10	R.O.W. Europe	Australia	Total
Central America	300[a]	3199					3499
Brazil	500[a]	3868					4368
Other South America		3835					3835
EEC-10		4500					4500[a]
Other W. Europe		2200					2200[a]
Eastern Europe	3201	2099					5300[a]
Soviet Union	3200[a]	8900	3000[a]				15100[a]
China	2800[a]	6248	200[a]	500[a]		2000[a]	11748
Japan	1300[a]	3300				900[a]	5500[a]
East Asia		2840				3402	6243
Southeast Asia						784	784
South Asia						3470	3470
West Asia	1450		200[a]	4950		400	7000
North Africa	350[a]	2000[a]		6850	800	1000[a]	11000[a]
Central Africa	3270		719				3989
South Africa						100[a]	100[a]
Total	16372	42988	4119	12300[a]	800[a]	12056	88635

Note: [a] indicates a binding constraint.

trade flows, however, differed substantially from the base period. During the base period each of the major wheat exporters shipped wheat to nearly all of the world's importing regions. The model, however, suggests more specialization, a result one now expects of spatial price equilibrium models, i.e., see Shei and Thompson (1977).

Some Results

Twenty-one competitive equilibrium solutions to the wheat trade model are obtained. For these solutions, the United States excess supply schedule was replaced with a fixed quantity beginning with 25 million metric tons and increased in 2 million ton increments in the remaining solutions, to a maximum of 65 million tons.

As one would expect, as the quantity of wheat exported by the United States increases, the U.S. wheat export price drops. The twenty-one competitive U.S. export quantities are plotted in Figure 12.1 and connected by line segments to represent the short-run U.S. export demand curve for wheat. Also plotted in Figure 12.1 are the corresponding quantity adjustments made by other exporting regions and the importing regions to the change in U.S. exports. As U.S. exports increase and wheat prices fall around the world, other exporters decrease exports, increase stocks and increase domestic consumption. Those importers who have foreign exchange constraints buy more wheat at the lower price. Importers with administered domestic wheat prices and adequate reserves make no adjustments to the lower price. The U.S. export demand curve in Figure 12.1 is equivalent to the quantity difference between the excess demand curve of the importing regions and the excess supply curve of the other exporting regions.

During the base period the United States exported about 43 million tons of wheat. The U.S. export demand curve (Figure 12.1) in that vicinity has a price elasticity of about -.7. In contrast, an elasticity estimate obtained by forcing all importers to import the fixed base period quantities is -.3. Additional sensitivity analysis with the wheat trade model shows that the bilateral trade agreements and other constraints on individual trade flows have no perceptible impact n the elasticity of demand for U.S. wheat exports at the base period export quantity of 43 million tons. The trade flow constraints, however, have an impact upon the U.S. export demand curve below 39 million tons. At that point the Chinese import price is high enough that "desired" imports

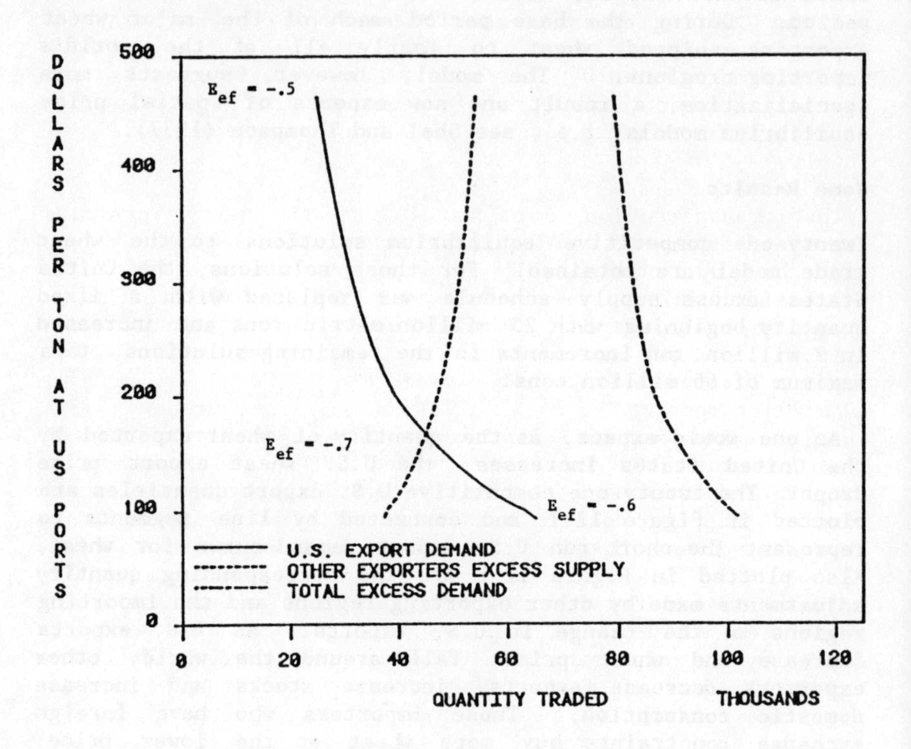

Figure 12.1
COMPUTED EXCESS SUPPLY
AND DEMAND SCHEDULES
BASE SOLUTION

are less than the sum of the Chinese bilateral agreements, and the Chinese excess demand becomes perfectly inelastic. The model generates similar results for Canada with very high U.S. exports. When U.S. exports exceed 63 million tons, the Candadian export price is low enough that the Canadian bilateral commitments exceed their price responsive excess supply.

The transportation cost matrix in the model contains constant rates, but as the United States increases the volume exported, the average shipping cost per ton goes up. The marginal additions to U.S. exports are shipped to higher transport-cost destinations. For example, the average shipping cost per ton is $19.36 for 43 million tons of wheat exports but the average cost increased to $20.33 per ton for 53 million tons. The marginal 10 million tons are over more costly routes and have an average shipping cost of $24.47. Thus, as the U.S. export price decreases, the increase in quantity exported is less than it would be with a model which ignores shipping costs, because the marginal shipping costs go up as volume shipped by the United States goes up.

The U.S. export demand curve becomes less elastic for quantities above 40 million tons (Figure 12.1). This is caused by the expansion of U.S. wheat exports (Q_{ef}) relative to the imports (Q_{mi}) or exports (Q_{xj}) of other counties, i.e., see equation (2).

If U.S. exports of wheat in the base period would have increased, which regions would adjust their trade to absorb it? An estimate is obtained by comparing solutions with U.S. exports of 43 and 45 million tons. With larger U.S. exports, the world price (at U.S. ports) decreases from $177 per ton to $166 per ton. Given all the model's assumptions, the largest adjustment to expanded U.S. exports is in Canada where exports decrease 691 thousand tons. As a result of the reduced export price, Canadian stocks increase 594 thousand tons and consumption increases 98 thousand tons (Table 12.8). Very little adjustment is made in the exports of Australia and Argentina.

Among importers, wheat imports increase in those regions in which scarce foreign exchange is assumed to curtail imports. The largest quantity increases are in China, Central Africa, South Asia, and East Asia. Canada plus these four importing regions absorb 84 percent of the effects of the increase in U.S. exports. The other fiteen regions account for only 16 percent.

Table 12.8

REGIONAL ADJUSTMENTS TO A TWO MILLION TON INCREASE IN U.S. WHEAT EXPORTS[a]
(1000 Metric Tons)

Item	Quantity Change	Percent Change
Increase in:		
Canadian Stocks	594	29.7
Imports - China	524	26.2
- Central Africa	170	8.5
- South Asia	150	7.5
- East Asia	136	6.8
Canadian Use	98	4.9
Imports - Other S. America	89	4.5
Australian Stocks	80	4.0
Imports - Brazil	51	2.6
- Central America	41	2.1
- Southeast Asia	35	1.8
Argentina - Use	27	1.4
- Stocks	6	0.3
Increase in U.S. Exports	2000	100.0
Decreased Imports in Rest of World	1195	59.8
Decreased Exports - Canada	691	34.6
- Australia	80	4.0
- Argentina	33	1.7
Increase in U.S. Exports	2000	100.0

[a]Comparison of model results with U.S. exports of 43 and 45 million metric tons.

These results give further evidence of the importance of

(1) the estimate of the world-price elasticity of demand for Canadian stocks,

(2) the assumed impact of scarce foreign exchange on wheat imports, and

(3) the level and enforcement, if any, of bilateral agreements.

Affect of a Hypothesized EEC Policy Change

Recently there has been much discussion among politicians, farm groups, and others interested in U.S. agricultural pertaining to the Common Agricultural Policy of the European Economic Community. In particular, U.S. agricultural leaders have expressed concern regarding wheat export levels and subsidies. U.S. interests maintain that the increased EEC wheat exports are due solely to CAP, and are displacing U.S. wheat exports thus lowering U.S. farm income. As the EEC wheat exports have increased, the cost of CAP has increased. It is possible that the EEC could alter CAP in response to budgetary considerations and U.S. political pressure.

Sharples and Paarlberg (1982) have suggested that EEC could achieve domestic agricultural goals and reduce CAP expenditures by employing a two-price production quota system. In this scheme the EEC would divide their wheat market into domestic and export components. Wheat producers would receive a high domestic price for domestic quota wheat, and any other quota wheat would move into trade channels at the prevailing world price. This type of program would maintain producer income, insure adequate domestic supply, and potentially reduce CAP wheat costs. Further, the concerns of U.S. wheat interest groups would lessen since the EEC would likely export much less wheat.

An EEC two-price policy would increase E_{ef} since EEC exports would be price responsive. The primary EEC price response is expected to be in the holding of speculative stocks, since the over quota wheat would either be exported or placed in storage. To investigate the change in E_{ef} resulting from the hypothesized pricing scheme, the model's EEC excess supply schedule was altered by adding an EEC stockholding schedule with an assumed elasticity of -1.0. The model was then solved for equilibria with various levels of fixed U.S. exports to trace out the export demand faced by the U.S. (Figure 12.2). The estimated value of E_{ef} is -.9 at the U.S. base export quantity of 43 million tons. The curves are very similar for the base solution and the alternative EEC domestic policy solutions, except as expected, the latter solution leads to more elastic U.S. export demand.

Conclusions

What is an appropriate estimate of the elasticity of demand for U.S. exports, known as E_{ef}, to use in short-run models? Different assumptions about the real world wheat market lead to different estimates of E_{ef}. For the base period, 1979/80 to 1981/82, the twenty-region model yields an elasticity estimate of -.7. Bilateral agreements appear to have no impact upon the estimate of E_{ef} at the quantities traded in the base period, but do show an impact at slightly lower volumes.

Two characteristics of the wheat trade model suggest that -.7 overestimates the true elasticity of demand for U.S. wheat exports. First, the model includes the assumption that trade flows will adjust immediately to a new equilibrium in response to a change in U.S. exports. To the extent that trading patterns tend to be more stable than modeled, adjustments to a change in U.S. exports would be fewer, i.e., it would take a larger price increase to induce a given quantity change. This is likely to be a significant factor. Trade channels once established tend to persist because of political reasons as well as for economic reasons omitted from this study. The United States, for example, shipped some wheat to each of the importing regions during the base period. This may reflect the desire of importers to diversify their sources, it may indicate that wheat from the United States has some unique characteristics, or it may reflect wheat shipments under PL-480, i.e, see Grennes, et al. (1977). Each factor would make short-run demand for U.S. wheat exports less elastic.

Second, the transportation rates are assumed constant no matter what the volume transported. If transportation rates were to increase with increased volume shipped, then a larger price drop to the exporter would accompany a given increase in world wheat trade, because the price wedge between the exporter and importer would increase. Both these factors, if put into the model, would make the U.S. export demand curve less elastic than shown here.

Examination of Tables 12.2 and 12.8 gives guidance on which

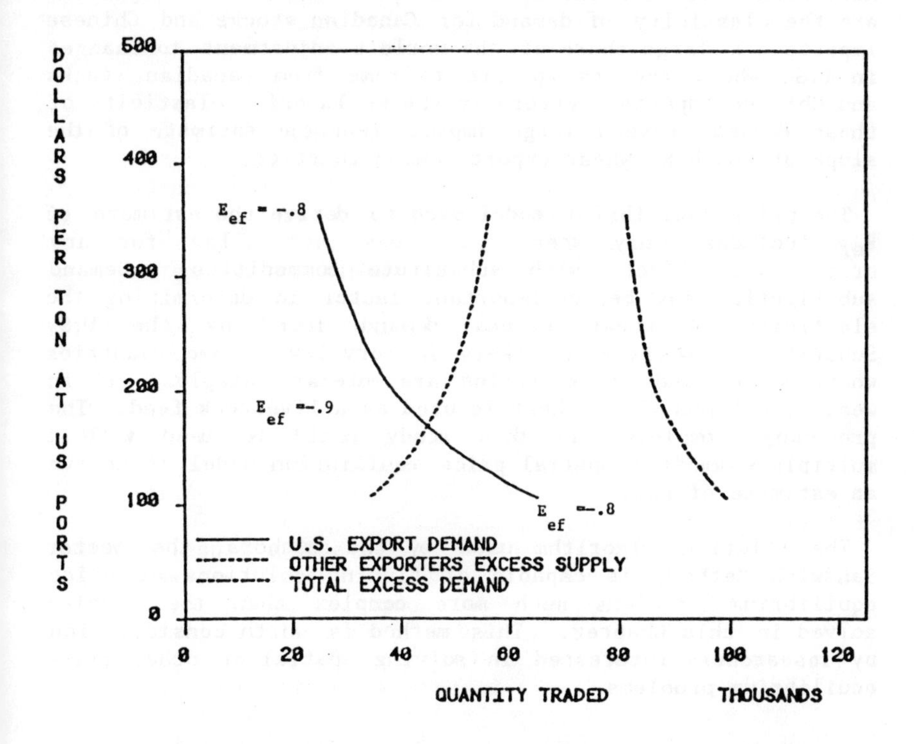

Figure 12.2

COMPUTED EXCESS SUPPLY
AND DEMAND SCHEDULES
ALTERNATIVE EEC DOMESTIC POLICY

Examination of Tables 12.2 and 12.8 gives guidance on which parameters play the most important role in determining the elasticity of the short-run excess demand function. Additional research should focus upon them. Most important are the elasticity of demand for Canadian stocks and Chinese imports. A large share of the world's adjustment to changes in U.S. wheat exports appears to come from Canadian stocks and Chinese imports. Errors in the world price elasticity of these demands have a large impact upon the estimate of the slope of the U.S. wheat export demand function.

The price equilibrium model used to derive the estimate of E_{ef} includes only wheat; it does not allow for any cross-price effects with substitute commodities. Demand substitution may be an important factor in determining the elasticity of wheat excess demand faced by the U.S. Substitution seems most likely in very low income countries where wheat and other grains are dietary staples and in wealthy nations where wheat is used as a livestock feed. The procedures employed in this study could be used with a multiple commodity spatial price equilibrium model to derive an estimate of E_{ef}.

The solution algorithm used by the authors, the Vector Sandwich Method, is capable of finding solutions of price equilibrium problems much more complex than the problem solved in this Chapter. This method is worth consideration by researchers interested in solving spatial or other price equilibrium problems.

Authors
Forest D. Holland
Jerry A Sharples
School of Agriculture Economics
Purdue University
West Lafayette, IN 47907
and the Economic Research Service
U.S. Department of Agriculture
Washington, D.C. 20520

References

Abbott, P.C., (1976). "Developing Countries and International Grain Trade," Ph.D. thesis, Massachusetts Institute of Technology.

Abbott, P.C., (1979). "Modeling International Grain Trade with Government Controlled Markets," American Journal of Agricultural Economics, 61: 22-31.

Bredahl, M., W.H. Meyers and K. Collins, (1979). "The Elasticity of Foreign Demand for U.S. Agricultural Products: The Importance of the Price Transmission Elasticity," American Journal of Agricultural Economics, 61: 58-63.

Gallagher, P., M. Lancaster, M. Bredahl and T.J. Ryan, (1981). The U.S. Wheat Economy in an International Setting: An Econometric Investigation, Technical Bulletin 1644, Economics and Statistics Service, U.S. Department of Agriculture.

Grennes, T., P.R. Johnson and M. Thursby, (1977). The Economics of World Grain Trade, New York: Praeger Publishers.

Harrer, B. and J. Binkley, (1979). International Transport Rates for Grain and Their Determinants, Station Bulletin No. 264, Department of Agricultural Economics, Purdue University.

International Wheat Council, (1980). "World Wheat Statistics," 1976 through 1980 issues.

Islam, B, (1978). "Price, Income, and Foreign Exchange Reserve Elasticity for Asian Rice Imports," American Journal of Agricultural Economics, 60: 532-535.

Jabara, C.L., (1982). Wheat Import Demand Among Middle-Income Developing Countries: A Cross Sectional Analysis, ERS Staff Report, International Economics Division, Economic Research Service, U.S. Department of Agriculture.

Johnson, P.R. (1977). "The Elasticity of Foreign Demand for U.S. Agricultural Products," American Journal of Agricultural Economics, 59: 735-736.

King, R.A. and J. Gunn, (1981). "Reactive Programming User Manual: A Market Simulating Spatial Equilibrium Algorithm," Economics Research Report, North Carolina State University.

Kuhn, H.W. and J.G. MacKinnon, (1975). "Sandwich Method for Finding Fixed Points," Journal of Optimization Theory and Applications, 17: 189-204.

Lattimore, R. and A.C. Zwart, (1978). "Medium Term World Wheat Forecasting Model," Commodity Forecsting Models for Canadian Agriculture, 2.

MacKinnon, J.G., (1975). "An Algorithm for the Generalized Transportation Problem," Regional Science and Urban Economics, 5: 445-464.

McKinzie, L.D., III, (1979). "An Econometric Model of the Canadian Wheat Market," M.S. Thesis, Department of Agricultural Economics, Purdue University.

Ray, D.E. and J.W. Richardson, (1978). Detailed Descriptive of POLYSIM, Technical Bulletin, Oklahoma State University.

Rowse, J., (1981). "Solving the Generalized Transportation Problem," Regional Science and Urban Economics, 11: 57-68.

Schmitz, A., A.F. McCalla, D.O. Mitchell and C.A. Carter, (1981). Grain Export Cartels, Cambridge, MA: Ballinger Publishing Company.

Sharples, J.A., (1980). An Examination of U.S. Wheat Policy Since 1977 with Emphasis on the Farmer-Owned Reserve, IED Staff Report No. 1981-5, International Economics Division, Economic Research Service, U.S. Department of Agriculture.

Sharples, J.A. and P.L. Paarlberg, (1982). Japanese and European Community Agricultural Trade Policies: Some U.S. Strategies, Economic Research Service, U.S. Department of Agriculture.

Shei, S.Y. and R. L. Thompson, (1977). "The Impact of Trade Restrictions on Price Stability in the World Wheat Market," American Journal of Agricultural Economics, 59: 628-38.

Spriggs, J., (1978). An Econometric Analysis of Export Supply of Grains in Australia, FAER No. 150, Economics, Statistics, and Cooperatives Service, U.S. Department of Agriculture.

Takayama, T. and G.G. Judge, (1971). Spatial and Temporal Price and Allocation Models, Amsterdam: North Holland.

Tang, A.M. and B. Stone, (1980). Food Production in the People's Republic of China, Research report 15, International Food Policy Research Institute.

Tweeten, L., (1967). "The Demand for United States Farm Output," Food Research Institute Studies, 7: 343-369.

Vogt, D.U., C.K. Jabara and D.A. Linse, (1982). Barter of Agricultural Commodities ERS Staff Report No. AGES820413, International Economics Division, Economic Research Service, U.S. Department of Agricluture.

Webb, A.J. and E.C. Wilson, (1981). An Overview of Bilateral Trade Agreements for Agricultural Commodities in International Markets, Staff Report, Trade Policy Branch, Economics and Statistics Service, U.S. Department of Agriculture.

Zangwill, W.I. and C.B. Garcia, (1981). Pathways to Solutions, FIxed Points, and Equilibria. Englewood Cliffs, NJ: Prentice-Hall.

Zwart, A.C. and K.D. Meilke, (1979). "The Influence of Domestic Pricing Policies and Buffer Stocks on Price Stability in the World Wheat Industry," American Journal of Agricultural Economics, 61: 434-447.

Sarris, A.H. [illegible] European Economic Agriculture [illegible] Statistics, Economic Research Service, U.S. Department of Agriculture.

Shei, S.Y. and R.L. Thompson (1977). "The Impact of Trade Restrictions on Price Stability in the World Wheat Market," American Journal of Agricultural Economics, 59, 628-38.

Spriggs, J. (1978). An Econometric Analysis of Export Supply of Grains in Australia, FAER No. 150, Economics, Statistics and Cooperatives Service, U.S. Department of Agriculture.

Takayama, T. and G.G. Judge. (1971). Spatial and Temporal Price and Allocation Models, Amsterdam: North Holland.

Tang, A.M. and B. Stone. (1980). Food Production in the People's Republic of China, Research Report 15, International Food Policy Research Institute.

Tweeten, L. (1967). "The Demand for United States Farm Output," Food Research Institute Studies, 7, [illegible].

Vogt, D.U., C.K. Jabara and D.A. Liese. (1982). [illegible] Agricultural Commodities ERS Staff Report No. [illegible] International Economics Division, Economic Research Service, U.S. Department of Agriculture.

Webb, A.J. and R.G. Wilson. (1983). An Overview of Bilateral Trade Agreements for Agricultural Commodities in International Markets, Staff Report, Trade Policy Branch, Economics and Statistics Service, U.S. Department of Agriculture.

Zangwill, W.I. and C.B. Garcia. (1981). Pathways to Solutions, Fixed Points, and Equilibria. Englewood Cliffs, NJ: Prentice-Hall.

Zwart, A.C. and K.D. Meilke. (1979). "The Influence of Domestic Pricing Policies and Buffer Stocks on Price Stability in the World Wheat Industry," American Journal of Agricultural Economics, 61, 434-447.